Hyacinths of Knowledge and Wisdom

Bahá'í
Publications
Australia

Hyacinths of Knowledge and Wisdom

Published by Bahá'í Publications Australia

ISBN : 1 876322 89 6

Distributed by :
Bahá'í Distribution Services
P.O. Box 300
Bundoora Vic 3083
Australia

Email: bds@bahai.org.au
www.bahaibooks.com

Cover design: Douglas Jenkyns (douglas@jenkyns.org)
Book layout: Massoud Tahzib

A Resource for Teaching, Deepening and Personal Transformation

Selections From The
Writings of Bahá'u'lláh

Compiled by Curt Creager

Contents

Hearken to the delightsome words of My honeyed tongue, and quaff the stream of mystic holiness from My sugar-shedding lips. Sow the seeds of My divine wisdom in the pure soil of thy heart, and water them with the water of certitude, that the hyacinths of My knowledge and wisdom may spring up fresh and green in the sacred city of thy heart.

Bahá'u'lláh

Introduction

We live in an era in which God is openly denied and religion is frequently discredited as being out-of-date or a waste of time. Paradoxically, we live in an age that has witnessed the appearance of the most recent of God's Prophets, Bahá'u'lláh, with His Message for this day—proffering solutions to the array of problems afflicting humanity in every corner of our planet.

A Prophet of God has appeared in our age! Such is His claim, and such is the claim of those who have responded to His call to build a new world order on the foundation of world peace and brotherhood. His life, His teachings and His Writings, all testify to the authenticity of His station. Little more than; *"one hundred years ago, Bahá'u'lláh, Founder of the Bahá'í Faith, proclaimed in clear and unmistakable language, to the kings and rulers of the world, to its religious leaders, and to mankind in general that the long-promised age of world peace and brotherhood had at last dawned and that He Himself was the Bearer of the new message and power from God which would transform the prevailing system of antagonism and enmity between men and create the spirit and form of the destined world order."[1]*

Reflective study of His Writings takes the seeker of truth and student of religion on a fascinating and wide-ranging exploration of spiritual reality. All He asks is that we keep an open mind and make our own independent search after truth.

From the earliest days of Bahá'u'lláh's Revelation to the present hour, leaders of thought and impartial observers[2] have voiced their tributes to His Divinely-inspired Writings. For example, expressing his view of Bahá'u'lláh's teachings, one of the world's leading social scientists, has stated; *"The Bahá'í call for peace comes at a crucial moment in the history of humanity. Peace in the contemporary world is no longer an option but a necessity. All leaders and peoples of the world must come to realize this fact, and achieve the maturity which the Bahá'í Faith foresees for the coming of age of humanity."[3]*

Voicing his views of the Bahá'í Faith, an acclaimed US journalist and former news anchor for the CBS Evening News[4] has noted; "... Bahá'u'lláh taught, to put it in simple terms, that God is too great for any one religion to fully contain. Each, however, has contributed to humankind's understanding and progress. To the Bahá'í, the teachings of Abraham, Moses, the Buddha, Zoroaster, Jesus, Krishna, and Mohammed are all pieces of a vast universal puzzle. All have made equal contributions to morality and civilization, and all are studied closely by Bahá'í."

The Writings of Bahá'u'lláh may be likened to a well of spiritual knowledge and understanding, from which one may draw the live-giving waters of His Revelation. Study of His Writings takes the reader on a fascinating and wide-ranging journey.

Structure and Use of This Book

Hyacinths of Knowledge and Wisdom is an in-depth resource for your personal exploration of the Writings of Bahá'u'lláh. It amply illustrates the power and scope of His Revelation, and is designed to complement your times of study, prayer, and meditation. It contains 683 quotations drawn from 25 sources, arranged in 123 topical headings, ranging from the practical to the mystical. You will find the volume a helpful resource for expanding your knowledge and appreciation of the teachings and principles of the Bahá'í Faith.

Drawing inspiration from the wealth of Bahá'u'lláh's utterances is an essential component of daily deepening. For Bahá'ís, such study and meditation provides courage and enthusiasm for teaching the Faith to others. It is also a valuable tool for such activities as developing lesson plans, assembling the scriptural readings for a community event, or researching the topics to be discussed in a study group.

Topics are arranged under six headings: God, Manifestations of God, Bahá'u'lláh, The Spiritual Reality of Mankind, A New World Order, and Personal Character, Conduct and Spiritual Transformation. *"It is now incumbent upon them who are endowed with a hearing ear and a seeing eye to ponder these sublime words, in each of which the oceans of inner meaning and explanation are hidden, that haply the words uttered by Him Who is the Lord of Revelation may enable His servants to attain, with the utmost joy and radiance, unto the Supreme Goal and Most Sublime Summit—the dawning-place of this Voice."[5]*

The Nature of Deepening

The power and scope of Baha'u'llah's Writings provide a lustrous vision of spiritual reality. Deepening in the Cause of God reveals the passageway leading to communion with the Holy Spirit. Immersion in the Holy Writings is an action by which one's character is purified. Prayer, deepening and meditation opens the gate of the mystical pathway that leads to an understanding and appreciation of the historic, spiritual and social consequences of the Revelation, and results in a life dedicated to the servitude to humanity.

Shoghi Effendi tells us; *"To strive to obtain a more adequate understanding of the significance of Bahá'u'lláh's stupendous Revelation must, it is my unalterable conviction, remain the first obligation and the object of the constant endeavor of each one of its loyal adherents. An exact and thorough comprehension of so vast a system, so sublime a revelation, so sacred a trust, is for obvious reasons beyond the reach and ken of our finite minds. We can, however, and it is our bounden duty to seek to derive fresh inspiration and added sustenance as we labor for the propagation of His Faith through a clearer apprehension of the truths it enshrines and the principles on which it is based."[6]*

The Mystery

Bahá'ís believe that a mystical process is set in motion when a person declares his or her belief in Bahá'u'lláh, the Promised One of God, and acknowledges their recognition of the Báb, His Forerunner, and 'Abdu'l-Bahá[7], the Center of His Covenant. One pledges their obedience to the sacred principles, laws, and institutions of the Faith. From that moment of affirmation, until one's body is finally *"...laid to rest beneath a canopy of dust,"*[8] one embarks on a life-journey unique in the annals of religious history.

The Writings of Bahá'u'lláh possess a creative and transforming power. With the birth of each new Revelation from God, humanity becomes the beneficiary of the fresh release of spiritual power released from the Heaven of God's Will.

For a mysterious reason known only to the Ancient Being (God), you have become acquainted with the Revelation of Bahá'u'lláh. You are among the first people on the planet to read and study His Writings, and with an open mind investigate the inner meanings of His Teachings. *"Verily, God has chosen you for His love and knowledge; God has chosen you for the worthy service of unifying mankind; God has chosen you for the purpose of investigating reality and promulgating international peace; God has chosen you for the progress and development of humanity, for spreading and proclaiming true education, for the expression of love toward your fellow creatures and the removal of prejudice; God has chosen you to blend together human hearts and give light to the human world."*[9]

In another tablet, Bahá'u'lláh states: *"...ye are the first among men to be re-created by His Spirit, the first to adore and bow the knee before Him, the first to circle round His throne of glory. I swear by Him Who hath caused Me to reveal whatever hath pleased Him! Ye are better known to the inmates of the Kingdom on high than ye are known to your own selves."*[10] Pause for a moment and ask yourself the question; "Why me?" Out of the world's entire population, only about 1 in every 1,000 are Bahá'ís. Even when you add the number of scholars and students of religion, the total is meager. You, however, represent a unique minority. Did you find the Message, or did the Message find you? Why you? Why indeed.

The Deepening Process

Studying the Writings of Bahá'u'lláh is much like being a detective. As we read, re-read, and meditate on His Words, hints and clues are revealed that we would not have otherwise discovered. Insights are drawn and our minds are illumined. Step-by-step one's character is transformed. *"As repeatedly emphasized in Bahá'u'lláh's exposition of the Báb's message, the primary purpose of God in revealing His will is to effect a transformation in the character of humankind, to develop within those who respond the moral and spiritual qualities that are latent within human nature."*[11]

When a person acknowledges the station of Bahá'u'lláh, and commits to the overarching objective of firmness in His Covenant, he or she enters upon an infinite spiritual journey. Of great comfort is the knowledge that Bahá'u'lláh is your companion during every step of your journey. *"If ye follow Me, ye shall behold that which ye were promised, and I will make you My companions in the dominion of My majesty and the intimates of My beauty in the heaven of My power forevermore."*[12]

As one's character is transformed the seeker becomes progressively better fit to serve at His Holy Threshold. Bahá'u'lláh offers to guide you through this journey. He holds out His arms and embraces you with Words of mystery and love.

Deepening in the Writings of Bahá'u'lláh is a decidedly personal and subjective process. There are countless lamps of guidance that illumine the spiritual path. As you traverse the pathway you uncover the gems of mystery that lie hidden within the forest of wonder. Your journey transcends physical reality, and Bahá'u'lláh so loves your service that He says; *"I would love to lay My face upon every single spot of Thine earth, that perchance it might be honored by touching a spot ennobled by the footsteps of Thy loved ones!"*[13] Can you imagine?

The Covenant between Bahá'u'lláh and His Followers

We must never be discouraged. We must be forever steadfast. The Covenant of Bahá'u'lláh is the prime vehicle that transports us to the arena of service and teaching. *"May the brightness of His glory shining above the horizon of bounty rest upon you, O people of Bahá, upon every one who standeth firm and steadfast and upon those that are well grounded in the Faith and are endued with true understanding."*[14] In another verse He again addresses this steadfastness; *"Thus with steadfast steps we may tread the Path of certitude, that perchance the breeze that bloweth from the meads of the good-pleasure of God may waft upon us the sweet savours of divine acceptance, and cause us, vanishing mortals that we are, to attain unto the Kingdom of everlasting glory."*[15]

Sometimes our efforts seem meager and ineffectual. We make mention of the Faith and our family, friends, coworkers, neighbors or contacts often seem neutral or disinterested. Even the founder of the Faith, Bahá'u'lláh, found people non-responsive; *"My signs have encompassed the earth, and My power enveloped all mankind, and yet the people are wrapped in a strange sleep!"*[16] Perhaps those chosen to serve at the Holy Threshold, are those that have the capacity and courage to embark on the journey, and remain so engaged in all the worlds of God.

Unqualified love, obedience, vision, patience and steadfastness are essential guiding factors of our lives. *"Nowhere doth your true and abiding glory reside except in your firm adherence unto the precepts of God, your wholehearted observance of His laws, your resolution to see that they do not remain unenforced, and to pursue steadfastly the right course."*[17]

An amazing characteristic relating to spiritual transformation—that is systematic prayer, meditation, deepening, and arising to serve—is that every day you make progress. You are awake and attuned to spiritual realities. Each step of your journey is constructive and beneficial, and yet there stretches before you a path that is ever-advancing, repetitively-beneficial, and forever-expanding. At every turn something marvelous is awaiting discovery. You become increasingly aware that you will never come to an end of the journey, but are in no way discouraged. Contentment abounds.

Regarding the necessity of deepening every day and being faithful to the Covenant, Bahá'u'lláh states; *"Recite ye the verses of God every morn and eventide. Whoso faileth to recite them hath not been faithful to the Covenant of God and His Testament, and whoso turneth away from these holy verses in this Day is of those who throughout eternity have turned away from God."*[18]

Recognition of, and firmness in, the Covenant brings unfathomed joy. You entreat God to accept your meager gifts, and offer your continual thanks for being permitted to be of service. Your humble efforts in His cause bring forth life-giving waters to the whole of humanity. A joyful heart is the inevitable result of a heart burning with love. *"Live then the days of thy life, that are less than a fleeting moment, with thy mind stainless, thy heart unsullied, thy thoughts pure, and thy nature sanctified, so that, free and content, thou mayest put away this mortal frame, and repair unto the mystic paradise and abide in the eternal kingdom for evermore."*[19]

The Heart of the Matter

The Writings of Bahá'u'lláh are, in every reality, Messages from God revealed through His Supreme Manifestation. Listen, as Bahá'u'lláh defines the purpose and function of your spiritual heart; *"O friend, the heart is the dwelling of eternal mysteries, make it not the home of fleeting fancies; waste not the treasure of thy precious life in employment with this swiftly passing world. Thou comest from the world of holiness—bind not thine heart to the earth; thou art a dweller in the court of nearness—choose not the homeland of the dust."*[20] Bahá'u'lláh also reveals this injunction in *the Hidden Words; "O SON OF BEING! Thy heart is My home; sanctify it for My descent. Thy spirit is My place of revelation; cleanse it for My manifestation."*[21] To open one's heart is to welcome Bahá'u'lláh into His home.

The Promise

"O My brother! Sanctify thy heart, illumine thy soul, and sharpen thy sight, that thou mayest perceive the sweet accents of the Birds of Heaven and the melodies of the Doves of Holiness warbling in the Kingdom of eternity, and perchance apprehend the inner meaning of these utterances and their hidden mysteries."[22]

Bon Voyage!

We wish you an amazing journey to your personal and unique spiritual destination.

Dennis R. Jenkyns

God

God: The Unknowable Essence

Exalted, immeasurably exalted art Thou, O my Beloved, above the strivings of any of Thy creatures, however learned, to know Thee; exalted, immensely exalted art Thou above every human attempt, no matter how searching, to describe Thee! For the highest thought of men, however deep their contemplation, can never hope to outsoar the limitations imposed upon Thy creation, nor ascend beyond the state of the contingent world, nor break the bounds irrevocably set for it by Thee. How can, then, a thing that hath been created by Thy will that overruleth the whole of creation, a thing that is itself a part of the contingent world, have the power to soar into the holy atmosphere of Thy knowledge, or reach unto the seat of Thy transcendent power?

High, immeasurably high art Thou above the endeavors of the evanescent creature to soar unto the throne of Thine eternity, or of the poor and wretched to attain the summit of Thine all-sufficing glory! From eternity Thou didst Thyself describe Thine own Self unto Thy Self, and extol, in Thine own Essence, Thine Essence unto Thine Essence. I swear by Thy glory, O my Best-Beloved! Who is there besides Thee that can claim to know Thee, and who save Thyself can make fitting mention of Thee? Thou art He Who, from eternity, abode in His realm, in the glory of His transcendent unity, and the splendors of His holy grandeur.[1]

Lauded and glorified art Thou, O Lord, my God! How can I make mention of Thee, assured as I am that no tongue, however deep its wisdom, can befittingly magnify Thy name, nor can the bird of the human heart, however great its longing, ever hope to ascend into the heaven of Thy majesty and knowledge.

If I describe Thee, O my God, as Him Who is the All-Perceiving, I find myself compelled to admit that They Who are the highest Embodiments of perception have been created by virtue of Thy behest. And if I extol Thee as Him Who is the All-Wise, I, likewise, am forced to recognize that the Well Springs of wisdom have themselves been generated through the operation of Thy Will. And if I proclaim Thee as the Incomparable One, I soon discover that they Who are the inmost essence of oneness have been sent down by Thee and are but the evidences of Thine handiwork. And if I acclaim Thee as the Knower of all things, I must confess that they Who are the Quintessence of knowledge are but the creation and instruments of Thy Purpose.

Exalted, immeasurably exalted, art Thou above the strivings of mortal man to unravel Thy mystery, to describe Thy glory, or even to hint at the nature of Thine Essence.[2]

Praise be to God, the All-Possessing, the King of incomparable glory, a praise which is immeasurably above the understanding of all created things, and is exalted beyond the grasp of the minds of men. None else besides Him hath ever been able to sing adequately His praise, nor will any man succeed at any time in describing the full measure of His glory. Who is it that can claim to have attained the heights of His exalted Essence, and what mind can measure the depths of His unfathomable mystery? From each and every revelation emanating from the Source of His glory, holy and never-ending evidences of unimaginable splendor have appeared, and out of every manifestation of His invincible power oceans of eternal light have outpoured. How immensely exalted are the wondrous testimonies of His almighty sovereignty, a glimmer of which, if it but touched them, would utterly consume all that are in the heavens and in the earth! How indescribably lofty are the tokens of His consummate power, a single sign of which, however inconsiderable, must transcend the comprehension of whatsoever hath, from the beginning that hath no beginning, been brought into being, or will be created in the future till the end that hath no end. All the Embodiments of His Names wander in the wilderness of search, athirst and eager to discover His Essence, and all the Manifestations of His Attributes implore Him, from the Sinai of Holiness, to unravel His mystery.[3]

To every discerning and illumined heart it is evident that God, the unknowable Essence, the divine Being, is immensely exalted beyond every human attribute, such as corporeal existence, ascent and descent, egress and regress. Far be it from His glory that human tongue should adequately recount His praise, or that human heart comprehend His fathomless mystery. He is and hath ever been veiled in the ancient eternity of His Essence, and will remain in His Reality everlastingly hidden from the sight of men.[4]

The conceptions of the devoutest of mystics, the attainments of the most accomplished amongst men, the highest praise which human tongue or pen can render are all the product of man's finite mind and are conditioned by its limitations. Ten thousand Prophets, each a Moses, are thunderstruck upon the Sinai of their search at His forbidding voice, "Thou shalt never behold Me!"; whilst a myriad Messengers, each as great as Jesus, stand dismayed upon their heavenly thrones by the interdiction, "Mine Essence thou shalt never apprehend!" From time immemorial He hath been veiled in the ineffable sanctity of His exalted Self, and will everlastingly continue to be wrapt in the impenetrable mystery of His unknowable Essence. Every attempt to attain to an understanding of His inaccessible Reality hath ended in complete bewilderment, and every effort to approach His exalted Self and envisage His Essence hath resulted in hopelessness and failure.[5]

I swear by Thy Beauty, O King of eternity Who sittest on Thy most glorious Throne! He Who is the Day-Spring of Thy signs and the Revealer of Thy clear tokens hath, notwithstanding the immensity of His wisdom and the loftiness of His knowledge, confessed His powerlessness to comprehend the least of Thine utterances, in their relation to Thy most exalted Pen,—how much more is He incapable of apprehending the nature of Thine all-glorious Self and of Thy most august Essence![6]

Unity of God

God testifieth to the unity of His Godhood and to the singleness of His own Being. On the throne of eternity, from the inaccessible heights of His station, His tongue proclaimeth that there is none other God but Him. He Himself, independently of all else, hath ever been a witness unto His own oneness, the revealer of His own nature, the glorifier of His own essence. He, verily, is the All-Powerful, the Almighty, the Beauteous.[7]

How wondrous is the unity of the Living, the Ever-Abiding God, a unity which is exalted above all limitations, that transcendeth the comprehension of all created things! He hath, from everlasting, dwelt in His inaccessible habitation of holiness and glory, and will unto everlasting continue to be enthroned upon the heights of His independent sovereignty and grandeur. How lofty hath been His incorruptible Essence, how completely independent of the knowledge of all created things, and how immensely exalted will it remain above the praise of all the inhabitants of the heavens and the earth![8]

The one true God hath everlastingly existed, and will everlastingly continue to exist. His creation, likewise, hath had no beginning, and will have no end. All that is created, however, is preceded by a cause. This fact, in itself, establisheth, beyond the shadow of a doubt, the unity of the Creator.[9]

Regard thou the one true God as One Who is apart from, and immeasurably exalted above, all created things. The whole universe reflecteth His glory, while He is Himself independent of, and transcendeth His creatures. This is the true meaning of Divine unity. He Who is the Eternal Truth is the one Power Who exerciseth undisputed sovereignty over the world of being, Whose image is reflected in the mirror of the entire creation. All existence is dependent upon Him, and from Him is derived the source of the sustenance of all things. This is what is meant by Divine unity; this is its fundamental principle.[10]

He is a true believer in Divine unity who, far from confusing duality with oneness, refuseth to allow any notion of multiplicity to becloud his conception of the singleness of God, who will regard the Divine Being as One Who, by His very nature, transcendeth the limitations of numbers.[11]

And now concerning thy reference to the existence of two Gods. Beware, beware, lest thou be led to join partners with the Lord, thy God. He is, and hath from everlasting been, one and alone, without peer or equal, eternal in the past, eternal in the future, detached from all things, ever-abiding, unchangeable, and self-subsisting. He hath assigned no associate unto Himself in His Kingdom, no counsellor to counsel Him, none to compare unto Him, none to rival His glory. To this every atom of the universe beareth witness, and beyond it the inmates of the realms on high, they that occupy the most exalted seats, and whose names are remembered before the Throne of Glory.

Bear thou witness in thine inmost heart unto this testimony which God hath Himself and for Himself pronounced, that there is none other God but Him, that all else besides Him have been created by His behest, have been fashioned by His leave, are subject to His law, are as a thing forgotten when compared to the glorious evidences of His oneness, and are as nothing when brought face to face with the mighty revelations of His unity.

He, in truth, hath, throughout eternity, been one in His Essence, one in His attributes, one in His works. Any and every comparison is applicable only to His creatures, and all conceptions of association are conceptions that belong solely to those that serve Him. Immeasurably exalted is His Essence above the descriptions of His creatures. He, alone, occupieth the Seat of transcendent majesty, of supreme and inaccessible glory. The birds of men's hearts, however high they soar, can never hope to attain the heights of His unknowable Essence.[12]

God: The Creator

As to thy question concerning the origin of creation. Know
assuredly that God's creation hath existed from eternity, and will
continue to exist forever. Its beginning hath had no beginning,
and its end knoweth no end. His name, the Creator, presupposeth
a creation, even as His title, the Lord of Men, must involve the
existence of a servant.[13]

All praise to the unity of God, and all honor to Him, the
sovereign Lord, the incomparable and all-glorious Ruler of the
universe, Who, out of utter nothingness, hath created the reality
of all things, Who, from naught, hath brought into being the most
refined and subtle elements of His creation, and Who, rescuing
His creatures from the abasement of remoteness and the perils
of ultimate extinction, hath received them into His kingdom of
incorruptible glory. Nothing short of His all-encompassing grace,
His all-pervading mercy, could have possibly achieved it.[14]

A drop of the billowing ocean of His endless mercy hath
adorned all creation with the ornament of existence, and a breath
wafted from His peerless Paradise hath invested all beings with the
robe of His sanctity and glory. A sprinkling from the unfathomed
deep of His sovereign and all-pervasive Will hath, out of utter
nothingness, called into being a creation which is infinite in its
range and deathless in its duration. The wonders of His bounty
can never cease, and the stream of His merciful grace can never be
arrested. The process of His creation hath had no beginning, and
can have no end.[15]

So perfect and comprehensive is His creation that no mind
nor heart, however keen or pure, can ever grasp the nature of
the most insignificant of His creatures; much less fathom the
mystery of Him Who is the Day Star of Truth, Who is the invisible
and unknowable Essence.[16]

As to thy question concerning the worlds of God. Know thou of a truth that the worlds of God are countless in their number, and infinite in their range. None can reckon or comprehend them except God, the All-Knowing, the All-Wise...Verily I say, the creation of God embraceth worlds besides this world, and creatures apart from these creatures. In each of these worlds He hath ordained things which none can search except Himself, the All-Searching, the All-Wise.[17]

As regards thine assertions about the beginning of creation, this is a matter on which conceptions vary by reason of the divergences in men's thoughts and opinions. Wert thou to assert that it hath ever existed and shall continue to exist, it would be true; or wert thou to affirm the same concept as is mentioned in the sacred Scriptures, no doubt would there be about it, for it hath been revealed by God, the Lord of the worlds. Indeed He was a hidden treasure. This is a station that can never be described nor even alluded to. And in the station of 'I did wish to make Myself known', God was, and His creation had ever existed beneath His shelter from the beginning that hath no beginning, apart from its being preceded by a Firstness which cannot be regarded as firstness and originated by a Cause inscrutable even unto all men of learning.[18]

Every thing must needs have an origin and every building a builder. Verily, the Word of God is the Cause which hath preceded the contingent world—a world which is adorned with the splendours of the Ancient of Days, yet is being renewed and regenerated at all times. Immeasurably exalted is the God of Wisdom Who hath raised this sublime structure.[19]

Say: Nature in its essence is the embodiment of My Name, the Maker, the Creator. Its manifestations are diversified by varying causes, and in this diversity there are signs for men of discernment. Nature is God's Will and is its expression in and through the contingent world. It is a dispensation of Providence ordained by the Ordainer, the All-Wise. Were anyone to affirm that it is the Will of God as manifested in the world of being, no one should question this assertion. It is endowed with a power whose reality men of learning fail to grasp. Indeed a man of insight can perceive naught therein save the effulgent splendour of Our Name, the Creator. Say: This is an existence which knoweth no decay, and Nature itself is lost in bewilderment before its revelations, its compelling evidences and its effulgent glory which have encompassed the universe [20]

And now, concerning thy question regarding the creation of man. Know thou that all men have been created in the nature made by God, the Guardian, the Self-Subsisting. Unto each one hath been prescribed a pre-ordained measure, as decreed in God's mighty and guarded Tablets. All that which ye potentially possess can, however, be manifested only as a result of your own volition.[21]

Know thou that, according to what thy Lord, the Lord of all men, hath decreed in His Book, the favors vouchsafed by Him unto mankind have been, and will ever remain, limitless in their range. First and foremost among these favors, which the Almighty hath conferred upon man, is the gift of understanding. His purpose in conferring such a gift is none other except to enable His creature to know and recognize the one true God—exalted be His glory. This gift giveth man the power to discern the truth in all things, leadeth him to that which is right, and helpeth him to discover the secrets of creation.[22]

He is supreme over His servants, and standeth over His creatures. In His hand is the source of authority and truth. He maketh men alive by His signs, and causeth them to die through His wrath. He shall not be asked of His doings and His might is equal unto all things. He is the Potent, the All-Subduing. He holdeth within His grasp the empire of all things, and on His right hand is fixed the Kingdom of His Revelation. His power, verily, embraceth the whole of creation. Victory and overlordship are His; all might and dominion are His; all glory and greatness are His. He, of a truth, is the All-Glorious, the Most Powerful, the Unconditioned.[23]

Word of God

O friend of mine! The Word of God is the king of words and its pervasive influence is incalculable. It hath ever dominated and will continue to dominate the realm of being. The Great Being saith: The Word is the master key for the whole world, inasmuch as through its potency the doors of the hearts of men, which in reality are the doors of heaven, are unlocked. No sooner had but a glimmer of its effulgent splendour shone forth upon the mirror of love than the blessed word 'I am the Best-Beloved' was reflected therein. It is an ocean inexhaustible in riches, comprehending all things. Every thing which can be perceived is but an emanation therefrom. High, immeasurably high is this sublime station, in whose shadow moveth the essence of loftiness and splendour, wrapt in praise and adoration. [24]

The entire creation hath been called into being through the Will of God, magnified be His glory, and peerless Adam hath been fashioned through the agency of His all-compelling Word, a Word which is the source, the wellspring, the repository, and the dawning-place of the intellect. From it all creation hath proceeded, and it is the channel of God's primal grace. None can grasp the reality of the origin of creation save God, exalted be His glory, Whose knowledge embraceth all things both before and after they come into being. Creation hath neither beginning nor end, and none hath ever unravelled its mystery. Its knowledge hath ever been, and shall remain, hidden and preserved with those Who are the Repositories of divine knowledge. [25]

Know thou, moreover, that the Word of God—exalted be His glory—is higher and far superior to that which the senses can perceive, for it is sanctified from any property or substance. It transcendeth the limitations of known elements and is exalted above all the essential and recognized substances. It became manifest without any syllable or sound and is none but the Command of God which pervadeth all created things. It hath never been withheld from the world of being. It is God's all-pervasive grace, from which all grace doth emanate. It is an entity far removed above all that hath been and shall be.[26]

Every word that proceedeth out of the mouth of God is endowed with such potency as can instill new life into every human frame, if ye be of them that comprehend this truth. All the wondrous works ye behold in this world have been manifested through the operation of His supreme and most exalted Will, His wondrous and inflexible Purpose. Through the mere revelation of the word "Fashioner," issuing forth from His lips and proclaiming His attribute to mankind, such power is released as can generate, through successive ages, all the manifold arts which the hands of man can produce. This, verily, is a certain truth. No sooner is this resplendent word uttered, than its animating energies, stirring within all created things, give birth to the means and instruments whereby such arts can be produced and perfected. All the wondrous achievements ye now witness are the direct consequences of the Revelation of this Name. In the days to come, ye will, verily, behold things of which ye have never heard before. Thus hath it been decreed in the Tablets of God, and none can comprehend it except them whose sight is sharp. In like manner, the moment the word expressing My attribute "The Omniscient" issueth forth from My mouth, every created thing will, according to its capacity and limitations, be invested with the power to unfold the knowledge of the most marvelous sciences, and will be empowered to manifest them in the course of time at the bidding of Him Who is the Almighty, the All-Knowing. Know thou of a certainty that the Revelation of every other Name is accompanied by a similar manifestation of Divine power.[27]

It hath been decreed by Us that the Word of God and all the potentialities thereof shall be manifested unto men in strict conformity with such conditions as have been foreordained by Him Who is the All-Knowing, the All-Wise. We have, moreover, ordained that its veil of concealment be none other except its own Self. Such indeed is Our Power to achieve Our Purpose. Should the

Word be allowed to release suddenly all the energies latent within it, no man could sustain the weight of so mighty a Revelation. Nay, all that is in heaven and on earth would flee in consternation before it.[28]

Praise be to the all-perceiving, the ever-abiding Lord Who, from a dewdrop out of the ocean of His grace, hath reared the firmament of existence, adorned it with the stars of knowledge, and admitted man into the lofty court of insight and understanding. This dewdrop, which is the Primal Word of God, is at times called the Water of Life, inasmuch as it quickeneth with the waters of knowledge them that have perished in the wilderness of ignorance. Again it is called the Primal Light, a light born of the Sun of divine knowledge, through whose effulgence the first stirrings of existence were made plain and manifest. Such manifestations are the expressions of the grace of Him Who is the Peerless, the All-Wise. He it is who knoweth and bestoweth all. He it is who transcendeth all that hath been said or heard. His knowledge will remain forever above the grasp of human vision and understanding and beyond the reach of human words and deeds. To the truth of this utterance existence itself and all that hath appeared therefrom bear eloquent testimony.

It is clear and evident, therefore, that the first bestowal of God is the Word, and its discoverer and recipient is the power of understanding. This Word is the foremost instructor in the school of existence and the revealer of Him Who is the Almighty. All that is seen is visible only through the light of its wisdom. All that is manifest is but a token of its knowledge. All names are but its name, and the beginning and end of all matters must needs depend upon it.[29]

Know assuredly that just as thou firmly believest that the Word of God, exalted be His glory, endureth for ever, thou must, likewise, believe with undoubting faith that its meaning can never be exhausted. They who are its appointed interpreters, they whose hearts are the repositories of its secrets, are, however, the only ones who can comprehend its manifold wisdom.[30]

Signs of God

Every created thing in the whole universe is but a door leading into His knowledge, a sign of His sovereignty, a revelation of His names, a symbol of His majesty, a token of His power, a means of admittance into His straight Path....[31]

In every age and cycle He hath, through the splendorous light shed by the Manifestations of His wondrous Essence, recreated all things, so that whatsoever reflecteth in the heavens and on the earth the signs of His glory may not be deprived of the outpourings of His mercy, nor despair of the showers of His favors. How all-encompassing are the wonders of His boundless grace! Behold how they have pervaded the whole of creation. Such is their virtue that not a single atom in the entire universe can be found which doth not declare the evidences of His might, which doth not glorify His holy Name, or is not expressive of the effulgent light of His unity.[32]

I am well aware, O my Lord, that I have been so carried away by the clear tokens of Thy loving-kindness, and so completely inebriated with the wine of Thine utterance, that whatever I behold I readily discover that it maketh Thee known unto me, and it remindeth me of Thy signs, and of Thy tokens, and of Thy testimonies. By Thy glory! Every time I lift up mine eyes unto Thy heaven, I call to mind Thy highness and Thy loftiness, and Thine incomparable glory and greatness; and every time I turn my gaze to Thine earth, I am made to recognize the evidences of Thy power and the tokens of Thy bounty. And when I behold the sea, I find that it speaketh to me of Thy majesty, and of the potency of Thy might, and of Thy sovereignty and Thy grandeur. And at whatever time I contemplate the mountains, I am led to discover the ensigns of Thy victory and the standards of Thine omnipotence.[33]

Know thou that every created thing is a sign of the revelation of God. Each, according to its capacity, is, and will ever remain, a token of the Almighty. Inasmuch as He, the sovereign Lord of all, hath willed to reveal His sovereignty in the kingdom of names and attributes, each and every created thing hath, through the act of the Divine Will, been made a sign of His glory. So pervasive and general is this revelation that nothing whatsoever in the whole universe can be discovered that doth not reflect His splendor. Under such conditions every consideration of proximity and remoteness is obliterated.... Were the Hand of Divine power to divest of this high endowment all created things, the entire universe would become desolate and void.[34]

From the exalted source, and out of the essence of His favor and bounty He hath entrusted every created thing with a sign of His knowledge, so that none of His creatures may be deprived of its share in expressing, each according to its capacity and rank, this knowledge. This sign is the mirror of His beauty in the world of creation.[35]

He hath endowed every soul with the capacity to recognize the signs of God. How could He, otherwise, have fulfilled His testimony unto men, if ye be of them that ponder His Cause in their hearts. He will never deal unjustly with any one, neither will He task a soul beyond its power. He, verily, is the Compassionate, the All-Merciful.[36]

Let no one imagine that by Our assertion that all created things are the signs of the revelation of God is meant that, God forbid, all men, be they good or evil, pious or infidel, are equal in the sight of God. Nor doth it imply that the Divine Being, magnified be His name and exalted be His glory, is, under any circumstances, comparable unto men, or can, in any way, be associated with His creatures. Such an error hath been committed by certain foolish ones who, after having ascended into the heavens of their idle fancies, have interpreted Divine Unity to mean that all created things are the signs of God, and that, consequently, there is no distinction whatsoever between them. Some have even outstripped them by maintaining that these signs are peers and partners of God Himself. Gracious God! He, verily, is one and indivisible; one in His essence, one in His attributes. Everything besides Him is as nothing when brought face to face with the resplendent revelation of but one of His names, with no more than the faintest intimation of His glory, how much less when confronted with His own Self! [37]

How great is Thy power! How exalted Thy sovereignty! How lofty Thy might! How excellent Thy majesty! How supreme is Thy grandeur, a grandeur which He Who is Thy Manifestation hath made known and wherewith Thou hast invested Him as a sign of Thy generosity and bountiful favor. I bear witness, O my God, that through Him Thy most resplendent signs have been uncovered, and Thy mercy hath encompassed the entire creation. But for Him, how could the Celestial Dove have uttered its songs or the Heavenly Nightingale, according to the decree of God, have warbled its melody? [38]

Love Between God and Mankind

O SON OF MAN! I loved thy creation, hence I created thee. Wherefore, do thou love Me, that I may name thy name and fill thy soul with the spirit of life.[39]

O SON OF MAN! Veiled in My immemorial being and in the ancient eternity of My essence, I knew My love for thee; therefore I created thee, have engraved on thee Mine image and revealed to thee My beauty.[40]

O SON OF BEING! Love Me, that I may love thee. If thou lovest Me not, My love can in no wise reach thee. Know this, O servant.[41]

O SON OF BEING! My love is My stronghold; he that entereth therein is safe and secure, and he that turneth away shall surely stray and perish.[42]

O SON OF MAN! If thou lovest Me, turn away from thyself; and if thou seekest My pleasure, regard not thine own; that thou mayest die in Me and I may eternally live in thee.[43]

O SON OF UTTERANCE! Thou art My stronghold; enter therein that thou mayest abide in safety. My love is in thee, know it, that thou mayest find Me near unto thee.[44]

O SON OF THE WONDROUS VISION! I have breathed within thee a breath of My own Spirit, that thou mayest be My lover. Why hast thou forsaken Me and sought a beloved other than Me?[45]

O SON OF SPIRIT! My claim on thee is great, it cannot be forgotten. My grace to thee is plenteous, it cannot be veiled. My love has made in thee its home, it cannot be concealed. My light is manifest to thee, it cannot be obscured.[46]

O SON OF MAN! My majesty is My gift to thee, and My grandeur the token of My mercy unto thee. That which beseemeth Me none shall understand, nor can anyone recount. Verily, I have preserved it in My hidden storehouses and in the treasuries of My command, as a sign of My loving-kindness unto My servants and My mercy unto My people.[47]

O CHILDREN OF THE DIVINE AND INVISIBLE ESSENCE! Ye shall be hindered from loving Me and souls shall be perturbed as they make mention of Me. For minds cannot grasp Me nor hearts contain Me.[48]

O SON OF JUSTICE! Whither can a lover go but to the land of his beloved? and what seeker findeth rest away from his heart's desire? To the true lover reunion is life, and separation is death. His breast is void of patience and his heart hath no peace. A myriad lives he would forsake to hasten to the abode of his beloved.[49]

O SON OF LOVE! Thou art but one step away from the glorious heights above and from the celestial tree of love. Take thou one pace and with the next advance into the immortal realm and enter the pavilion of eternity. Give ear then to that which hath been revealed by the pen of glory.[50]

O DWELLERS OF MY PARADISE! With the hands of loving-kindness I have planted in the holy garden of paradise the young tree of your love and friendship, and have watered it with the goodly showers of My tender grace; now that the hour of its fruiting is come, strive that it may be protected, and be not consumed with the flame of desire and passion.[51]

O CHILDREN OF NEGLIGENCE AND PASSION! Ye have suffered My enemy to enter My house and have cast out My friend, for ye have enshrined the love of another than Me in your hearts. Give ear to the sayings of the Friend and turn towards His paradise. Worldly friends, seeking their own good, appear to love one the other, whereas the true Friend hath loved and doth love you for your own sakes; indeed He hath suffered for your guidance countless afflictions. Be not disloyal to such a Friend, nay rather hasten unto Him. Such is the daystar of the word of truth and faithfulness, that hath dawned above the horizon of the pen of the Lord of all names. Open your ears that ye may hearken unto the word of God, the Help in peril, the Self-existent.[52]

O people of Bahá! Ye are the dawning-places of the love of God and the daysprings of His loving-kindness.[53]

For every one of you his paramount duty is to choose for himself that on which no other may infringe and none usurp from him. Such a thing and to this the Almighty is My witness, is the love of God, could ye but perceive it.[54]

That which beseemeth you is the love of God, and the love of Him Who is the Manifestation of His Essence, and the observance of whatsoever He chooseth to prescribe unto you, did ye but know it.[55]

The essence of love is for man to turn his heart to the Beloved One, and sever himself from all else but Him, and desire naught save that which is the desire of his Lord.[56]

O My servant, who hast sought the good-pleasure of God and clung to His love on the Day when all except a few who were endued with insight have broken away from Him! May God, through His grace, recompense thee with a generous, an incorruptible and everlasting reward, inasmuch as thou hast sought Him on the Day when eyes were blinded.[57]

Manifestations of God

Manifestations of God

The door of the knowledge of the Ancient of Days being thus closed in the face of all beings, the Source of infinite grace, according to His saying: "His grace hath transcended all things; My grace hath encompassed them all" hath caused those luminous Gems of Holiness to appear out of the realm of the spirit, in the noble form of the human temple, and be made manifest unto all men, that they may impart unto the world the mysteries of the unchangeable Being, and tell of the subtleties of His imperishable Essence. These sanctified Mirrors, these Day-springs of ancient glory are one and all the Exponents on earth of Him Who is the central Orb of the universe, its Essence and ultimate Purpose. From Him proceed their knowledge and power; from Him is derived their sovereignty. The beauty of their countenance is but a reflection of His image, and their revelation a sign of His deathless glory. They are the Treasuries of divine knowledge, and the Repositories of celestial wisdom. Through them is transmitted a grace that is infinite, and by them is revealed the light that can never fade....

These Tabernacles of holiness, these primal Mirrors which reflect the light of unfading glory, are but expressions of Him Who is the Invisible of the Invisibles. By the revelation of these gems of divine virtue all the names and attributes of God, such as knowledge and power, sovereignty and dominion, mercy and wisdom, glory, bounty and grace, are made manifest.[58]

And since there can be no tie of direct intercourse to bind the one true God with His creation, and no resemblance whatever can exist between the transient and the Eternal, the contingent and the Absolute, He hath ordained that in every age and dispensation a pure and stainless Soul be made manifest in the kingdoms of earth and heaven. Unto this subtle, this mysterious and ethereal Being He hath assigned a twofold nature; the physical, pertaining to the world of matter, and the spiritual, which is born of the substance of God Himself.[59]

From the foregoing passages and allusions it hath been made indubitably clear that in the kingdoms of earth and heaven there must needs be manifested a Being, an Essence Who shall act as a Manifestation and Vehicle for the transmission of the grace of the Divinity Itself, the Sovereign Lord of all. Through the Teachings of this Day Star of Truth every man will advance and develop until he attaineth the station at which he can manifest all the potential forces with which his inmost true self hath been endowed. It is for this very purpose that in every age and dispensation the Prophets of God and His chosen Ones have appeared amongst men, and have evinced such power as is born of God and such might as only the Eternal can reveal.[60]

These ancient Beings, though delivered from the womb of their mother, have in reality descended from the heaven of the will of God. Though they be dwelling on this earth, yet their true habitations are the retreats of glory in the realms above. Whilst walking amongst mortals, they soar in the heaven of the divine presence. Without feet they tread the path of the spirit, and without wings they rise unto the exalted heights of divine unity.[61]

From that which hath been said it becometh evident that all things, in their inmost reality, testify to the revelation of the names and attributes of God within them. Each according to its capacity, indicateth, and is expressive of, the knowledge of God. So potent and universal is this revelation, that it hath encompassed all things, visible and invisible. Thus hath He revealed: "Hath aught else save Thee a power of revelation which is not possessed by Thee, that it could have manifested Thee? Blind is the eye which doth not perceive Thee." Likewise, hath the eternal King spoken: "No thing have I perceived, except that I perceived God within it, God before it, or God after it." Also in the tradition of Kumayl it is written: "Behold, a light hath shone forth out of the Morn of eternity, and lo! its waves have penetrated the inmost reality of all men." Man, the noblest and most perfect of all created things, excelleth them all in the intensity of this revelation, and is a fuller expression of its glory. And of all men, the most accomplished, the most distinguished and the most excellent are the Manifestations of the Sun of Truth. Nay, all else besides these Manifestations, live by the operation of their Will, and move and have their being through the outpourings of their grace. "But for Thee, I would have not created the heavens." Nay, all in their holy presence fade into utter nothingness, and are a thing forgotten. Human tongue can never befittingly sing their praise, and human speech can never unfold their mystery.[62]

Station of the Manifestation

When I contemplate, O my God, the relationship that bindeth me to Thee, I am moved to proclaim to all created things "verily I am God"; and when I consider my own self, lo, I find it coarser than clay! [63]

Know verily that whenever this Youth turneth His eyes towards His own self, he findeth it the most insignificant of all creation. When He contemplates, however, the bright effulgences He hath been empowered to manifest, lo, that self is transfigured before Him into a sovereign Potency permeating the essence of all things visible and invisible. Glory be to Him Who, through the power of truth, hath sent down the Manifestation of His own Self and entrusted Him with His message unto all mankind.[64]

He hath, moreover, conferred upon Him a double station. The first station, which is related to His innermost reality, representeth Him as One Whose voice is the voice of God Himself. To this testifieth the tradition: "Manifold and mysterious is My relationship with God. I am He, Himself, and He is I, Myself, except that I am that I am, and He is that He is." And in like manner, the words: "Arise, O Muhammad, for lo, the Lover and the Beloved are joined together and made one in Thee." He similarly saith: "There is no distinction whatsoever between Thee and Them, except that They are Thy Servants." The second station is the human station, exemplified by the following verses: "I am but a man like you." "Say, praise be to my Lord! Am I more than a man, an apostle?" These Essences of Detachment, these resplendent Realities are the channels of God's all-pervasive grace. Led by the light of unfailing guidance, and invested with supreme sovereignty, They are commissioned to use the inspiration of Their words, the effusions of Their infallible grace and the sanctifying breeze of Their Revelation for the cleansing of every longing heart and receptive spirit from the dross and dust of earthly cares and limitations. Then, and only then, will the Trust of God, latent in the reality of man, emerge, as resplendent as the rising Orb of Divine Revelation, from behind the veil of concealment, and implant the ensign of its revealed glory upon the summits of men's hearts.[65]

Were any of the all-embracing Manifestations of God to declare: "I am God," He, verily, speaketh the truth, and no doubt attacheth thereto. For it hath been repeatedly demonstrated that through their Revelation, their attributes and names, the Revelation of God, His names and His attributes, are made manifest in the world...And were any of them to voice the utterance, "I am the Messenger of God," He, also, speaketh the truth, the indubitable truth...Viewed in this light, they are all but Messengers of that ideal King, that unchangeable Essence...And were they to say, "We are the Servants of God," this also is a manifest and indisputable fact. For they have been made manifest in the uttermost state of servitude, a servitude the like of which no man can possibly attain. Thus in moments in which these Essences of Being were deep immersed beneath the oceans of ancient and everlasting holiness, or when they soared to the loftiest summits of Divine mysteries, they claimed their utterances to be the Voice of Divinity, the Call of God Himself...

By virtue of this station they have claimed for themselves the Voice of Divinity and the like, whilst by virtue of their station of Messengership, they have declared themselves the Messengers of God. In every instance they have voiced an utterance that would conform to the requirements of the occasion, and have ascribed all these declarations to Themselves, declarations ranging from the realm of Divine Revelation to the realm of creation, and from the domain of Divinity even unto the domain of earthly existence. Thus it is that whatsoever be their utterance, whether it pertain to the realm of Divinity, Lordship, Prophethood, Messengership, Guardianship, Apostleship, or Servitude, all is true, beyond the shadow of a doubt.[66]

The Bearers of the Trust of God are made manifest unto the peoples of the earth as the Exponents of a new Cause and the Revealers of a new Message. Inasmuch as these Birds of the celestial Throne are all sent down from the heaven of the Will of God, and as they all arise to proclaim His irresistible Faith, they, therefore, are regarded as one soul and the same person. For they all drink from the one Cup of the love of God, and all partake of the fruit of the same Tree of Oneness.

These Manifestations of God have each a twofold station. One is the station of pure abstraction and essential unity. In this respect, if thou callest them all by one name, and dost ascribe to them the same attributes, thou hast not erred from the truth. Even as He hath revealed: "No distinction do We make between any of His Messengers." For they, one and all, summon the people of the earth to acknowledge the unity of God, and herald unto them the Kawthar of an infinite grace and bounty. They are all invested with the robe of prophethood, and are honored with the mantle of glory...

It is clear and evident to thee that all the Prophets are the Temples of the Cause of God, Who have appeared clothed in divers attire. If thou wilt observe with discriminating eyes, thou wilt behold Them all abiding in the same tabernacle, soaring in the same heaven, seated upon the same throne, uttering the same speech, and proclaiming the same Faith. Such is the unity of those Essences of Being, those Luminaries of infinite and immeasurable splendor! Wherefore, should one of these Manifestations of Holiness proclaim saying: "I am the return of all the Prophets," He, verily, speaketh the truth. In like manner, in every subsequent Revelation, the return of the former Revelation is a fact, the truth of which is firmly established....

The other station is the station of distinction, and pertaineth to the world of creation, and to the limitations thereof. In this respect, each Manifestation of God hath a distinct individuality, a definitely prescribed mission, a predestined revelation, and specially designated limitations. Each one of them is known by a different name, is characterized by a special attribute, fulfils a definite mission, and is entrusted with a particular Revelation. Even as He saith: "Some of the Apostles We have caused to excel the others. To some God hath spoken, some He hath raised and exalted. And to Jesus, Son of Mary, We gave manifest signs, and We strengthened Him with the Holy Spirit."

It is because of this difference in their station and mission that the words and utterances flowing from these Well Springs of Divine knowledge appear to diverge and differ. Otherwise, in the eyes of them that are initiated into the mysteries of Divine wisdom, all their utterances are, in reality, but the expressions of one Truth. As most of the people have failed to appreciate those stations to which We have referred, they, therefore, feel perplexed and dismayed at the varying utterances pronounced by Manifestations that are essentially one and the same.[67]

Divine Presence

In all the Divine Books the promise of the Divine Presence hath been explicitly recorded. By this Presence is meant the Presence of Him Who is the Dayspring of the signs, and the Dawning-Place of the clear tokens, and the Manifestation of the Excellent Names, and the Source of the attributes, of the true God, exalted be His glory. God in His Essence and in His own Self hath ever been unseen, inaccessible, and unknowable. By Presence, therefore, is meant the Presence of the One Who is His Vicegerent amongst men. He, moreover, hath never had, nor hath He, any peer or likeness. For were He to have any peer or likeness, how could it then be demonstrated that His being is exalted above, and His essence sanctified from, all comparison and likeness? [68]

The knowledge of Him, Who is the Origin of all things, and attainment unto Him, are impossible save through knowledge of, and attainment unto, these luminous Beings who proceed from the Sun of Truth. By attaining, therefore, to the presence of these holy Luminaries, the "Presence of God" Himself is attained. From their knowledge, the knowledge of God is revealed, and from the light of their countenance, the splendour of the Face of God is made manifest. Through the manifold attributes of these Essences of Detachment, Who are both the first and the last, the seen and the hidden, it is made evident that He Who is the Sun of Truth is "the First and the Last, the Seen, and the Hidden." [69] Likewise the other lofty names and exalted attributes of God. Therefore, whosoever, and in whatever Dispensation, hath recognized and attained unto the presence of these glorious, these resplendent and most excellent Luminaries, hath verily attained unto the "Presence of God" Himself, and entered the city of eternal and immortal life. Attainment unto such presence is possible only in the Day of Resurrection, which is the Day of the rise of God Himself through His all-embracing Revelation. [70]

Say: Naught is seen in My temple but the Temple of God, and in My beauty but His Beauty, and in My being but His Being, and in My self but His Self, and in My movement but His Movement, and in My acquiescence but His Acquiescence, and in My pen but His Pen, the Mighty, the All-Praised. There hath not been in My soul but the Truth, and in Myself naught could be seen but God.[71]

Unity of God's Religion and His Prophets

The Purpose of the one true God, exalted be His glory, in revealing Himself unto men is to lay bare those gems that lie hidden within the mine of their true and inmost selves. That the divers communions of the earth, and the manifold systems of religious belief, should never be allowed to foster the feelings of animosity among men, is, in this Day, of the essence of the Faith of God and His Religion. These principles and laws, these firmly-established and mighty systems, have proceeded from one Source, and are the rays of one Light. That they differ one from another is to be attributed to the varying requirements of the ages in which they were promulgated.[72]

In thine esteemed letter thou hadst inquired which of the Prophets of God should be regarded as superior to others. Know thou assuredly that the essence of all the Prophets of God is one and the same. Their unity is absolute. God, the Creator, saith: There is no distinction whatsoever among the Bearers of My Message. They all have but one purpose; their secret is the same secret. To prefer one in honor to another, to exalt certain ones above the rest, is in no wise to be permitted. Every true Prophet hath regarded His Message as fundamentally the same as the Revelation of every other Prophet gone before Him...

The measure of the revelation of the Prophets of God in this world, however, must differ. Each and every one of them hath been the Bearer of a distinct Message, and hath been commissioned to reveal Himself through specific acts. It is for this reason that they appear to vary in their greatness.[73]

Beware, O believers in the Unity of God, lest ye be tempted to make any distinction between any of the Manifestations of His Cause, or to discriminate against the signs that have accompanied and proclaimed their Revelation. This indeed is the true meaning of Divine Unity, if ye be of them that apprehend and believe this truth. Be ye assured, moreover, that the works and acts of each and every one of these Manifestations of God, nay whatever pertaineth unto them, and whatsoever they may manifest in the future, are all ordained by God, and are a reflection of His Will and Purpose.[74]

God's Purpose in Sending His Messengers

He hath sent forth His Messengers, and sent down His Books, that they may announce unto His creatures the Straight Path.[75]

God's purpose in sending His Prophets unto men is twofold. The first is to liberate the children of men from the darkness of ignorance, and guide them to the light of true understanding. The second is to ensure the peace and tranquillity of mankind, and provide all the means by which they can be established.[76]

Moreover He hath in every age and cycle, in conformity with His transcendent wisdom, sent forth a divine Messenger to revive the dispirited and despondent souls with the living waters of His utterance, One Who is indeed the Expounder, the true Interpreter, inasmuch as man is unable to comprehend that which hath streamed forth from the Pen of Glory and is recorded in His heavenly Books. Men at all times and under all conditions stand in need of one to exhort them, guide them and to instruct and teach them. Therefore He hath sent forth His Messengers, His Prophets and chosen ones that they might acquaint the people with the divine purpose underlying the revelation of Books and the raising up of Messengers, and that everyone may become aware of the trust of God which is latent in the reality of every soul.[77]

The Prophets and Messengers of God have been sent down for the sole purpose of guiding mankind to the straight Path of Truth. The purpose underlying Their revelation hath been to educate all men, that they may, at the hour of death, ascend, in the utmost purity and sanctity and with absolute detachment, to the throne of the Most High.[78]

God hath sent down His Messengers to succeed to Moses and Jesus, and He will continue to do so till 'the end that hath no end'; so that His grace may, from the heaven of Divine bounty, be continually vouchsafed to mankind.[79]

Divine Physicians

The Prophets of God should be regarded as physicians whose task is to foster the well-being of the world and its peoples, that, through the spirit of oneness, they may heal the sickness of a divided humanity. To none is given the right to question their words or disparage their conduct, for they are the only ones who can claim to have understood the patient and to have correctly diagnosed its ailments. No man, however acute his perception, can ever hope to reach the heights which the wisdom and understanding of the Divine Physician have attained. Little wonder, then, if the treatment prescribed by the physician in this day should not be found to be identical with that which he prescribed before. How could it be otherwise when the ills affecting the sufferer necessitate at every stage of his sickness a special remedy? In like manner, every time the Prophets of God have illumined the world with the resplendent radiance of the Day Star of Divine knowledge, they have invariably summoned its peoples to embrace the light of God through such means as best befitted the exigencies of the age in which they appeared. They were thus able to scatter the darkness of ignorance, and to shed upon the world the glory of their own knowledge. It is towards the inmost essence of these Prophets, therefore, that the eye of every man of discernment must be directed, inasmuch as their one and only purpose hath always been to guide the erring, and give peace to the afflicted.... These are not days of prosperity and triumph. The whole of mankind is in the grip of manifold ills. Strive, therefore, to save its life through the wholesome medicine which the almighty hand of the unerring Physician hath prepared.[80]

The All-Knowing Physician hath His finger on the pulse of mankind. He perceiveth the disease, and prescribeth, in His unerring wisdom, the remedy. Every age hath its own problem, and every soul its particular aspiration. The remedy the world needeth in its present-day afflictions can never be the same as that which a subsequent age may require. Be anxiously concerned with the needs of the age ye live in, and centre your deliberations on its exigencies and requirements.

We can well perceive how the whole human race is encompassed with great, with incalculable afflictions. We see it languishing on its bed of sickness, sore-tried and disillusioned. They that are intoxicated by self-conceit have interposed themselves between it and the Divine and infallible Physician. Witness how they have entangled all men, themselves included, in the mesh of their devices. They can neither discover the cause of the disease, nor have they any knowledge of the remedy. They have conceived the straight to be crooked, and have imagined their friend an enemy.[81]

Witness how the world is being afflicted with a fresh calamity every day. Its tribulation is continually deepening. From the moment the Súriy-i-Ra'ís (Tablet to Ra'ís) was revealed until the present day, neither hath the world been tranquillized, nor have the hearts of its peoples been at rest. At one time it hath been agitated by contentions and disputes, at another it hath been convulsed by wars, and fallen a victim to inveterate diseases. Its sickness is approaching the stage of utter hopelessness, inasmuch as the true Physician is debarred from administering the remedy, whilst unskilled practitioners are regarded with favor, and are accorded full freedom to act.... The dust of sedition hath clouded the hearts of men, and blinded their eyes. Erelong, they will perceive the consequences of what their hands have wrought in the Day of God. Thus warneth you He Who is the All-Informed, as bidden by One Who is the Most Powerful, the Almighty.[82]

Divine Revelation

That which is preeminent above all other gifts, is incorruptible in nature, and pertaineth to God Himself, is the gift of Divine Revelation. Every bounty conferred by the Creator upon man, be it material or spiritual, is subservient unto this. It is, in its essence, and will ever so remain, the Bread which cometh down from Heaven. It is God's supreme testimony, the clearest evidence of His truth, the sign of His consummate bounty, the token of His all-encompassing mercy, the proof of His most loving providence, the symbol of His most perfect grace. He hath, indeed, partaken of this highest gift of God who hath recognized His Manifestation in this Day.

Render thanks unto thy Lord for having vouchsafed unto thee so great a bounty. Lift up thy voice and say: All praise be to Thee, O Thou, the Desire of every understanding heart! [83]

That the heart is the throne, in which the Revelation of God the All-Merciful is centered, is attested by the holy utterances which We have formerly revealed. Among them is this saying: "Earth and heaven cannot contain Me; what can alone contain Me is the heart of him that believeth in Me, and is faithful to My Cause."[84]

Incline your hearts, O people of God, unto the counsels of your true, your incomparable Friend. The Word of God may be likened unto a sapling, whose roots have been implanted in the hearts of men. It is incumbent upon you to foster its growth through the living waters of wisdom, of sanctified and holy words, so that its root may become firmly fixed and its branches may spread out as high as the heavens and beyond.[85]

Progressive Revelation

Know of a certainty that in every Dispensation the light of Divine Revelation hath been vouchsafed unto men in direct proportion to their spiritual capacity. Consider the sun. How feeble its rays the moment it appeareth above the horizon. How gradually its warmth and potency increase as it approacheth its zenith, enabling meanwhile all created things to adapt themselves to the growing intensity of its light. How steadily it declineth until it reacheth its setting point. Were it, all of a sudden, to manifest the energies latent within it, it would, no doubt, cause injury to all created things.... In like manner, if the Sun of Truth were suddenly to reveal, at the earliest stages of its manifestation, the full measure of the potencies which the providence of the Almighty hath bestowed upon it, the earth of human understanding would waste away and be consumed; for men's hearts would neither sustain the intensity of its revelation, nor be able to mirror forth the radiance of its light. Dismayed and overpowered, they would cease to exist.[86]

And now concerning thy question regarding the nature of religion. Know thou that they who are truly wise have likened the world unto the human temple. As the body of man needeth a garment to clothe it, so the body of mankind must needs be adorned with the mantle of justice and wisdom. Its robe is the Revelation vouchsafed unto it by God. Whenever this robe hath fulfilled its purpose, the Almighty will assuredly renew it. For every age requireth a fresh measure of the light of God. Every Divine Revelation hath been sent down in a manner that befitted the circumstances of the age in which it hath appeared.[87]

God witnesseth that there is no God but Him, the Gracious, the Best-Beloved. All grace and bounty are His. To whomsoever He will He giveth whatsoever is His wish. He, verily, is the All-Powerful, the Almighty, the Help in Peril, the Self-Subsisting. We, verily, believe in Him Who, in the person of the Báb, hath been sent down by the Will of the one true God, the King of Kings, the

All-Praised. We, moreover, swear fealty to the One Who, in the time of Mustag̲h̲áth, is destined to be made manifest, as well as to those Who shall come after Him till the end that hath no end. We recognize in the manifestation of each one of them, whether outwardly or inwardly, the manifestation of none but God Himself, if ye be of those that comprehend. Every one of them is a mirror of God, reflecting naught else but His Self, His Beauty, His Might and Glory, if ye will understand. All else besides them are to be regarded as mirrors capable of reflecting the glory of these Manifestations Who are themselves the Primary Mirrors of the Divine Being, if ye be not devoid of understanding. No one hath ever escaped them, neither are they to be hindered from achieving their purpose. These Mirrors will everlastingly succeed each other, and will continue to reflect the light of the Ancient of Days. They that reflect their glory will, in like manner, continue to exist for evermore, for the Grace of God can never cease from flowing. This is a truth that none can disprove.

Contemplate with thine inward eye the chain of successive Revelations that hath linked the Manifestation of Adam with that of the Báb. I testify before God that each one of these Manifestations hath been sent down through the operation of the Divine Will and Purpose, that each hath been the bearer of a specific Message, that each hath been entrusted with a divinely-revealed Book and been commissioned to unravel the mysteries of a mighty Tablet. The measure of the Revelation with which every one of them hath been identified had been definitely fore-ordained. This, verily, is a token of Our favor unto them, if ye be of those that comprehend this truth.[88]

Wherefore, O my friend, it behooveth Us to exert the highest endeavour to attain unto that City, and, by the grace of God and His loving-kindness, rend asunder the "veils of glory"; so that, with inflexible steadfastness, we may sacrifice our drooping souls in the path of the New Beloved. We should with tearful eyes, fervently and repeatedly, implore Him to grant us the favour of that grace.

That city is none other than the Word of God revealed in every age and dispensation. In the days of Moses it was the Pentateuch; in the days of Jesus the Gospel; in the days of Muhammad the Messenger of God the Qur'án; in this day the Bayán; and in the dispensation of Him Whom God will make manifest His own Book, the Book unto which all the Books of former Dispensations must needs be referred, the Book which standeth amongst them all transcendent and supreme.[89]

Language of the Messengers

It is evident unto thee that the Birds of Heaven and Doves of Eternity speak a twofold language. One language, the outward language, is devoid of allusions, is unconcealed and unveiled; that it may be a guiding lamp and a beaconing light whereby wayfarers may attain the heights of holiness, and seekers may advance into the realm of eternal reunion. Such are the unveiled traditions and the evident verses already mentioned. The other language is veiled and concealed, so that whatever lieth hidden in the heart of the malevolent may be made manifest and their innermost being be disclosed. Thus hath Sadiq, son of Muhammad, spoken: "God verily will test them and sift them." This is the divine standard, this is the Touchstone of God, wherewith He proveth His servants. None apprehendeth the meaning of these utterances except them whose hearts are assured, whose souls have found favour with God, and whose minds are detached from all else but Him. In such utterances, the literal meaning, as generally understood by the people, is not what hath been intended.[90]

Proofs of Prophethood

The first and foremost testimony establishing His truth is His own Self. Next to this testimony is His Revelation. For whoso faileth to recognize either the one or the other He hath established the words He hath revealed as proof of His reality and truth. This is, verily, an evidence of His tender mercy unto men.[91]

He Who is everlastingly hidden from the eyes of men can never be known except through His Manifestation, and His Manifestation can adduce no greater proof of the truth of His Mission than the proof of His own Person.[92]

It hath therefore become manifest and evident that within the tabernacles of these Prophets and chosen Ones of God the light of His infinite names and exalted attributes hath been reflected, even though the light of some of these attributes may or may not be outwardly revealed from these luminous Temples to the eyes of men. That a certain attribute of God hath not been outwardly manifested by these Essences of Detachment doth in no wise imply that they Who are the Daysprings of God's attributes and the Treasuries of His holy names did not actually possess it. Therefore, these illuminated Souls, these beauteous Countenances have, each and every one of them, been endowed with all the attributes of God, such as sovereignty, dominion, and the like, even though to outward seeming they be shorn of all earthly majesty.[93]

Twin Duties Prescribed by God

The first duty prescribed by God for His servants is the recognition of Him Who is the Dayspring of His Revelation and the Fountain of His laws, Who representeth the Godhead in both the Kingdom of His Cause and the world of creation. Whoso achieveth this duty hath attained unto all good; and whoso is deprived thereof hath gone astray, though he be the author of every righteous deed. It behoveth every one who reacheth this most sublime station, this summit of transcendent glory, to observe every ordinance of Him Who is the Desire of the world. These twin duties are inseparable. Neither is acceptable without the other. Thus hath it been decreed by Him Who is the Source of Divine inspiration.[94]

Rejection and Persecution of God's Manifestations

Consider the past. How many, both high and low, have, at all times, yearningly awaited the advent of the Manifestations of God in the sanctified persons of His chosen Ones. How often have they expected His coming, how frequently have they prayed that the breeze of divine mercy might blow, and the promised Beauty step forth from behind the veil of concealment, and be made manifest to all the world. And whensoever the portals of grace did open, and the clouds of divine bounty did rain upon mankind, and the light of the Unseen did shine above the horizon of celestial might, they all denied Him, and turned away from His face, the face of God Himself.[95]

It is evident that the changes brought about in every Dispensation constitute the dark clouds that intervene between the eye of man's understanding and the divine Luminary which shineth forth from the dayspring of the divine Essence. Consider how men for generations have been blindly imitating their fathers, and have been trained according to such ways and manners as have been laid down by the dictates of their Faith. Were these men, therefore, to discover suddenly that a Man, Who hath been living in their midst, Who, with respect to every human limitation, hath been their equal, had risen to abolish every established principle imposed by their Faith—principles by which for centuries they have been disciplined, and every opposer and denier of which they have come to regard as infidel, profligate and wicked,—they would of a certainty be veiled and hindered from acknowledging His truth.[96]

Consider the former generations. Witness how every time the Day Star of Divine bounty hath shed the light of His Revelation upon the world, the people of His Day have arisen against Him, and repudiated His truth. They who were regarded as the leaders of men have invariably striven to hinder their followers from turning unto Him Who is the Ocean of God's limitless bounty.

Behold how the people, as a result of the verdict pronounced by the divines of His age, have cast Abraham, the Friend of God, into fire; how Moses, He Who held converse with the Almighty, was denounced as liar and slanderer. Reflect how Jesus, the Spirit of God, was, notwithstanding His extreme meekness and perfect tender-heartedness, treated by His enemies. So fierce was the opposition which He, the Essence of Being and Lord of the visible and invisible, had to face, that He had nowhere to lay His head. He wandered continually from place to place, deprived of a permanent abode. Ponder that which befell Muhammad, the Seal of the Prophets, may the life of all else be a sacrifice unto Him. How severe the afflictions which the leaders of the Jewish people and of the idol-worshipers caused to rain upon Him, Who is the sovereign Lord of all, in consequence of His proclamation of the unity of God and of the truth of His Message! By the righteousness of My Cause! My Pen groaneth, and all created things weep with a great weeping, as a result of the woes He suffered at the hands of them that have broken the Covenant of God, violated His Testament, rejected His proofs, and disputed His signs. Thus recount We unto thee the tale of that which happened in days past, haply thou mayest comprehend.

Thou hast known how grievously the Prophets of God, His Messengers and Chosen Ones, have been afflicted. Meditate a while on the motive and reason which have been responsible for such a persecution. At no time, in no Dispensation, have the Prophets of God escaped the blasphemy of their enemies, the cruelty of their oppressors, the denunciation of the learned of their age, who appeared in the guise of uprightness and piety. Day and night they passed through such agonies as none can ever measure, except the knowledge of the one true God, exalted be His glory.[97]

Praise be to Thee, O Lord My God, for the wondrous revelations of Thy inscrutable decree and the manifold woes and trials Thou hast destined for Myself. At one time Thou didst deliver Me into the hands of Nimrod; at another Thou hast allowed Pharaoh's rod to persecute Me. Thou, alone, canst estimate, through Thine all-encompassing knowledge and the operation of Thy Will, the incalculable afflictions I have suffered at their hands. Again Thou didst cast Me into the prison-cell of the ungodly, for no reason except that I was moved to whisper into the ears of the well-favored denizens of Thy Kingdom an intimation of the vision with which Thou hadst, through Thy knowledge, inspired Me, and revealed to Me its meaning through the potency of Thy might. And again Thou didst decree that I be beheaded by the sword of the infidel. Again I was crucified for having unveiled to men's eyes the hidden gems of Thy glorious unity, for having revealed to them the wondrous signs of Thy sovereign and everlasting power. How bitter the humiliations heaped upon Me, in a subsequent age, on the plain of Karbila! How lonely did I feel amidst Thy people! To what a state of helplessness I was reduced in that land! Unsatisfied with such indignities, My persecutors decapitated Me, and, carrying aloft My head from land to land paraded it before the gaze of the unbelieving multitude, and deposited it on the seats of the perverse and faithless. In a later age, I was suspended, and My breast was made a target to the darts of the malicious cruelty of My foes. My limbs were riddled with bullets, and My body was torn asunder. Finally, behold how, in this Day, My treacherous enemies have leagued themselves against Me, and are continually plotting to instill the venom of hate and malice into the souls of Thy servants. With all their might they are scheming to accomplish their purpose.... Grievous as is My plight, O God, My Well-Beloved, I render thanks unto Thee, and My Spirit is grateful for whatsoever hath befallen me in the path of Thy good-pleasure. I am well pleased with that which Thou didst ordain for Me, and welcome, however calamitous, the pains and sorrows I am made to suffer.[98]

Forerunners of Manifestations

From all that We have stated it hath become clear and manifest that before the revelation of each of the Mirrors reflecting the divine Essence, the signs heralding their advent must needs be revealed in the visible heaven as well as in the invisible, wherein is the seat of the sun of knowledge, of the moon of wisdom, and of the stars of understanding and utterance. The sign of the invisible heaven must needs be revealed in the person of that perfect man who, before each Manifestation appeareth, educateth, and prepareth the souls of men for the advent of the divine Luminary, the Light of the unity of God amongst men.[99]

Prophets Before Adam

And now regarding thy question, "How is it that no records are to be found concerning the Prophets that have preceded Adam, the Father of Mankind, or of the kings that lived in the days of those Prophets?" Know thou that the absence of any reference to them is no proof that they did not actually exist. That no records concerning them are now available, should be attributed to their extreme remoteness, as well as to the vast changes which the earth hath undergone since their time.

Moreover such forms and modes of writing as are now current amongst men were unknown to the generations that were before Adam. There was even a time when men were wholly ignorant of the art of writing, and had adopted a system entirely different from the one which they now use.[100]

Abraham

That which thou hast heard concerning Abraham, the Friend of the All-Merciful, is the truth, and no doubt is there about it. The Voice of God commanded Him to offer up Ishmael as a sacrifice, so that His steadfastness in the Faith of God and His detachment from all else but Him may be demonstrated unto men. The purpose of God, moreover, was to sacrifice him as a ransom for the sins and iniquities of all the peoples of the earth. This same honor, Jesus, the Son of Mary, besought the one true God, exalted be His name and glory, to confer upon Him. For the same reason was Husayn offered up as a sacrifice by Muhammad, the Apostle of God.[101]

Later, the beauty of the countenance of the Friend of God[102] appeared from behind the veil, and another standard of divine guidance was hoisted. He invited the people of the earth to the light of righteousness. The more passionately He exhorted them, the fiercer waxed the envy and waywardness of the people, except those who wholly detached themselves from all save God, and ascended on the wings of certainty to the station which God hath exalted beyond the comprehension of men. It is well known what a host of enemies besieged Him, until at last the fires of envy and rebellion were kindled against Him. And after the episode of the fire came to pass, He, the lamp of God amongst men, was, as recorded in all books and chronicles, expelled from His city.[103]

Moses

And when His day was ended, there came the turn of Moses. Armed with the rod of celestial dominion, adorned with the white hand of divine knowledge, and proceeding from the Paran of the love of God, and wielding the serpent of power and everlasting majesty, He shone forth from the Sinai of light upon the world. He summoned all the peoples and kindreds of the earth to the kingdom of eternity, and invited them to partake of the fruit of the tree of faithfulness. Surely you are aware of the fierce opposition of Pharaoh and his people, and of the stones of idle fancy which the hands of infidels cast upon that blessed Tree. So much so that Pharaoh and his people finally arose and exerted their utmost endeavor to extinguish with the waters of falsehood and denial the fire of that sacred Tree, oblivious of the truth that no earthly water can quench the flame of divine wisdom, nor mortal blasts extinguish the lamp of everlasting dominion. Nay, rather, such water cannot but intensify the burning of the flame, and such blasts cannot but ensure the preservation of the lamp, were ye to observe with the eye of discernment, and walk in the way of God's holy will and pleasure.[104]

Call thou to mind the days when He Who conversed with God tended, in the wilderness, the sheep of Jethro, His father-in-law. He hearkened unto the Voice of the Lord of mankind coming from the Burning Bush which had been raised above the Holy Land, exclaiming, 'O Moses! Verily I am God, thy Lord and the Lord of thy forefathers, Abraham, Isaac and Jacob.' He was so carried away by the captivating accent of the Voice that He detached Himself from the world and set out in the direction of Pharaoh and his people, invested with the power of thy Lord Who exerciseth sovereignty over all that hath been and shall be. The people of the world are now hearing that which Moses did hear, but they understand not.[105]

Christir

And when the days of Moses were ended, and the light of Jesus, shining forth from the dayspring of the Spirit, encompassed the world, all the people of Israel arose in protest against Him. They clamoured that He Whose advent the Bible had foretold must needs promulgate and fulfil the laws of Moses, whereas this youthful Nazarene, who laid claim to the station of the divine Messiah, had annulled the law of divorce and of the sabbath day, the most weighty of all the laws of Moses. Moreover, what of the signs of the Manifestation yet to come? These people of Israel are even unto the present day still expecting that Manifestation which the Bible hath foretold! [106]

Thus Jesus, Son of Mary, whilst seated one day and speaking in the strain of the Holy Spirit, uttered words such as these: "O people! My food is the grass of the field, wherewith I satisfy my hunger. My bed is the dust, my lamp in the night the light of the moon, and my steed my own feet. Behold, who on earth is richer than I?" By the righteousness of God! Thousands of treasures circle round this poverty, and a myriad kingdoms of glory yearn for such abasement! Shouldst thou attain to a drop of the ocean of the inner meaning of these words, thou wouldst surely forsake the world and all that is therein, and, as the Phoenix wouldst consume thyself in the flames of the undying Fire. [107]

Know thou that when the Son of Man yielded up His breath to God, the whole creation wept with a great weeping. By sacrificing Himself, however, a fresh capacity was infused into all created things. Its evidences, as witnessed in all the peoples of the earth, are now manifest before thee. The deepest wisdom which the sages have uttered, the profoundest learning which any mind hath unfolded, the arts which the ablest hands have produced, the influence exerted by the most potent of rulers, are but manifestations of the quickening power released by His transcendent, His all-pervasive, and resplendent Spirit.

We testify that when He came into the world, He shed the splendor of His glory upon all created things. Through Him the leper recovered from the leprosy of perversity and ignorance. Through Him, the unchaste and wayward were healed. Through His power, born of Almighty God, the eyes of the blind were opened, and the soul of the sinner sanctified.[108]

Call thou to mind the day when the Jews, who had surrounded Jesus, Son of Mary, were pressing Him to confess His claim of being the Messiah and Prophet of God, so that they might declare Him an infidel and sentence Him to death. Then, they led Him away, He Who was the Day-star of the heaven of divine Revelation, unto Pilate and Caiaphas, who was the leading divine of that age. The chief priests were all assembled in the palace, also a multitude of people who had gathered to witness His sufferings, to deride and injure Him. Though they repeatedly questioned Him, hoping that He would confess His claim, yet Jesus held His peace and spake not. Finally, an accursed of God arose and, approaching Jesus, adjured Him saying: "Didst thou not claim to be the Divine Messiah? Didst thou not say, 'I am the King of Kings, My word is the Word of God, and I am the breaker of the Sabbath day?'" Thereupon Jesus lifted up His head and said: "Beholdest thou not the Son of Man sitting on the right hand of power and might?" These were His words, and yet consider how to outward seeming He was devoid of all power except that inner power which was of God and which had encompassed all that is in heaven and on earth. How can I relate all that befell Him after He spoke these words? How shall I describe their heinous behaviour towards Him? They at last heaped on His blessed Person such woes that He took His flight unto the fourth Heaven.[109]

In the sayings of Him Who is the Spirit (Jesus) unnumbered significances lie concealed. Unto many things did He refer, but as He found none possessed of a hearing ear or a seeing eye He chose to conceal most of these things. Even as He saith: "But ye cannot bear them now." That Dawning-Place of Revelation saith that on that Day He Who is the Promised One will reveal the things which are to come.[110]

To them that are endowed with understanding, it is clear and manifest that when the fire of the love of Jesus consumed the veils of Jewish limitations, and His authority was made apparent and partially enforced, He the Revealer of the unseen Beauty, addressing one day His disciples, referred unto His passing, and, kindling in their hearts the fire of bereavement, said unto them: "I go away and come again unto you." And in another place He said: "I go and another will come Who will tell you all that I have not told you, and will fulfil all that I have said." Both these sayings have but one meaning, were you to ponder upon the Manifestations of the Unity of God with divine insight.[111]

Muhammad

In like manner, when Muhammad, the Prophet of God, may all men be a sacrifice unto Him, appeared, the learned men of Mecca and Medina arose, in the early days of His Revelation, against Him and rejected His Message, while they who were destitute of all learning recognized and embraced His Faith.[112]

You are well aware of what befell His Faith in the early days of His dispensation. What woeful sufferings did the hand of the infidel and erring, the divines of that age and their associates, inflict upon that spiritual Essence, that most pure and holy Being! How abundant the thorns and briars which they have strewn over His path....For this reason did Muhammad cry out: "No Prophet of God hath suffered such harm as I have suffered."[113]

Every discerning observer will recognize that in the Dispensation of the Qur'án both the Book and the Cause of Jesus were confirmed. As to the matter of names, Muhammad, Himself, declared: "I am Jesus." He recognized the truth of the signs, prophecies, and words of Jesus, and testified that they were all of God. In this sense, neither the person of Jesus nor His writings hath differed from that of Muhammad and of His holy Book, inasmuch as both have championed the Cause of God, uttered His praise, and revealed His commandments.[114]

Consider that which hath been sent down unto Muhammad, the Apostle of God. The measure of the Revelation of which He was the bearer had been clearly foreordained by Him Who is the Almighty, the All-Powerful. They that heard Him, however, could apprehend His purpose only to the extent of their station and spiritual capacity. He, in like manner, uncovered the Face of Wisdom in proportion to their ability to sustain the burden of His Message.[115]

Hath not Muhammad, Himself, declared: "I am all the Prophets?" Hath He not said as We have already mentioned: "I am Adam, Noah,

Moses, and Jesus?" Why should Muhammad, that immortal Beauty, Who hath said: "I am the first Adam" be incapable of saying also: "I am the last Adam"? For even as He regarded Himself to be the "First of the Prophets" that is Adam in like manner, the "Seal of the Prophets" is also applicable unto that Divine Beauty. It is admittedly obvious that being the "First of the Prophets," He likewise is their "Seal."[116]

"Muhammad, the Seal of the Prophets, and the most distinguished of God's chosen Ones, hath likened the Dispensation of the Qur'án unto heaven, by reason of its loftiness, its paramount influence, its majesty, and the fact that it comprehendeth all religions. And as the sun and moon constitute the brightest and most prominent luminaries in the heavens, similarly in the heaven of the religion of God two shining orbs have been ordained fasting and prayer. 'Islám is heaven; fasting is its sun, prayer, its moon.'"[117]

Muhammad, Himself, as the end of His mission drew nigh, spoke these words: "Verily, I leave amongst you My twin weighty testimonies: The Book of God and My Family."[118]

PERUSED ye not the Qur'án? Read it, that haply ye may find the Truth, for this Book is verily the Straight Path. This is the Way of God unto all who are in the heavens and all who are on the earth.[119]

All the things that people required in connection with the Revelation of Muhammad and His laws were to be found revealed and manifest in that Riḍván of resplendent glory. That Book constitutes an abiding testimony to its people after Muhammad, inasmuch as its decrees are indisputable, and its promise unfailing. All have been enjoined to follow the precepts of that Book until "the year sixty"[120] the year of the advent of God's wondrous Manifestation.[121]

The Báb

No sooner had mankind attained the stage of maturity, than the Word revealed to men's eyes the latent energies with which it had been endowed energies which manifested themselves in the plenitude of their glory when the Ancient Beauty appeared, in the year sixty, in the person of 'Alí-Muhammad, the Báb.[122]

Ages rolled away, until they attained their consummation in this, the Lord of days, the Day whereon the Day Star of the Bayán manifested itself above the horizon of mercy, the Day in which the Beauty of the All-Glorious shone forth in the exalted person of 'Alí-Muhammad, the Báb. No sooner did He reveal Himself, than all the people rose up against Him. By some He was denounced as one that hath uttered slanders against God, the Almighty, the Ancient of Days. Others regarded Him as a man smitten with madness, an allegation which I, Myself, have heard from the lips of one of the divines. Still others disputed His claim to be the Mouthpiece of God, and stigmatized Him as one who had stolen and used as his the words of the Almighty, who had perverted their meaning, and mingled them with his own. The Eye of Grandeur weepeth sore for the things which their mouths have uttered, while they continue to rejoice upon their seats.

"God," said He, "is My witness, O people! I am come to you with a Revelation from the Lord, your God, the Lord of your fathers of old. Look not, O people, at the things ye possess. Look rather at the things God hath sent down unto you. This, surely, will be better for you than the whole of creation, could ye but perceive it. Repeat the gaze, O people, and consider the testimony of God and His proof which are in your possession, and compare them unto the Revelation sent down unto you in this Day, that the truth, the infallible truth, may be indubitably manifested unto you. Follow not, O people, the steps of the Evil One; follow ye the Faith of the All-Merciful, and be ye of them that truly believe."[123]

No understanding can grasp the nature of His Revelation, nor can any knowledge comprehend the full measure of His Faith.... Knowledge is twenty and seven letters. All that the Prophets have revealed are two letters thereof. No man thus far hath known more than these two letters. But when the Qá'im shall arise, He will cause the remaining twenty and five letters to be made manifest.

Behold...how great and lofty is His station! His rank excelleth that of all the Prophets and His Revelation transcendeth the comprehension and understanding of all their chosen ones.

Of His Revelation...the Prophets of God, His saints and chosen ones, have either not been informed, or, in pursuance of God's inscrutable decree, they have not disclosed.[124]

And among the evidences of the truth of His manifestation were the ascendancy, the transcendent power, and supremacy which He, the Revealer of being and Manifestation of the Adored, hath, unaided and alone, revealed throughout the world. No sooner had that eternal Beauty revealed Himself in Shíráz, in the year sixty, and rent asunder the veil of concealment, than the signs of the ascendancy, the might, the sovereignty, and power, emanating from that Essence of Essences and Sea of Seas, were manifest in every land. So much so, that from every city there appeared the signs, the evidences, the tokens, the testimonies of that divine Luminary. How many were those pure and kindly hearts which faithfully reflected the light of that eternal Sun, and how manifold the emanations of knowledge from that Ocean of divine wisdom which encompassed all beings! In every city, all the divines and dignitaries rose to hinder and repress them, and girded up the loins of malice, of envy, and tyranny for their suppression. How great the number of those holy souls, those essences of justice, who, accused of tyranny, were put to death! And how many embodiments of purity, who showed forth naught but true knowledge and stainless deeds, suffered an agonizing death! Notwithstanding all this, each of these holy beings, up to his last moment, breathed the Name of

God, and soared in the realm of submission and resignation. Such
was the potency and transmuting influence which He exercised
over them, that they ceased to cherish any desire but His will, and
wedded their soul to His remembrance.[125]

Magnify Thou, O Lord my God, Him Who is the Primal Point, the
Divine Mystery, the Unseen Essence, the Day-Spring of Divinity,
and the Manifestation of Thy Lordship, through Whom all the
knowledge of the past and all the knowledge of the future were
made plain, through Whom the pearls of Thy hidden wisdom were
uncovered, and the mystery of Thy treasured name disclosed, Whom
Thou hast appointed as the Announcer of the One through Whose
name the letter B and the letter E have been joined and united,
through Whom Thy majesty, Thy sovereignty and Thy might were
made known, through Whom Thy words have been sent down, and
Thy laws set forth with clearness, and Thy signs spread abroad, and
Thy Word established, through Whom the hearts of Thy chosen
ones were laid bare, and all that were in the heavens and all that
were on the earth were gathered together, Whom Thou hast called
'Alí-Muhammad in the kingdom of Thy names, and the Spirit of
Spirits in the Tablets of Thine irrevocable decree, Whom Thou hast
invested with Thine own title, unto Whose name all other names
have, at Thy bidding and through the power of Thy might, been
made to return, and in Whom Thou hast caused all Thine attributes
and titles to attain their final consummation. To Him also belong
such names as lay hid within Thy stainless tabernacles, in Thine
invisible world and Thy sanctified cities.

Magnify Thou, moreover, such as have believed in Him and
in His signs and have turned towards Him, from among those
that have acknowledged Thy unity in His Latter Manifestation, a
Manifestation whereof He hath made mention in His Tablets, and in
His Books, and in His Scriptures, and in all the wondrous verses and
gem-like utterances that have descended upon Him. It is this same
Manifestation Whose covenant Thou hast bidden Him establish
ere He had established His own covenant. He it is Whose praise

the Bayán hath celebrated. In it His excellence hath been extolled, and His truth established, and His sovereignty proclaimed, and His Cause perfected. Blessed is the man that hath turned unto Him, and fulfilled the things He hath commanded, O Thou Who art the Lord of the worlds and the Desire of all them that have known Thee!

Praised be Thou, O my God, inasmuch as Thou hast aided us to recognize and love Him. I, therefore, beseech Thee by Him and by Them Who are the Day-Springs of Thy Divinity, and the Manifestations of Thy Lordship, and the Treasuries of Thy Revelation, and the Depositories of Thine inspiration, to enable us to serve and obey Him, and to empower us to become the helpers of His Cause and the dispersers of His adversaries. Powerful art Thou to do all that pleaseth Thee. No God is there beside Thee, the Almighty, the All-Glorious, the One Whose help is sought by all men! [126]

In the year sixty He Who heralded the light of Divine Guidance, may all creation be a sacrifice unto Him, arose to announce a fresh revelation of the Divine Spirit, and was followed, twenty years later, by Him through Whose coming the world was made the recipient of this promised glory, this wondrous favour.[127]

That so brief a span...should have separated this most mighty and wondrous Revelation from Mine own previous Manifestation, is a secret that no man can unravel and a mystery such as no mind can fathom. Its duration had been foreordained, and no man shall ever discover its reason unless and until he be informed of the contents of My Hidden Book.[128]

Bahá'u'lláh

GOD testifieth that there is none other God but Him and that He Who hath appeared is the Hidden Mystery, the Treasured Symbol, the Most Great Book for all peoples, and the Heaven of bounty for the whole world. He is the Most Mighty Sign amongst men and the Dayspring of the most august attributes in the realm of creation. Through Him hath appeared that which had been hidden from time immemorial and been veiled from the eyes of men. He is the One Whose Manifestation was announced by the heavenly Scriptures, in former times and more recently. Whoso acknowledgeth belief in Him and in His signs and testimonies hath in truth acknowledged that which the Tongue of Grandeur uttered ere the creation of earth and heaven and the revelation of the Kingdom of Names. Through Him the ocean of knowledge hath surged amidst mankind and the river of divine wisdom hath gushed out at the behest of God, the Lord of Days.

Well is it with the man of discernment who hath recognized and perceived the Truth, and the one possessed of a hearing ear who hath hearkened unto His sweet Voice, and the hand that hath received His Book with such resolve as is born of God, the Lord of this world and of the next, and the earnest wayfarer who hath hastened unto His glorious Horizon, and the one endued with strength whom neither the overpowering might of the rulers, nor the tumult raised by the leaders of religion hath been able to shake. And woe betide him who hath rejected the grace of God and His bounty, and hath denied His tender mercy and authority; such a man is indeed reckoned with those who have throughout eternity repudiated the testimony of God and His proof.[129]

The light that is shed from the heaven of bounty, and the benediction that shineth from the dawning-place of the will of God, the Lord of the Kingdom of Names, rest upon Him Who is the Supreme Mediator, the Most Exalted Pen, Him Whom God hath made the Dawning-Place of His most excellent names and the Dayspring of His most exalted attributes. Through Him the light of unity hath shone forth above the horizon of the world, and the law of oneness hath been revealed amidst the nations, who, with radiant faces, have turned towards the Supreme Horizon, and acknowledged that which the Tongue of Utterance hath spoken in the kingdom of His knowledge: "Earth and heaven, glory and dominion, are God's, the Omnipotent, the Almighty, the Lord of grace abounding!"[130]

I testify before God to the greatness, the inconceivable greatness of this Revelation.... In this most mighty Revelation all the Dispensations of the past have attained their highest, their final consummation. That which hath been made manifest in this preeminent, this most exalted Revelation, stands unparalleled in the annals of the past, nor will future ages witness its like. He it is Who in the Old Testament hath been named Jehovah, Who in the Gospel hath been designated as the Spirit of Truth, and in the Qur'án acclaimed as the Great Announcement. But for Him no Divine Messenger would have been invested with the robe of prophethood, nor would any of the sacred scriptures have been revealed. To this bear witness all created things.

Had Muhammad, the Apostle of God, attained this Day ... He would have exclaimed: "I have truly recognized Thee, O Thou the Desire of the Divine Messengers!" Had Abraham attained it, He too, falling prostrate upon the ground, and in the utmost lowliness before the Lord thy God, would have cried: "Mine heart is filled with peace, O Thou Lord of all that is in heaven and on earth! I testify that Thou hast unveiled before mine eyes all the glory of Thy power and the full majesty of Thy law!"... Had Moses Himself attained it, He, likewise, would have raised His voice saying: "All praise be to Thee for having lifted upon me the light of Thy countenance and enrolled me among them that have been privileged to behold Thy face!"

Be fair, ye peoples of the world; ... is it meet and seemly for you to question the authority of one Whose presence 'He Who conversed with God' (Moses) hath longed to attain, the beauty of Whose countenance 'God's Well-beloved' (Muhammad) had yearned to behold, through the potency of Whose love the 'Spirit of God' (Jesus) ascended to heaven, for Whose sake the 'Primal Point' (the Báb) offered up His life? [131]

O Jews! If ye be intent on crucifying once again Jesus, the Spirit of God, put Me to death, for He hath once more, in My person, been made manifest unto you. Deal with Me as ye wish, for I have vowed to lay down My life in the path of God. I will fear no one, though the powers of earth and heaven be leagued against Me. Followers of the Gospel! If ye cherish the desire to slay Muhammad, the Apostle of God, seize Me and put an end to My life, for I am He, and My Self is His Self. Do unto Me as ye like, for the deepest longing of Mine heart is to attain the presence of My Best-Beloved in His Kingdom of Glory. Such is the Divine decree, if ye know it. Followers of Muhammad! If it be your wish to riddle with your shafts the breast of Him Who hath caused His Book the Bayán to be sent down unto you, lay hands on Me and persecute Me, for I am His Well-Beloved, the revelation of His own Self, though My name be not His name. I have come in the shadows of the clouds of glory, and am invested by God with invincible sovereignty. He, verily, is the Truth, the Knower of things unseen. I, verily, anticipate from you the treatment ye have accorded unto Him that came before Me. To this all things, verily, witness, if ye be of those who hearken. O people of the Bayán! If ye have resolved to shed the blood of Him Whose coming the Báb hath proclaimed, Whose advent Muhammad hath prophesied, and Whose Revelation Jesus Christ Himself hath announced, behold Me standing, ready and defenseless, before you. Deal with Me after your own desires.[132]

The Pen of Holiness, I solemnly affirm before God, hath writ upon My snow-white brow and in characters of effulgent glory these glowing, these musk-scented and holy words: "Behold ye that dwell on earth, and ye denizens of heaven, bear witness, He in truth is your Well-Beloved. He it is Whose like the world of creation hath not seen, He Whose ravishing beauty hath delighted the eye of God, the Ordainer, the All-Powerful, the Incomparable!"[133]

Next Manifestation

Whoso layeth claim to a Revelation direct from God, ere the expiration of a full thousand years, such a man is assuredly a lying impostor. We pray God that He may graciously assist him to retract and repudiate such claim. Should he repent, God will, no doubt, forgive him. If, however, he persisteth in his error, God will, assuredly, send down one who will deal mercilessly with him. Terrible, indeed, is God in punishing! Whosoever interpreteth this verse otherwise than its obvious meaning is deprived of the Spirit of God and of His mercy which encompasseth all created things. Fear God, and follow not your idle fancies. Nay, rather, follow the bidding of your Lord, the Almighty, the All-Wise.[134]

I am not apprehensive for My own self ... My fears are for Him Who will be sent down unto you after Me, Him Who will be invested with great sovereignty and mighty dominion. By those words which I have revealed, Myself is not intended, but rather He Who will come after Me. To it is witness God, the All-Knowing. Deal not with Him ... as ye have dealt with Me.[135]

Bahá'u'lláh

Ṭihrán

Let nothing grieve thee, O Land of Tá[136,] for God hath chosen thee to be the source of the joy of all mankind.

Rejoice with great joy, for God hath made thee "the Dayspring of His light", inasmuch as within thee was born the Manifestation of His Glory. Be thou glad for this name that hath been conferred upon thee—a name through which the Day-Star of grace hath shed its splendour, through which both earth and heaven have been illumined.

Erelong will the state of affairs within thee be changed, and the reins of power fall into the hands of the people. Verily, thy Lord is the All-Knowing. His authority embraceth all things. Rest thou assured in the gracious favour of thy Lord. The eye of His loving-kindness shall everlastingly be directed towards thee. The day is approaching when thy agitation will have been transmuted into peace and quiet calm. Thus hath it been decreed in the wondrous Book.[137]

Call thou to remembrance, O Land of Tá (Ṭihrán), the former days in which thy Lord had made thee the seat of His throne, and had enveloped thee with the effulgence of His glory. How vast the number of those sanctified beings, those symbols of certitude, who, in their great love for thee, have laid down their lives and sacrificed their all for thy sake! Joy be to thee, and blissfulness to them that inhabit thee. I testify that out of thee, as every discerning heart knoweth, proceedeth the living breath of Him Who is the Desire of the world. In thee the Unseen hath been revealed, and out of thee hath gone forth that which lay hid from the eyes of men. Which one of the multitude of thy sincere lovers shall We remember, whose blood hath been shed within thy gates, and whose dust is now concealed beneath thy soil? The sweet savors of God have unceasingly been wafted, and shall everlastingly continue to be wafted upon thee. Our Pen is moved to commemorate thee, and to extol the victims of tyranny, those men and women that sleep beneath thy dust.[138]

Imprisonment in the Siyáh-Chál

God witnesseth that there is no God but Him, the Gracious, the Best-Beloved. All grace and bounty are His. To whomsoever He will He giveth whatsoever is His wish. He, verily, is the All-Powerful, the Almighty, the Help in Peril, the Self-Subsisting. We, verily, believe in Him Who, in the person of the Báb, hath been sent down by the Will of the one true God, the King of Kings, the All-Praised.[139]

In Ṭihrán We were twice imprisoned as a result of Our having risen to defend the cause of the innocent against a ruthless oppressor. The first confinement to which We were subjected followed the slaying of Mullá Taqíy-i-Qazvíní, and was occasioned by the assistance We were moved to extend to those upon whom a severe punishment had been undeservedly inflicted. Our second imprisonment, infinitely more severe, was precipitated by the attempt which irresponsible followers of the Faith made on the life of the Sháh.[140]

At the time when His Majesty the Sháh, may God, his Lord, the Most Merciful, aid him through His strengthening grace, was planning a journey to Isfahán, this Wronged One, having obtained his permission, visited the holy and luminous resting-places of the Imáms, may the blessings of God be upon them! Upon Our return, We proceeded to Lavásán on account of the excessive heat prevailing in the capital. Following Our departure, there occurred the attempt upon the life of His Majesty, may God, exalted and glorified be He, assist him. Those days were troublous days, and the fires of hatred burned high. Many were arrested, among them this Wronged One. By the righteousness of God! We were in no wise connected with that evil deed, and Our innocence was indisputably established by the tribunals. Nevertheless, they apprehended Us, and from Níyávarán, which was then the residence of His Majesty, conducted Us, on foot and in chains, with bared head and bare feet, to the dungeon of Ṭihrán. A brutal man, accompanying Us on horseback, snatched off Our hat, whilst We were being hurried along by a troop of executioners and officials. We were consigned for four months to a place foul beyond comparison. As to the dungeon in which this Wronged One and others similarly wronged were confined, a dark and narrow pit were preferable. Upon Our arrival We were first conducted along a pitch-black corridor, from whence We descended three steep flights of stairs to the place of confinement assigned to Us. The dungeon was wrapped in thick darkness, and Our fellow prisoners numbered nearly a hundred and fifty souls: thieves, assassins and highwaymen. Though crowded, it had no other outlet than the passage by which We entered. No pen can depict that place, nor any tongue describe its loathsome smell. Most of these men had neither clothes nor bedding to lie on. God alone knoweth what befell Us in that most foul-smelling and gloomy place!

Day and night, while confined in that dungeon, We meditated upon the deeds, the condition, and the conduct of the Bábís, wondering what could have led a people so high-minded, so noble, and of such intelligence, to perpetrate such an audacious and outrageous act against the person of His Majesty. This Wronged One, thereupon, decided to arise, after His release from prison, and undertake, with the utmost vigor, the task of regenerating this people.[141]

O Shaykh! That which hath touched this Wronged One is beyond compare or equal. We have borne it all with the utmost willingness and resignation, so that the souls of men may be edified, and the Word of God be exalted. While confined in the prison of the Land of Mím (Mázindarán) We were one day delivered into the hands of the divines. Thou canst well imagine what befell Us. Shouldst thou at some time happen to visit the dungeon of His Majesty the Sháh, ask the director and chief jailer to show thee those two chains, one of which is known as Qará-Guhar, and the other as Salásil. I swear by the Daystar of Justice that for four months this Wronged One was tormented and chained by one or the other of them. "My grief exceedeth all the woes to which Jacob gave vent, and all the afflictions of Job are but a part of My sorrows!"[142]

Dawning of Revelation

During the days I lay in the prison of Ṭihrán, though the galling weight of the chains and the stench-filled air allowed Me but little sleep, still in those infrequent moments of slumber I felt as if something flowed from the crown of My head over My breast, even as a mighty torrent that precipitateth itself upon the earth from the summit of a lofty mountain. Every limb of My body would, as a result, be set afire. At such moments My tongue recited what no man could bear to hear.[143]

While engulfed in tribulations I heard a most wondrous, a most sweet voice, calling above My head. Turning My face, I beheld a Maiden, the embodiment of the remembrance of the name of My Lord, suspended in the air before Me. So rejoiced was she in her very soul that her countenance shone with the ornament of the good pleasure of God, and her cheeks glowed with the brightness of the All-Merciful. Betwixt earth and heaven she was raising a call which captivated the hearts and minds of men. She was imparting to both My inward and outer being tidings which rejoiced My soul, and the souls of God's honoured servants.

Pointing with her finger unto My head, she addressed all who are in heaven and all who are on earth, saying: By God! This is the Best-Beloved of the worlds, and yet ye comprehend not. This is the Beauty of God amongst you, and the power of His sovereignty within you, could ye but understand. This is the Mystery of God and His Treasure, the Cause of God and His glory unto all who are in the kingdoms of Revelation and of creation, if ye be of them that perceive.[144]

One night, in a dream, these exalted words were heard on every side: "Verily, We shall render Thee victorious by Thyself and by Thy Pen. Grieve Thou not for that which hath befallen Thee, neither be Thou afraid, for Thou art in safety. Erelong will God raise up the treasures of the earth, men who will aid Thee through Thyself and through Thy Name, wherewith God hath revived the hearts of such as have recognized Him."[145]

O King! I was but a man like others, asleep upon My couch, when lo, the breezes of the All-Glorious were wafted over Me, and taught Me the knowledge of all that hath been. This thing is not from Me, but from One Who is Almighty and All-Knowing. And He bade Me lift up My voice between earth and heaven, and for this there befell Me what hath caused the tears of every man of understanding to flow. The learning current amongst men I studied not; their schools I entered not. Ask of the city wherein I dwelt, that thou mayest be well assured that I am not of them who speak falsely. This is but a leaf which the winds of the will of thy Lord, the Almighty, the All-Praised, have stirred. Can it be still when the tempestuous winds are blowing? Nay, by Him Who is the Lord of all Names and Attributes! They move it as they list. The evanescent is as nothing before Him Who is the Ever-Abiding. His all-compelling summons hath reached Me, and caused Me to speak His praise amidst all people. I was indeed as one dead when His behest was uttered. The hand of the will of thy Lord, the Compassionate, the Merciful, transformed Me.[146]

Praised be Thou, O my God! How can I thank Thee for having singled me out and chosen me above all Thy servants to reveal Thee, at a time when all had turned away from Thy beauty! I testify, O my God, that if I were given a thousand lives by Thee, and offered them up all in Thy path, I would still have failed to repay the least of the gifts which, by Thy grace, Thou hast bestowed upon me.

I lay asleep on the bed of self when lo, Thou didst waken me with the divine accents of Thy voice, and didst unveil to me Thy beauty, and didst enable me to listen to Thine utterances, and to recognize Thy Self, and to speak forth Thy praise, and to extol Thy virtues, and to be steadfast in Thy love. Finally I fell a captive into the hands of the wayward among Thy servants.[147]

Consider the hour at which the supreme Manifestation of God revealeth Himself unto men. Ere that hour cometh, the Ancient Being, Who is still unknown of men and hath not as yet given utterance to the Word of God, is Himself the All-Knower in a world devoid of any man that hath known Him. He is indeed the Creator without a creation. For at the very moment preceding His Revelation, each and every created thing shall be made to yield up its soul to God. This is indeed the Day of which it hath been written: "Whose shall be the Kingdom this Day?" And none can be found ready to answer! [148]

Exiled to 'Iráq

My God, My Master, My Desire! ... Thou hast created this atom of dust through the consummate power of Thy might, and nurtured Him with Thine hands which none can chain up.... Thou hast destined for Him trials and tribulations which no tongue can describe, nor any of Thy Tablets adequately recount. The throat Thou didst accustom to the touch of silk Thou hast, in the end, clasped with strong chains, and the body Thou didst ease with brocades and velvets Thou hast at last subjected to the abasement of a dungeon. Thy decree hath shackled Me with unnumbered fetters, and cast about My neck chains that none can sunder. A number of years have passed during which afflictions have, like showers of mercy, rained upon Me.... How many the nights during which the weight of chains and fetters allowed Me no rest, and how numerous the days during which peace and tranquillity were denied Me, by reason of that wherewith the hands and tongues of men have afflicted Me! Both bread and water which Thou hast, through Thy all-embracing mercy, allowed unto the beasts of the field, they have, for a time, forbidden unto this servant, and the things they refused to inflict upon such as have seceded from Thy Cause, the same have they suffered to be inflicted upon Me, until, finally, Thy decree was irrevocably fixed, and Thy behest summoned this servant to depart out of Persia, accompanied by a number of frail-bodied men and children of tender age, at this time when the cold is so intense that one cannot even speak, and ice and snow so abundant that it is impossible to move.[149]

And when this Wronged One went forth out of His prison, We journeyed, in pursuance of the order of His Majesty the Sháh, may God, exalted be He, protect him, to Iráq, escorted by officers in the service of the esteemed and honored governments of Persia and Russia. After Our arrival, We revealed, as a copious rain, by the aid of God and His Divine Grace and mercy, Our verses, and sent them to various parts of the world. We exhorted all men, and particularly this people, through Our wise counsels and loving admonitions, and forbade them to engage in sedition, quarrels, disputes and conflict. As a result of this, and by the grace of God, waywardness and folly were changed into piety and understanding, and weapons converted into instruments of peace.[150]

From the Land of Tá (Ṭihrán), after countless afflictions, We reached Iráq, at the bidding of the Tyrant of Persia, where, after the fetters of Our foes, We were afflicted with the perfidy of Our friends. God knoweth what befell Me thereafter! [151]

Upon Our arrival in Iráq We found the Cause of God sunk in deep apathy and the breeze of divine revelation stilled. Most of the believers were faint and dispirited, nay utterly lost and dead. Hence there was a second blast on the Trumpet, whereupon the Tongue of Grandeur uttered these blessed words: We have sounded the Trumpet for the second time. Thus the whole world was quickened through the vitalizing breaths of divine revelation and inspiration.[152]

We enjoin the servants of God and His handmaidens to be pure and to fear God, that they may shake off the slumber of their corrupt desires, and turn toward God, the Maker of the heavens and of the earth. Thus have We commanded the faithful when the Daystar of the world shone forth from the horizon of Iráq. My imprisonment doeth Me no harm, neither the tribulations I suffer, nor the things that have befallen Me at the hands of My oppressors. That which harmeth Me is the conduct of those who, though they bear My name, yet commit that which maketh My heart and My pen to lament. They that spread disorder in the land, and lay hands on the property of others, and enter a house without leave of its owner, We, verily, are clear of them, unless they repent and return unto God, the Ever-Forgiving, the Most Merciful.[153]

We fain would hope that the people of the Bayán will be enlightened, will soar in the realm of the spirit and abide therein, will discern the Truth, and recognize with the eye of insight dissembling falsehood. In these days, however, such odours of jealousy are diffused, that I swear by the Educator of all beings, visible and invisible, from the beginning of the foundation of the world though it hath no beginning until the present day, such malice, envy, and hate have in no wise appeared, nor will they ever be witnessed in the future. For a number of people who have never inhaled the fragrance of justice, have raised the standard of sedition, and have leagued themselves against Us. On every side We witness the menace of their spears, and in all directions We recognize the shafts of their arrows. This, although We have never gloried in any thing, nor did We seek preference over any soul. To everyone We have been a most kindly companion, a most forbearing and affectionate friend. In the company of the poor We have sought their fellowship, and amidst the exalted and learned We have been submissive and resigned. I swear by God, the one true God! grievous as have been the woes and sufferings which the hand of the enemy and the people of the Book inflicted upon Us, yet all these fade into utter nothingness when compared with that which hath befallen Us at the hand of those who profess to be Our friends.[154]

Withdrawal to the Wilderness of Kurdistán

In the early days of Our arrival in this land, when We discerned the signs of impending events, We decided, ere they happened, to retire. We betook Ourselves to the wilderness, and there, separated and alone, led for two years a life of complete solitude. From Our eyes there rained tears of anguish, and in Our bleeding heart there surged an ocean of agonizing pain. Many a night We had no food for sustenance, and many a day Our body found no rest. By Him Who hath My being between His hands! notwithstanding these showers of afflictions and unceasing calamities, Our soul was wrapt in blissful joy, and Our whole being evinced an ineffable gladness. For in Our solitude We were unaware of the harm or benefit, the health or ailment, of any soul. Alone, We communed with Our spirit, oblivious of the world and all that is therein. We knew not, however, that the mesh of divine destiny exceedeth the vastest of mortal conceptions, and the dart of His decree transcendeth the boldest of human designs. None can escape the snares He setteth, and no soul can find release except through submission to His will. By the righteousness of God! Our withdrawal contemplated no return, and Our separation hoped for no reunion. The one object of Our retirement was to avoid becoming a subject of discord among the faithful, a source of disturbance unto Our companions, the means of injury to any soul, or the cause of sorrow to any heart. Beyond these, We cherished no other intention, and apart from them, We had no end in view. And yet, each person schemed after his own desire, and pursued his own idle fancy, until the hour when, from the Mystic Source, there came the summons bidding Us return whence We came. Surrendering Our will to His, We submitted to His injunction.[155]

Return to Baghdád

What pen can recount the things We beheld upon Our return! Two years have elapsed during which Our enemies have ceaselessly and assiduously contrived to exterminate Us, whereunto all witness. Nevertheless, none amongst the faithful hath risen to render Us any assistance, nor did any one feel inclined to help in Our deliverance. Nay, instead of assisting Us, what showers of continuous sorrows, their words and deeds have caused to rain upon Our soul! [156]

We found no more than a handful of souls, faint and dispirited, nay utterly lost and dead. The Cause of God had ceased to be on any one's lips, nor was any heart receptive to its message. [157]

By God besides Whom there is none other God! But for My recognition of the fact that the blessed Cause of the Primal Point was on the verge of being completely obliterated, and all the sacred blood poured out in the path of God would have been shed in vain, I would in no wise have consented to return to the people of the Bayán, and would have abandoned them to the worship of the idols their imaginations had fashioned. [158]

Upon Our return to Baghdád, We found, to Our great astonishment, that the Cause of the Báb had been sorely neglected, that its influence had waned, that its very name had almost sunk into oblivion. We arose to revive His Cause and to save it from decay and corruption. At the time when ear and perplexity had taken fast hold of Our companions, We reasserted, with fearlessness and determination, its essential verities, and summoned all those who had become lukewarm to espouse with enthusiasm the Faith they had so grievously neglected. We sent forth Our appeal to the peoples of the world, and invited them to fix their gaze upon the light of His Revelation. [159]

Tell out to the nations, O Pen of the Ancient of Days, the things that have happened in Iraq. Tell them of the messenger whom the congregation of the divines of that land had delegated to meet Us, who, when attaining Our presence, questioned Us concerning certain sciences, and whom We answered by virtue of the knowledge We inherently possess. Thy Lord is, verily, the Knower of things unseen. "We testify," said he, "that the knowledge Thou dost possess is such as none can rival. Such a knowledge, however, is insufficient to vindicate the exalted station which the people ascribe to Thee. Produce, if Thou speakest the truth, what the combined forces of the peoples of the earth are powerless to produce." Thus was it irrevocably decreed in the court of the presence of thy Lord, the All-Glorious, the Loving.

"Witness! What is it thou seest?" He was dumbfounded. And when he came to himself, he said: "I truly believe in God, the All-Glorious, the All-Praised." "Go thou to the people, and tell them: 'Ask whatsoever ye please. Powerful is He to do what He willeth. Nothing whatsoever, be it of the past or of the future, can frustrate His Will.' Say: 'O ye congregation of the divines! Choose any matter ye desire, and ask your Lord, the God of Mercy, to reveal it unto you. If He fulfil your wish, by virtue of His sovereignty, believe ye then in Him, and be not of those that reject His truth.'" "The dawn of understanding hath now broken," said he, "and the testimony of the All-Merciful is fulfilled." He arose and returned unto them that sent him, at the bidding of God, the All-Glorious, the Well-Beloved.

Days passed and he failed to come back to Us. Eventually, there came another messenger who informed Us that the people had given up what they originally had purposed. They are indeed a contemptible people. This is what happened in Iraq, and to what I reveal I Myself am witness. This happening was noised abroad, yet none was found to comprehend its meaning. Thus did We ordain it. Would that ye knew this!

By My Self! Whoso hath in bygone ages asked Us to produce the signs of God, hath, no sooner We revealed them to him, repudiated God's truth. The people, however, have, for the most part, remained heedless. They whose eyes are illumined with the light of understanding will perceive the sweet savors of the All-Merciful, and will embrace His truth. These are they who are truly sincere.[160]

Ridván

Verily, all created things were immersed in the sea of purification when, on that first day of Ridván, We shed upon the whole of creation the splendours of Our most excellent Names and Our most exalted Attributes. This, verily, is a token of My loving providence, which hath encompassed all the worlds.[161]

The Divine Springtime is come, O Most Exalted Pen, for the Festival of the All-Merciful is fast approaching. Bestir thyself, and magnify, before the entire creation, the name of God, and celebrate His praise, in such wise that all created things may be regenerated and made new. Speak, and hold not thy peace. The day star of blissfulness shineth above the horizon of Our name, the Blissful, inasmuch as the kingdom of the name of God hath been adorned with the ornament of the name of thy Lord, the Creator of the heavens. Arise before the nations of the earth, and arm thyself with the power of this Most Great Name, and be not of those who tarry.

Methinks that thou hast halted and movest not upon My Tablet. Could the brightness of the Divine Countenance have bewildered thee, or the idle talk of the froward filled thee with grief and paralyzed thy movement? Take heed lest anything deter thee from extolling the greatness of this Day—the Day whereon the Finger of majesty and power hath opened the seal of the Wine of Reunion, and called all who are in the heavens and all who are on the earth. Preferrest thou to tarry when the breeze announcing the Day of God hath already breathed over thee, or art thou of them that are shut out as by a veil from Him?

No veil whatever have I allowed, O Lord of all names and Creator of the heavens, to shut me from the recognition of the glories of Thy Day—the Day which is the lamp of guidance unto the whole world, and the sign of the Ancient of Days unto all them that dwell therein. My silence is by reason of the veils that have blinded Thy creatures' eyes to Thee, and my muteness is because of the impediments that have hindered Thy people from recognizing Thy truth. Thou knowest what is in me, but I know not what is in Thee. Thou art the All-Knowing, the All-Informed. By Thy name that excelleth all other names! If Thy overruling and all-compelling behest should ever reach me, it would empower me to revive the souls of all men, through Thy most exalted Word, which I have heard uttered by Thy Tongue of power in Thy Kingdom of glory. It would enable me to announce the revelation of Thy effulgent countenance wherethrough that which lay hidden from the eyes of men hath been manifested in Thy name, the Perspicuous, the sovereign Protector, the Self-Subsisting.

Canst thou discover any one but Me, O Pen, in this Day? What hath become of the creation and the manifestations thereof? What of the names and their kingdom? Whither are gone all created things, whether seen or unseen? What of the hidden secrets of the universe and its revelations? Lo, the entire creation hath passed away! Nothing remaineth except My Face, the Ever-Abiding, the Resplendent, the All-Glorious.

This is the Day whereon naught can be seen except the splendors of the Light that shineth from the face of Thy Lord, the Gracious, the Most Bountiful. Verily, We have caused every soul to expire by virtue of Our irresistible and all-subduing sovereignty. We have, then, called into being a new creation, as a token of Our grace unto men. I am, verily, the All-Bountiful, the Ancient of Days.

This is the Day whereon the unseen world crieth out: "Great is thy blessedness, O earth, for thou hast been made the foot-stool of thy God, and been chosen as the seat of His mighty throne." The realm of glory exclaimeth: "Would that my life could be sacrificed for thee, for He Who is the Beloved of the All-Merciful hath established His sovereignty upon thee, through the power of His Name that hath been promised unto all things, whether of the past or of the future." This is the Day whereon every sweet smelling thing hath derived its fragrance from the smell of My garment—a garment that hath shed its perfume upon the whole of creation. This is the Day whereon the rushing waters of everlasting life have gushed out of the Will of the All-Merciful. Haste ye, with your hearts and souls, and quaff your fill, O Concourse of the realms above!

Say: He it is Who is the Manifestation of Him Who is the Unknowable, the Invisible of the Invisibles, could ye but perceive it. He it is Who hath laid bare before you the hidden and treasured Gem, were ye to seek it. He it is Who is the one Beloved of all things, whether of the past or of the future. Would that ye might set your hearts and hopes upon Him!

We have heard the voice of thy pleading, O Pen, and excuse thy silence. What is it that hath so sorely bewildered thee?

The inebriation of Thy presence, O Well-Beloved of all worlds, hath seized and possessed me.

Arise, and proclaim unto the entire creation the tidings that He Who is the All-Merciful hath directed His steps towards the Riḍván and entered it. Guide, then, the people unto the garden of delight which God hath made the Throne of His Paradise. We have chosen thee to be our most mighty Trumpet, whose blast is to signalize the resurrection of all mankind.

Say: This is the Paradise on whose foliage the wine of utterance hath imprinted the testimony: "He that was hidden from the eyes of men is revealed, girded with sovereignty and power!" This is the Paradise, the rustling of whose leaves proclaims: "O ye that inhabit the heavens and the earth! There hath appeared what hath never previously appeared. He Who, from everlasting, had concealed His Face from the sight of creation is now come." From the whispering breeze that wafteth amidst its branches there cometh the cry: "He Who is the sovereign Lord of all is made manifest. The Kingdom is God's," while from its streaming waters can be heard the murmur: "All eyes are gladdened, for He Whom none hath beheld, Whose secret no one hath discovered, hath lifted the veil of glory, and uncovered the countenance of Beauty."

Within this Paradise, and from the heights of its loftiest chambers, the Maids of Heaven have cried out and shouted: "Rejoice, ye dwellers of the realms above, for the fingers of Him Who is the Ancient of Days are ringing, in the name of the All-Glorious, the Most Great Bell, in the midmost heart of the heavens. The hands of bounty have borne round the cup of everlasting life. Approach, and quaff your fill. Drink with healthy relish, O ye that are the very incarnations of longing, ye who are the embodiments of vehement desire!"

Forget the world of creation, O Pen, and turn thou towards the face of thy Lord, the Lord of all names. Adorn, then, the world with the ornament of the favors of thy Lord, the King of everlasting days. For We perceive the fragrance of the Day whereon He Who is the Desire of all nations hath shed upon the kingdoms of the unseen and of the seen the splendor of the light of His most excellent names, and enveloped them with the radiance of the luminaries of His most gracious favors—favors which none can reckon except Him, Who is the omnipotent Protector of the entire creation.

Look not upon the creatures of God except with the eye of kindliness and of mercy, for Our loving providence hath pervaded all created things, and Our grace encompassed the earth and the heavens. This is the Day whereon the true servants of God partake of the life-giving waters of reunion, the Day whereon those that are nigh unto Him are able to drink of the soft-flowing river of immortality, and they who believe in His unity, the wine of His Presence, through their recognition of Him Who is the Highest and Last End of all, in Whom the Tongue of Majesty and Glory voiceth the call: "The Kingdom is Mine. I, Myself, am, of Mine own right, its Ruler."

Attract the hearts of men, through the call of Him, the one alone Beloved. Say: This is the Voice of God, if ye do but hearken.

This is the Day Spring of the Revelation of God, did ye but know it. This is the Dawning-Place of the Cause of God, were ye to recognize it. This is the Source of the commandment of God, did ye but judge it fairly. This is the manifest and hidden Secret; would that ye might perceive it. O peoples of the world! Cast away, in My name that transcendeth all other names, the things ye possess, and immerse yourselves in this Ocean in whose depths lay hidden the pearls of wisdom and of utterance, an ocean that surgeth in My name, the All-Merciful. Thus instructeth you He with Whom is the Mother Book.

The Best-Beloved is come. In His right hand is the sealed Wine of His name. Happy is the man that turneth unto Him, and drinketh his fill, and exclaimeth: "Praise be to Thee, O Revealer of the signs of God!" By the righteousness of the Almighty! Every hidden thing hath been manifested through the power of truth. All the favors of God have been sent down, as a token of His grace. The waters of everlasting life have, in their fullness, been proffered unto men. Every single cup hath been borne round by the hand of the Well-Beloved. Draw near, and tarry not, though it be for one short moment.

Blessed are they that have soared on the wings of detachment and attained the station which, as ordained by God, overshadoweth the entire creation, whom neither the vain imaginations of the learned, nor the multitude of the hosts of the earth have succeeded in deflecting from His Cause. Who is there among you, O people, who will renounce the world, and draw nigh unto God, the Lord of all names? Where is he to be found who, through the power of My name that transcendeth all created things, will cast away the things that men possess, and cling, with all his might, to the things which God, the Knower of the unseen and of the seen, hath bidden him observe? Thus hath His bounty been sent down unto men, His testimony fulfilled, and His proof shone forth above the Horizon of mercy. Rich is the prize that shall be won by him who hath believed and exclaimed: "Lauded art Thou, O Beloved of all worlds! Magnified be Thy name, O Thou the Desire of every understanding heart!"

Rejoice with exceeding gladness, O people of Bahá, as ye call to remembrance the Day of supreme felicity, the Day whereon the Tongue of the Ancient of Days hath spoken, as He departed from His House, proceeding to the Spot from which He shed upon the whole of creation the splendors of His name, the All-Merciful. God is Our witness. Were We to reveal the hidden secrets of that Day, all they that dwell on earth and in the heavens would swoon away and die, except such as will be preserved by God, the Almighty, the All-Knowing, the All-Wise.

Such is the inebriating effect of the words of God upon Him Who is the Revealer of His undoubted proofs, that His Pen can move no longer. With these words He concludeth His Tablet: "No God is there but Me, the Most Exalted, the Most Powerful, the Most Excellent, the All-Knowing."[162]

Release yourselves, O nightingales of God, from the thorns and brambles of wretchedness and misery, and wing your flight to the rose-garden of unfading splendor. O My friends that dwell upon the dust! Haste forth unto your celestial habitation. Announce unto yourselves the joyful tidings: "He Who is the Best-Beloved is come! He hath crowned Himself with the glory of God's Revelation, and hath unlocked to the face of men the doors of His ancient Paradise." Let all eyes rejoice, and let every ear be gladdened, for now is the time to gaze on His beauty, now is the fit time to hearken to His voice. Proclaim unto every longing lover: "Behold, your Well-Beloved hath come among men!" and to the messengers of the Monarch of love impart the tidings: "Lo, the Adored One hath appeared arrayed in the fullness of His glory!" O lovers of His beauty! Turn the anguish of your separation from Him into the joy of an everlasting reunion, and let the sweetness of His presence dissolve the bitterness of your remoteness from His court.

Behold how the manifold grace of God, which is being showered from the clouds of Divine glory, hath, in this day, encompassed the world. For whereas in days past every lover besought and searched after his Beloved, it is the Beloved Himself Who now is calling His lovers and is inviting them to attain His presence. Take heed lest ye forfeit so precious a favor; beware lest ye belittle so remarkable a token of His grace. Abandon not the incorruptible benefits, and be not content with that which perisheth. Lift up the veil that obscureth your vision, and dispel the darkness with which it is enveloped, that ye may gaze on the naked beauty of the Beloved's face, may behold that which no eye hath beheld, and hear that which no ear hath heard.

Hear Me, ye mortal birds! In the Rose Garden of changeless splendor a Flower hath begun to bloom, compared to which every other flower is but a thorn, and before the brightness of Whose glory the very essence of beauty must pale and wither. Arise, therefore, and, with the whole enthusiasm of your hearts, with all the eagerness of your souls, the full fervor of your will, and the concentrated efforts of your entire being, strive to attain the paradise of His presence, and endeavor to inhale the fragrance of the incorruptible Flower, to breathe the sweet savors of holiness, and to obtain a portion of this perfume of celestial glory. Whoso followeth this counsel will break his chains asunder, will taste the abandonment of enraptured love, will attain unto his heart's desire, and will surrender his soul into the hands of his Beloved. Bursting through his cage, he will, even as the bird of the spirit, wing his flight to his holy and everlasting nest.

Night hath succeeded day, and day hath succeeded night, and the hours and moments of your lives have come and gone, and yet none of you hath, for one instant, consented to detach himself from that which perisheth. Bestir yourselves, that the brief moments that are still yours may not be dissipated and lost. Even as the swiftness of lightning your days shall pass, and your bodies shall be laid to rest beneath a canopy of dust. What can ye then achieve? How can ye atone for your past failure?

The everlasting Candle shineth in its naked glory. Behold how it hath consumed every mortal veil. O ye moth-like lovers of His light! Brave every danger, and consecrate your souls to its consuming flame. O ye that thirst after Him! Strip yourselves of every earthly affection, and hasten to embrace your Beloved. With a zest that none can equal make haste to attain unto Him. The Flower, thus far hidden from the sight of men, is unveiled to your eyes. In the open radiance of His glory He standeth before you. His voice summoneth all the holy and sanctified beings to come and be united with Him. Happy is he that turneth thereunto; well is it with him that hath attained, and gazed on the light of so wondrous a countenance.[163]

To Constantinople

O King! We were in Iráq, when the hour of parting arrived. At the bidding of the King of Islám (Sultán of Turkey) We set Our steps in his direction. Upon Our arrival, there befell Us at the hands of the malicious that which the books of the world can never adequately recount. Thereupon the inmates of Paradise, and they that dwell within the retreats of holiness, lamented; and yet the people are wrapped in a thick veil! [164]

O My companions ... I entrust to your keeping this city of Baghdád, in the state ye now behold it, when from the eyes of friends and strangers alike, crowding its housetops, its streets and markets, tears like the rain of spring are flowing down, and I depart. With you it now rests to watch lest your deeds and conduct dim the flame of love that gloweth within the breasts of its inhabitants.[165]

He (God) it was ... Who enabled Me to depart out of the city (Baghdád), clothed with such majesty as none, except the denier and the malicious, can fail to acknowledge.[166]

That the Spirit should depart out of the body of Iráq is indeed a wondrous sign unto all who are in heaven and all who are on earth. Erelong will ye behold this Divine Youth riding upon the steed of victory. Then will the hearts of the envious be seized with trembling.[167]

Call Thou to remembrance Thine arrival in the City (Constantinople), how the Ministers of the Sultán thought Thee to be unacquainted with their laws and regulations, and believed Thee to be one of the ignorant. Say: Yea, by My Lord! I am ignorant of all things except what God hath, through His bountiful favour, been pleased to teach Me. To this We assuredly testify, and unhesitatingly confess it.

Say: If the laws and regulations to which ye cleave be of your own making, We will, in no wise, follow them. Thus have I been instructed by Him Who is the All-Wise, the All-Informed. Such hath been My way in the past, and such will it remain in the future, through the power of God and His might. This, indeed, is the true and right way. If they be ordained by God, bring forth, then, your proofs, if ye be of them that speak the truth. Say: We have written down in a Book which leaveth not unrecorded the work of any man, however insignificant, all that they have imputed to Thee, and all that they have done unto Thee.[168]

Narrate, O Servant, the things Thou didst behold at the time of Thine arrival in the City, that Thy testimony may endure amongst men, and serve as a warning unto them that believe. We found, upon Our arrival in the City, its governors and elders as children gathered about and disporting themselves with clay. We perceived no one sufficiently mature to acquire from Us the truths which God hath taught Us, nor ripe for Our wondrous words of wisdom. Our inner eye wept sore over them, and over their transgressions and their total disregard of the thing for which they were created. This is what We observed in that city, and which We have chosen to note down in Our Book, that it may serve as a warning unto them, and unto the rest of mankind.[169]

O Spot that art situate on the shores of the two seas! The throne of tyranny hath, verily, been established upon thee, and the flame of hatred hath been kindled within thy bosom, in such wise that the Concourse on high and they who circle around the Exalted Throne have wailed and lamented. We behold in thee the foolish ruling over the wise, and darkness vaunting itself against the light. Thou art indeed filled with manifest pride. Hath thine outward splendour made thee vainglorious? By Him Who is the Lord of mankind! It shall soon perish, and thy daughters and thy widows and all the kindreds that dwell within thee shall lament. Thus informeth thee the All-Knowing, the All-Wise.[170]

Fear God, ye inhabitants of the City (Constantinople), and sow not the seeds of dissension amongst men. Walk not in the paths of the Evil One. Walk ye, during the few remaining days of your life, in the ways of the one true God. Your days shall pass away as have the days of them who were before you. To dust shall ye return, even as your fathers of old did return.[171]

Exiled to Adrianople: The Remote Prison

They expelled Us ... from thy city (Constantinople) with an abasement with which no abasement on earth can compare. Neither My family, nor those who accompanied ... Me had the necessary raiment to protect them from the cold in that freezing weather. ...The eyes of Our enemies wept over Us, and beyond them those of every discerning person.[172]

Be fair in your judgment, O ye Ministers of State! What is it that We have committed that could justify Our banishment? What is the offense that hath warranted Our expulsion? It is We Who have sought you, and yet, behold how ye refused to receive Us! By God! This is a sore injustice that ye have perpetrated—an injustice with which no earthly injustice can measure. To this the Almighty is Himself a witness....[173]

O Ahmad! Forget not My Bounties while I am absent. Remember My days during thy days, and My distress and banishment in this remote prison.[174]

Such are the outpourings...from the clouds of Divine Bounty that within the space of an hour the equivalent of a thousand verses hath been revealed. So great is the grace vouchsafed in this day that in a single day and night, were an amanuensis capable of accomplishing it to be found, the equivalent of the Persian Bayán would be sent down from the heaven of Divine holiness. I Swear by God! ... In those days the equivalent of all that hath been sent down aforetime unto the Prophets hath been revealed. That which hath already been revealed in this land (Adrianople) ... secretaries are incapable of transcribing. It has, therefore, remained for the most part untranscribed.[175]

The day is approaching when the Land of Mystery (Adrianople), and what is beside it shall be changed, and shall pass out of the hands of the King, and commotions shall appear, and the voice of lamentation shall be raised, and the evidences of mischief shall be revealed on all sides, and confusion shall spread by reason of that which hath befallen these captives at the hands of the hosts of oppression. The course of things shall be altered, and conditions shall wax so grievous, that the very sands on the desolate hills will moan, and the trees on the mountain will weep, and blood will flow out of all things. Then wilt thou behold the people in sore distress.[176]

Say: This Youth hath departed out of this country and deposited beneath every tree and every stone a trust, which God will erelong bring forth through the power of truth.[177]

Days of Stress

I am the one, O Lord, whose heart and soul, whose limbs, whose inner and outer tongue testify to Thy unity and Thy oneness, and bear witness that Thou art God and that there is no God but Thee. Thou didst bring mankind into being to know Thee and to serve Thy Cause, that their station might thereby be elevated upon Thine earth and their souls be uplifted by virtue of the things Thou hast revealed in Thy Scriptures, Thy Books and Thy Tablets. Yet no sooner didst Thou manifest Thyself and reveal Thy signs than they turned away from Thee and repudiated Thee and rejected that which Thou didst unveil before their eyes through the potency of Thy might and Thy power. They rose up to inflict harm upon Thee, to extinguish Thy light and to put out the flame that blazeth in Thy Burning Bush. Their iniquity waxed so grievous that they conspired to shed Thy blood and to violate Thy honour. And likewise acted he[178] whom Thou hadst nurtured with the hand of Thy loving-kindness, hadst protected from the mischief of the rebellious among Thy creatures and the froward amidst Thy servants, and whom Thou hadst set the task of writing Thy holy verses before Thy throne.

Alas! Alas! for the things he perpetrated in Thy days to such an extent that he violated Thy Covenant and Thy Testament, rejected Thy holy Writ, rose up in rebellion and committed that which caused the denizens of Thy Kingdom to lament. Then no sooner had he found his hopes shattered and had perceived the odour of utter failure than he raised his voice and gave tongue to that which caused Thy chosen ones, who are nigh unto Thee, and the inmates of the pavilion of glory, to be lost in bewilderment.

Thou seest me, O my God, writhing in anguish upon the dust, like unto a fish. Deliver me, have mercy upon me, O Thou Whose aid is invoked by all men, O Thou within Whose grasp lie the reins of power over all men and women.[179]

He who for months and years...I reared with the hand of loving-kindness hath risen to take My life. The cruelties inflicted by My oppressors...have bowed Me down, and turned My hair white. Shouldst thou present thyself before My throne, thou wouldst fail to recognize the Ancient Beauty, for the freshness of His countenance is altered, and its brightness hath faded, by reason of the oppression of the infidels. By God! No spot is left on My body that hath not been touched by the spears of thy machinations. Thou hast perpetrated against thy Brother what no man hath perpetrated against another. What hath proceeded from thy pen...hath caused the Countenances of Glory to be prostrated upon the dust, hath rent in twain the Veil of Grandeur in the Sublime Paradise, and lacerated the hearts of the favored ones established upon the loftiest seats.[180]

O Shaykh! My Pen, verily, lamenteth over Mine own Self, and My Tablet weepeth sore over what hath befallen Me at the hands of one (Mírzá Yahyá) over whom We watched for successive years, and who, day and night, served in My presence, until he was made to err by one of My servants, named Siyyid Muhammad. Unto this bear witness My believing servants who accompanied Me in My exile from Baghdád to this, the Most Great Prison. And there befell Me at the hands of both of them that which made every man of understanding to cry out, and he who is endued with insight to groan aloud, and the tears of the fair-minded to flow.[181]

Say: O Yahyá (Azal), produce a single verse, if thou dost possess divinely-inspired knowledge. These words were formerly spoken by My Herald Who at this hour proclaimeth: Verily, verily, I am the first to adore Him. Be fair, O My brother. Art thou able to express thyself when brought face to face with the billowing ocean of Mine utterance? Canst thou unloose thy tongue when confronted with the shrill voice of My Pen? Hast thou any power before the revelations of Mine omnipotence? Judge thou fairly, I adjure thee by God, and call to mind when thou didst stand in the presence of this Wronged One and We dictated to thee the verses of God, the Help in Peril, the Self-Subsisting. Beware lest the source of falsehood withhold thee from the manifest Truth.182

O Muhammad! He Who is the Spirit hath, verily, issued from His habitation, and with Him have come forth the souls of God's chosen ones and the realities of His Messengers. Behold, then, the dwellers of the realms on high above Mine head, and all the testimonies of the Prophets in My grasp. Say: Were all the divines, all the wise men, all the kings and rulers on earth to gather together, I, in very truth, would confront them, and would proclaim the verses of God, the Sovereign, the Almighty, the All-Wise. I am He Who feareth no one, though all who are in heaven and all who are on earth rise up against me.... This is Mine hand which God hath turned white for all the worlds to behold. This is My staff; were We to cast it down, it would, of a truth, swallow up all created things.[183]

Exiled to 'Akká: The Most Great Prison

O Shaykh! These perspicuous verses have been sent down in one of the Tablets by the Abhá Pen: "Hearken, O servant, unto the voice of this Wronged One, Who hath endured grievous vexations and trials in the path of God, the Lord of all Names, until such time as He was cast into prison, in the Land of Tá (Ṭihrán). He summoned men unto the most sublime Paradise, and yet they seized Him and paraded Him through cities and countries. How many the nights during which slumber fled from the eyes of My loved ones, because of their love for Me; and how numerous the days whereon I had to face the assaults of the peoples against Me! At one time I found Myself on the heights of mountains; at another in the depths of the prison of Tá (Ṭihrán), in chains and fetters. By the righteousness of God! I was at all times thankful unto Him, uttering His praise, engaged in remembering Him, directed towards Him, satisfied with His pleasure, and lowly and submissive before Him. So passed My days, until they ended in this Prison ('Akká) which hath made the earth to tremble and the heavens to sigh. Happy that one who hath cast away his vain imaginings, when He Who was hid came with the standards of His signs. We, verily, have announced unto men this Most Great Revelation, and yet the people are in a state of strange stupor."

Thereupon, a Voice was raised from the direction of Hijáz, calling aloud and saying: "Great is thy blessedness, O 'Akká, in that God hath made thee the dayspring of His Most Sweet Voice, and the dawn of His most mighty signs. Happy art thou in that the Throne of Justice hath been established upon thee, and the Daystar of God's loving-kindness and bounty hath shone forth above thy horizon. Well is it with every fair-minded person that hath judged fairly Him Who is the Most Great Remembrance, and woe betide him that hath erred and doubted."[184]

More grievous became Our plight from day to day, nay, from hour to hour, until they took Us forth from Our prison and made

Us, with glaring injustice, enter the Most Great Prison. And if anyone ask them: "For what crime were they imprisoned?", they would answer and say: "They, verily, sought to supplant the Faith with a new religion!" If that which is ancient be what ye prefer, wherefore, then, have ye discarded that which hath been set down in the Torah and the Evangel? Clear it up, O men! By My life! There is no place for you to flee to in this day. If this be My crime, then Muhammad, the Apostle of God, committed it before Me, and before Him He Who was the Spirit of God, and yet earlier He Who conversed with God. And if My sin be this, that I have exalted the Word of God and revealed His Cause, then indeed am I the greatest of sinners! Such a sin I will not barter for the kingdoms of earth and heaven.[185]

Upon Our arrival ... We were welcomed with banners of light, whereupon the Voice of the Spirit cried out saying: "Soon will all that dwell on earth be enlisted under these banners."

Know thou ... that upon Our arrival at this Spot, We chose to designate it as the Most Great Prison. Though previously subjected in another land (Ṭihrán) to chains and fetters, We yet refused to call it by that name. Say: Ponder thereon, O ye endued with understanding! [186]

Meditate on the world and the state of its people. He, for Whose sake the world was called into being, hath been imprisoned in the most desolate of cities,[187] by reason of that which the hands of the wayward have wrought. From the horizon of His prison-city He summoneth mankind unto the Dayspring of God, the Exalted, the Great.[188]

None ... knoweth what befell Us, except God, the Almighty, the All-Knowing ... From the foundation of the world until the present day a cruelty such as this hath neither been seen nor heard of.

He hath, during the greater part of His life ... been sore-tried in the clutches of His enemies. His sufferings have now reached their culmination in this afflictive Prison, into which His oppressors have so unjustly thrown Him.[189]

O my God! Thou beholdest the Lord of all mankind confined in His Most Great Prison, calling aloud Thy Name, gazing upon Thy face, proclaiming that which hath enraptured the denizens of Thy kingdoms of revelation and of creation. O my God! I behold Mine own Self captive in the hands of Thy servants, yet the light of Thy sovereignty and the revelations of Thine invincible power shine resplendent from His face, enabling all to know of a certainty that Thou art God, and that there is none other God but Thee. Neither can the power of the powerful frustrate Thee, nor the ascendancy of the rulers prevail against Thee. Thou doest whatsoever Thou willest by virtue of Thy sovereignty which encompasseth all created things, and ordainest that which Thou pleasest through the potency of Thy behest which pervadeth the entire creation.[190]

The instigators of this oppression are those very persons who, though so foolish, are reputed the wisest of the wise. Such is their blindness that, with unfeigned severity, they have cast into this fortified and afflictive Prison Him, for the servants of Whose Threshold the world hath been created. The Almighty, however, in spite of them and those that have repudiated the truth of this "Great Announcement," hath transformed this Prison House into the Most Exalted Paradise, the Heaven of Heavens.[191]

O Thou Who art the Ruler of earth and heaven and the Author of all names! Thou hearest the voice of my lamentation which from the fortress-town of 'Akká ascendeth towards Thee, and beholdest how my captive friends have fallen into the hands of the workers of iniquity.

We render Thee thanks, O our Lord, for all the troubles which have touched us in Thy path. Oh, that the span of my earthly life could be so extended as to embrace the lives of the former and the latter generations, or could even be so lengthened that no man on the face of the earth could measure it, and be afflicted every day and every moment with a fresh tribulation for love of Thee and for Thy pleasure's sake! [192]

Thou seest, O my God, how Thy servants have been cleaving fast to Thy names, and have been calling on them in the daytime and in the night season. No sooner, however, had He been made manifest through Whose word the kingdom of names and the heaven of eternity were created, than they broke away from Him and disbelieved in the greatest of Thy signs. They finally banished Him from the land of His birth, and caused Him to dwell within the most desolate of Thy cities, though all the world had been built up by Thee for His sake. Within this, the Most Great Prison, He hath established His seat. Though sore tried by trials, the like of which the eye of creation hath not seen, He summoneth the people unto Thee, O Thou Who art the Fashioner of the universe! [193]

O Carmel

ALL glory be to this Day, the Day in which the fragrances of mercy have been wafted over all created things, a Day so blest that past ages and centuries can never hope to rival it, a Day in which the countenance of the Ancient of Days hath turned towards His holy seat. Thereupon the voices of all created things, and beyond them those of the Concourse on High, were heard calling aloud: "Haste thee, O Carmel, for lo, the light of the countenance of God, the Ruler of the Kingdom of Names and Fashioner of the heavens, hath been lifted upon thee."

Seized with transports of joy, and raising high her voice, she thus exclaimed: "May my life be a sacrifice to Thee, inasmuch as Thou hast fixed Thy gaze upon me, hast bestowed upon me Thy bounty, and hast directed towards me Thy steps. Separation from Thee, O Thou Source of everlasting life, hath well nigh consumed me, and my remoteness from Thy presence hath burned away my soul. All praise be to Thee for having enabled me to hearken to Thy call, for having honoured me with Thy footsteps, and for having quickened my soul through the vitalizing fragrance of Thy Day and the shrilling voice of Thy Pen, a voice Thou didst ordain as Thy trumpet-call amidst Thy people...."

No sooner had her voice reached that most exalted Spot than We made reply: 'Render thanks unto thy Lord, O Carmel. The fire of thy separation from Me was fast consuming thee, when the ocean of My presence surged before thy face, cheering thine eyes and those of all creation, and filling with delight all things visible and invisible. Rejoice, for God hath in this Day established upon thee His throne, hath made thee the dawning-place of His signs and the dayspring of the evidences of His Revelation. Well is it with him that circleth around thee, that proclaimeth the revelation of thy glory, and recounteth that which the bounty of the Lord thy God hath showered upon thee. Seize thou the Chalice of Immortality in the name of thy Lord, the All-Glorious, and give thanks unto Him, inasmuch as He, in token of His mercy unto thee, hath turned thy sorrow into gladness, and transmuted thy grief into blissful joy. He, verily, loveth the spot which hath been made the seat of His throne, which His footsteps have trodden, which hath been honoured by His presence, from which He raised His call, and upon which He shed His tears.

"Call out to Zion, O Carmel, and announce the joyful tidings: He that was hidden from mortal eyes is come! His all-conquering sovereignty is manifest; His all-encompassing splendour is revealed.... Ere long will God sail His Ark upon thee, and will manifest the people of Bahá who have been mentioned in the Book of Names."[194]

Death of Mírzá Mihdí: The Purest Branch

Lauded be Thy name, O Lord my God! Thou seest me in this day shut up in my prison, and fallen into the hands of Thine adversaries, and beholdest my son (The Purest Branch) lying on the dust before Thy face. He is Thy servant, O my Lord, whom Thou hast caused to be related to Him Who is the Manifestation of Thyself and the Day-Spring of Thy Cause.

At his birth he was afflicted through his separation from Thee, according to what had been ordained for him through Thine irrevocable decree. And when he had quaffed the cup of reunion with Thee, he was cast into prison for having believed in Thee and in Thy signs. He continued to serve Thy Beauty until he entered into this Most Great Prison. Thereupon I offered him up, O my God, as a sacrifice in Thy path. Thou well knowest what they who love Thee have endured through this trial that hath caused the kindreds of the earth to wail, and beyond them the Concourse on high to lament.

I beseech Thee, O my Lord, by him and by his exile and his imprisonment, to send down upon such as loved him what will quiet their hearts and bless their works. Potent art Thou to do as Thou willest. No God is there but Thee, the Almighty, the Most Powerful.[195]

At this very moment ... My son is being washed before My face, after Our having sacrificed him in the Most Great Prison. Thereat have the dwellers of the Abhá Tabernacle wept with a great weeping, and such as have suffered imprisonment with this Youth in the path of God, the Lord of the promised Day, lamented. Under such conditions My Pen hath not been prevented from remembering its Lord, the Lord of all nations. It summoneth the people unto God, the Almighty, the All-Bountiful. This is the day whereon he that was created by the light of Bahá has suffered martyrdom, at a time when he lay imprisoned at the hands of his enemies.

Upon thee, O Branch of God! ... be the remembrance of God and His praise, and the praise of all that dwell in the Realm of Immortality, and of all the denizens of the Kingdom of Names. Happy art thou in that thou hast been faithful to the Covenant of God and His Testament, until Thou didst sacrifice thyself before the face of thy Lord, the Almighty, the Unconstrained. Thou, in truth, hast been wronged, and to this testifieth the Beauty of Him, the Self-Subsisting. Thou didst, in the first days of thy life, bear that which hath caused all things to groan, and made every pillar to tremble. Happy is the one that remembereth thee, and draweth nigh, through thee, unto God, the Creator of the Morn.[196]

I have, O my Lord, offered up that which Thou hast given Me, that Thy servants may be quickened, and all that dwell on earth be united.[1976]

Blessed art thou ... and blessed he that turneth unto thee, and visiteth thy grave, and draweth nigh, through thee, unto God, the Lord of all that was and shall be.... I testify that thou didst return in meekness unto thine abode. Great is thy blessedness and the blessedness of them that hold fast unto the hem of thy outspread robe.... Thou art, verily, the trust of God and His treasure in this land. Erelong will God reveal through thee that which He hath desired. He, verily, is the Truth, the Knower of things unseen. When thou wast laid to rest in the earth, the earth itself trembled in its longing to meet thee. Thus hath it been decreed, and yet the people perceive not.... Were We to recount the mysteries of thine ascension, they that are asleep would waken, and all beings would be set ablaze with the fire of the remembrance of My Name, the Mighty, the Loving.[198]

Life of Tribulations and Sorrows

Were I to recount to thee the tale of the things that have befallen Me, the souls and minds of men would be incapable of sustaining its weight. God Himself beareth Me witness ... Recall to mind My sorrows, ... My cares and anxieties, My woes and trials, the state of My captivity, the tears that I have shed, the bitterness of Mine anguish, and now Mine imprisonment in this far-off land... Couldst thou be told what hath befallen the Ancient Beauty, thou wouldst flee into the wilderness, and weep with a great weeping... Every morning I arose from my bed, I discovered the hosts of countless afflictions massed behind My door; and every night when I lay down, lo, My heart was torn with agony at what it had suffered from the fiendish cruelty of its foes.[199]

The cruelties inflicted by My oppressors have bowed Me down, and turned My hair white. Shouldst thou present thyself before My throne, thou wouldst fail to recognize the Ancient Beauty, for the freshness of His countenance is altered and its brightness hath faded, by reason of the oppression of the infidels. I swear by God! His heart, His soul, and His vitals are melted! Wert thou to hear with Mine ear thou wouldst hear how Alí [the Báb] bewaileth Me in the presence of the Glorious Companion, and how Muhammad weepeth over Me in the all-highest Horizon, and how the Spirit [Jesus] beateth Himself upon the head in the heaven of My decree, by reason of what hath befallen this Wronged One at the hands of every impious sinner.[200]

The Ancient Beauty hath consented to be bound with chains that mankind may be released from its bondage, and hath accepted to be made a prisoner within this most mighty Stronghold that the whole world may attain unto true liberty. He hath drained to its dregs the cup of sorrow, that all the peoples of the earth may attain unto abiding joy, and be filled with gladness. This is of the mercy of your Lord, the Compassionate, the Most Merciful. We have accepted to be abased, O believers in the Unity of God, that ye may be exalted, and have suffered manifold afflictions, that ye might prosper and flourish. He Who hath come to build anew the whole world, behold, how they that have joined partners with God have forced Him to dwell within the most desolate of cities!

I sorrow not for the burden of My imprisonment. Neither do I grieve over My abasement, or the tribulation I suffer at the hands of Mine enemies. By My life! They are My glory, a glory wherewith God hath adorned His own Self. Would that ye know it! [201]

Hearken unto My voice that calleth from My prison, that it may acquaint thee with the things that have befallen My Beauty, at the hands of them that are the manifestations of My glory, and that thou mayest perceive how great hath been My patience, notwithstanding My might, and how immense My forbearance, notwithstanding My power. By My life! Couldst thou but know the things sent down by My Pen, and discover the treasures of My Cause, and the pearls of My mysteries which lie hid in the seas of My names and in the goblets of My words, thou wouldst, in thy love for My name, and in thy longing for My glorious and sublime Kingdom, lay down thy life in My path. Know thou that though My body be beneath the swords of My foes, and My limbs be beset with incalculable afflictions, yet My spirit is filled with a gladness with which all the joys of the earth can never compare.[202]

The one true God well knoweth, and all the company of His trusted ones testify, that this Wronged One hath, at all times, been faced with dire peril. But for the tribulations that have touched Me in the path of God, life would have held no sweetness for Me, and My existence would have profited Me nothing. For them who are endued with discernment, and whose eyes are fixed upon the Sublime Vision, it is no secret that I have been, most of the days of My life, even as a slave, sitting under a sword hanging on a thread, knowing not whether it would fall soon or late upon him. And yet, notwithstanding all this We render thanks unto God, the Lord of the worlds.[203]

Grievous as is My plight, O God, My Well-Beloved, I render thanks unto Thee, and My Spirit is grateful for whatsoever hath befallen me in the path of Thy good-pleasure. I am well pleased with that which Thou didst ordain for Me, and welcome, however calamitous, the pains and sorrows I am made to suffer.[204]

I swear by the beauty of the Well-Beloved! This is the Mercy that hath encompassed the entire creation, the Day whereon the grace of God hath permeated and pervaded all things. The living waters of My mercy, O 'Alí, are fast pouring down, and Mine heart is melting with the heat of My tenderness and love. At no time have I been able to reconcile Myself to the afflictions befalling My loved ones, or to any trouble that could becloud the joy of their hearts.

Every time My name "the All-Merciful" was told that one of My lovers had breathed a word that runneth counter to My wish, it repaired, grief-stricken and disconsolate to its abode; and whenever My name "the Concealer" discovered that one of My followers had inflicted any shame or humiliation on his neighbor, it, likewise, turned back chagrined and sorrowful to its retreats of glory, and there wept and mourned with a sore lamentation. And whenever My name "the Ever-Forgiving" perceived that any one of My friends had committed any transgression, it cried out in its great distress, and, overcome with anguish, fell upon the dust, and was borne away by a company of the invisible angels to its habitation in the realms above.

By Myself, the True One, O 'Alí! The fire that hath inflamed the heart of Bahá is fiercer than the fire that gloweth in thine heart, and His lamentation louder than thy lamentation. Every time the sin committed by any one amongst them was breathed in the Court of His Presence, the Ancient Beauty would be so filled with shame as to wish He could hide the glory of His countenance from the eyes of all men, for He hath, at all times, fixed His gaze on their fidelity, and observed its essential requisites.[205]

How numerous the tribulations which have rained, and will soon rain, upon Me! I advance with My face set towards Him Who is the Almighty, the All-Bounteous, whilst behind Me glideth the serpent. Mine eyes have rained down tears until My bed is drenched.

I sorrow not for Myself, however. By God! Mine head yearneth for the spear out of love for its Lord. I never passed a tree, but Mine heart addressed it saying: "O would that thou wert cut down in My name, and My body crucified upon thee, in the path of My Lord!"...

By God! Though weariness lay Me low, and hunger consume Me, and the bare rock be My bed, and My fellows the beasts of the field, I will not complain, but will endure patiently as those endued with constancy and firmness have endured patiently, through the power of God, the Eternal King and Creator of the nations, and will render thanks unto God under all conditions. We pray that, out of His bounty—exalted be He—He may release, through this imprisonment, the necks of men from chains and fetters, and cause them to turn, with sincere faces, towards His face, Who is the Mighty, the Bounteous. Ready is He to answer whosoever calleth upon Him, and nigh is He unto such as commune with Him.[206]

Say: Tribulation is a horizon unto My Revelation. The day star of grace shineth above it, and sheddeth a light which neither the clouds of men's idle fancy nor the vain imaginations of the aggressor can obscure.[207]

On His Ascension

Be not dismayed, O peoples of the world, when the day-star of My beauty is set, and the heaven of My tabernacle is concealed from your eyes. Arise to further My Cause, and to exalt My Word amongst men. We are with you at all times, and shall strengthen you through the power of truth. We are truly almighty. Whoso hath recognized Me will arise and serve Me with such determination that the powers of earth and heaven shall be unable to defeat his purpose.[208]

Should differences arise amongst you over any matter, refer it to God while the Sun still shineth above the horizon of this Heaven and, when it hath set, refer ye to whatsoever hath been sent down by Him. This, verily, is sufficient unto the peoples of the world. Say: Let not your hearts be perturbed, O people, when the glory of My Presence is withdrawn, and the ocean of My utterance is stilled. In My presence amongst you there is a wisdom, and in My absence there is yet another, inscrutable to all but God, the Incomparable, the all-Knowing. Verily, We behold you from Our realm of glory, and shall aid whosoever will arise for the triumph of Our Cause with the hosts of the Concourse on high and a company of Our favoured angels.[209]

We remember every one of you, men and women, and from this Spot, the Scene of incomparable glory, regard you all as one soul and send you the joyous tidings of divine blessings which have preceded all created things, and of My remembrance that pervadeth everyone, whether young or old. The glory of God rest upon you, O people of Bahá. Rejoice with exceeding gladness through My remembrance, for He is indeed with you at all times.[210]

'Abdu'l-Bahá: Center of the Covenant

When the ocean of My presence hath ebbed and the Book of My Revelation is ended, turn your faces toward Him Whom God hath purposed, Who hath branched from this Ancient Root.[211]

O people of the world! When the Mystic Dove will have winged its flight from its Sanctuary of Praise and sought its far-off goal, its hidden habitation, refer ye whatsoever ye understand not in the Book to Him Who hath branched from this mighty Stock.[212]

The Will of the divine Testator is this: It is incumbent upon the Aghsán, the Afnán and My Kindred to turn, one and all, their faces towards the Most Mighty Branch. Consider that which We have revealed in Our Most Holy Book: When the ocean of My presence hath ebbed and the Book of My Revelation is ended, turn your faces toward Him Whom God hath purposed, Who hath branched from this Ancient Root. The object of this sacred verse is none other except the Most Mighty Branch ['Abdu'l-Bahá]. Thus have We graciously revealed unto you Our potent Will, and I am verily the Gracious, the All-Powerful.[213]

There hath branched from the Sadratu'l-Muntahá this sacred and glorious Being, this Branch of Holiness; well is it with him that hath sought His shelter and abideth beneath His shadow. Verily the Limb of the Law of God hath sprung forth from this Root which God hath firmly implanted in the Ground of His Will, and Whose Branch hath been so uplifted as to encompass the whole of creation. Magnified be He, therefore, for this sublime, this blessed, this mighty, this exalted Handiwork! ... A Word hath, as a token of Our grace, gone forth from the Most Great Tablet—a Word which God hath adorned with the ornament of His own Self, and made it sovereign over the earth and all that is therein, and a sign of His greatness and power among its people ... Render thanks unto God, O people, for His appearance; for verily He is the most great Favor unto you, the most perfect bounty upon you; and through

Him every mouldering bone is quickened. Whoso turneth towards Him hath turned towards God, and whoso turneth away from Him hath turned away from My beauty, hath repudiated My Proof, and transgressed against Me. He is the Trust of God amongst you, His charge within you, His manifestation unto you and His appearance among His favored servants ... We have sent Him down in the form of a human temple. Blest and sanctified be God Who createth whatsoever He willeth through His inviolable, His infallible decree. They who deprive themselves of the shadow of the Branch, are lost in the wilderness of error, are consumed by the heat of worldly desires, and are of those who will assuredly perish.

O Thou Who art the apple of Mine eye! ... My glory, the ocean of My loving-kindness, the sun of My bounty, the heaven of My mercy rest upon Thee. We pray God to illumine the world through Thy knowledge and wisdom, to ordain for Thee that which will gladden Thine heart and impart consolation to Thine eyes.

The glory of God rest upon Thee ... and upon whosoever serveth Thee and circleth around Thee. Woe, great woe, betide him that opposeth and injureth Thee. Well is it with him that sweareth fealty to Thee; the fire of hell torment him who is Thine enemy.

We have made Thee a shelter for all mankind, ... a shield unto all who are in heaven and on earth, a stronghold for whosoever hath believed in God, the Incomparable, the All-Knowing. God grant that through Thee He may protect them, may enrich and sustain them, that He may inspire Thee with that which shall be a wellspring of wealth unto all created things, an ocean of bounty unto all men, and the dayspring of mercy unto all peoples.

Thou knowest, O my God, ... that I desire for Him naught except that which Thou didst desire, and have chosen Him for no purpose save that which Thou hadst intended for Him. Render Him victorious, therefore, through Thy hosts of earth and heaven... Ordain, I beseech Thee, by the ardor of My love for Thee and My yearning to manifest Thy Cause, for Him, as well as for them that love Him, that which Thou hast destined for Thy Messengers and the Trustees of Thy Revelation. Verily, Thou art the Almighty, the All-Powerful.

... Blessed, doubly blessed, is the ground which His footsteps have trodden, the eye that hath been cheered by the beauty of His countenance, the ear that hath been honored by hearkening to His call, the heart that hath tasted the sweetness of His love, the breast that hath dilated through His remembrance, the pen that hath voiced His praise, the scroll that hath borne the testimony of His writings.[214]

Bahíyyih Khánum: The Greatest Holy Leaf

Let these exalted words be thy love-song on the tree of Bahá, O thou most holy and resplendent Leaf: 'God, besides Whom is none other God, the Lord of this world and the next!' Verily, We have elevated thee to the rank of one of the most distinguished among thy sex, and granted thee, in My court, a station such as none other woman hath surpassed. Thus have We preferred thee and raised thee above the rest, as a sign of grace from Him Who is the Lord of the throne on high and earth below. We have created thine eyes to behold the light of My countenance, thine ears to hearken unto the melody of My words, thy body to pay homage before My throne. Do thou render thanks unto God, thy Lord, the Lord of all the world.

How high is the testimony of the Sadratu'l-Muntahá for its leaf; how exalted the witness of the Tree of Life unto its fruit! Through My remembrance of her a fragrance laden with the perfume of musk hath been diffused; well is it with him that hath inhaled it and exclaimed: 'All praise be to Thee, O God, my Lord the most glorious!' How sweet thy presence before Me; how sweet to gaze upon thy face, to bestow upon thee My loving-kindness, to favour thee with My tender care, to make mention of thee in this, My Tablet—a Tablet which I have ordained as a token of My hidden and manifest grace unto thee.[215]

O My Leaf! Hearken thou unto My Voice: Verily there is none other God but Me, the Almighty, the All-Wise. I can well inhale from thee the fragrance of My love and the sweet-smelling savour wafting from the raiment of My Name, the Most Holy, the Most Luminous. Be astir upon God's Tree in conformity with thy pleasure and unloose thy tongue in praise of thy Lord amidst all mankind. Let not the things of the world grieve thee. Cling fast unto this divine Lote-Tree from which God hath graciously caused thee to spring forth. I swear by My life! It behoveth the lover to be closely joined to the loved one, and here indeed is the Best-Beloved of the world.[216]

Greatness of This Day

This is the King of Days ... the Day that hath seen the coming of the Best-beloved, Him Who through all eternity hath been acclaimed the Desire of the World. The world of being shineth in this Day with the resplendency of this Divine Revelation. All created things extol its saving grace and sing its praises. The universe is wrapt in an ecstasy of joy and gladness. The Scriptures of past Dispensations celebrate the great jubilee that must needs greet this most great Day of God. Well is it with him that hath lived to see this Day and hath recognized its station.[217]

This Day a door is open wider than both heaven and earth. The eye of the mercy of Him Who is the Desire of the worlds is turned towards all men. ... These days are God's days, a moment of which ages and centuries can never rival. An atom, in these days, is as the sun, a drop as the ocean. One single breath exhaled in the love of God and for His service is written down by the Pen of Glory as a princely deed. Were the virtues of this Day to be recounted, all would be thunderstruck, except those whom thy Lord hath exempted. ... Say, O men! This is a matchless Day. Matchless must, likewise, be the tongue that celebrateth the praise of the Desire of all nations, and matchless the deed that aspireth to be acceptable in His sight. The whole human race hath longed for this Day, that perchance it may fulfill that which well beseemeth its station and is worthy of its destiny.

Through the movement of Our Pen of Glory We have, at the bidding of the Omnipotent Ordainer, breathed a new life into every human frame, and instilled into every word a fresh potency. All created things proclaim the evidences of this worldwide regeneration.[218]

ALL glory be to this Day, the Day in which the fragrances of mercy have been wafted over all created things, a Day so blest that past ages and centuries can never hope to rival it....[219]

This is the Day, O my Lord, which Thou didst announce unto all mankind as the Day whereon Thou wouldst reveal Thy Self, and shed Thy radiance, and shine brightly over all Thy creatures. Thou hast, moreover, entered into a covenant with them, in Thy Books, and Thy Scriptures, and Thy Scrolls, and Thy Tablets, concerning Him Who is the Day-Spring of Thy Revelation, and hast appointed the Bayán to be the Herald of this Most Great and all-glorious Manifestation, and this most resplendent and most sublime Appearance.[220]

This is the Day in which God's most excellent favours have been poured out upon men, the Day in which His most mighty grace hath been infused into all created things. It is incumbent upon all the peoples of the world to reconcile their differences, and, with perfect unity and peace, abide beneath the shadow of the Tree of His care and loving-kindness. It behoveth them to cleave to whatsoever will, in this Day, be conducive to the exaltation of their stations, and to the promotion of their best interests.[221]

The potentialities inherent in the station of man, the full measure of his destiny on earth, the innate excellence of his reality, must all be manifested in this promised Day of God.[222]

It is evident that every age in which a Manifestation of God hath lived is divinely ordained, and may, in a sense, be characterized as God's appointed Day. This Day, however, is unique, and is to be distinguished from those that have preceded it. The designation "Seal of the Prophets" fully revealeth its high station.[223]

Behold how the manifold grace of God, which is being showered from the clouds of Divine glory, hath, in this day, encompassed the world. For whereas in days past every lover besought and searched after his Beloved, it is the Beloved Himself Who now is calling His lovers and is inviting them to attain His presence. Take heed lest ye forfeit so precious a favor; beware lest ye belittle so remarkable a token of His grace.[224]

These sublime words have streamed forth from the Pen of the Most High. He saith, exalted be His glory: "This is the day of vision, for the countenance of God is shining resplendent above the horizon of Manifestation. This is the day of hearing, for the call of God hath been raised. It behoveth everyone in this day to uphold and proclaim that which hath been revealed by Him Who is the Author of all scripture, the Dayspring of revelation, the Fount of knowledge and the Source of divine wisdom."[225]

For this day is the Lord of all days, and whatsoever hath been revealed therein by the Source of divine Revelation is the truth and the essence of all principles. This day may be likened to a sea and all other days to gulfs and channels that have branched therefrom. That which is uttered and revealed in this day is the foundation, and is accounted as the Mother Book and the Source of all utterance. Although every day is associated with God, magnified be His glory, yet these days have been singled out and adorned with the ornament of intimate association with Him, for they have been extolled in the books of the Chosen Ones of God, as well as of some of His Prophets, as the "Day of God".[226]

Had Muhammad, the Apostle of God, attained this Day, He would have exclaimed: "I have truly recognized Thee, O Thou the Desire of the Divine Messengers!" Had Abraham attained it, He too, falling prostrate upon the ground, and in the utmost lowliness before the Lord thy God, would have cried: "Mine heart is filled with peace, O Thou Lord of all that is in heaven and on earth! I testify that Thou hast unveiled before mine eyes all the glory of Thy power and the full majesty of Thy law! I bear witness, moreover, that through Thy Revelation the hearts of the faithful are well assured and contented." Had Moses Himself attained it, He, likewise, would have raised His voice saying: "All praise be to Thee for having lifted upon me the light of Thy countenance and enrolled me among them that have been privileged to behold Thy face!"[227]

North and South both vibrate to the call announcing the advent of our Revelation. We can hear the voice of Mecca acclaiming: "All praise be to Thee, O Lord my God, the All-Glorious, for having wafted over me the breath redolent with the fragrance of Thy presence!" Jerusalem, likewise, is calling aloud: "Lauded and magnified art Thou, O Beloved of earth and heaven, for having turned the agony of my separation from Thee into the joy of a life-giving reunion!"[228]

Promised One of all Religions

Go thou straight on and persevere in His service. Say: O people! The Day, promised unto you in all the Scriptures, is now come. Fear ye God, and withhold not yourselves from recognizing the One Who is the Object of your creation. Hasten ye unto Him. Better is this for you than the world and all that is therein. Would that ye could perceive it! [229]

All the Divine Books and Scriptures have predicted and announced unto men the advent of the Most Great Revelation. None can adequately recount the verses recorded in the Books of former ages which forecast this supreme Bounty, this most mighty Bestowal.[230]

The Revelation which, from time immemorial, hath been acclaimed as the Purpose and Promise of all the Prophets of God, and the most cherished Desire of His Messengers, hath now, by virtue of the pervasive Will of the Almighty and at His irresistible bidding, been revealed unto men. The advent of such a Revelation hath been heralded in all the sacred Scriptures. Behold how, notwithstanding such an announcement, mankind hath strayed from its path and shut out itself from its glory.[231]

VERILY I say, this is the Day in which mankind can behold the Face, and hear the Voice, of the Promised One. The Call of God hath been raised, and the light of His countenance hath been lifted up upon men. It behoveth every man to blot out the trace of every idle word from the tablet of his heart, and to gaze, with an open and unbiased mind, on the signs of His Revelation, the proofs of His Mission, and the tokens of His glory.

Great indeed is this Day! The allusions made to it in all the sacred Scriptures as the Day of God attest its greatness. The soul of every Prophet of God, of every Divine Messenger, hath thirsted for this wondrous Day. All the divers kindreds of the earth have, likewise, yearned to attain it. No sooner, however, had the Day Star of His Revelation manifested itself in the heaven of God's Will, than all, except those whom the Almighty was pleased to guide, were found dumbfounded and heedless.

... God grant that the light of unity may envelop the whole earth, and that the seal, 'the Kingdom is God's', may be stamped upon the brow of all its peoples.[232]

THE time fore-ordained unto the peoples and kindreds of the earth is now come. The promises of God, as recorded in the holy Scriptures, have all been fulfilled. Out of Zion hath gone forth the Law of God, and Jerusalem, and the hills and land thereof, are filled with the glory of His Revelation.[233]

O Lord! The tongue of my tongue and the heart of my heart and the spirit of my spirit and my outward and inmost beings bear witness to Thy unity and Thy oneness, Thy power and Thine omnipotence, Thy grandeur and Thy sovereignty, and attest Thy glory, loftiness and authority. I testify that Thou art God and that there is none other God besides Thee. From everlasting Thou hast been a treasure hidden from the sight and minds of men and shalt continue to remain the same for ever and ever. The powers of earth can never frustrate Thee, nor can the might of the nations alarm Thee. Thou art the One Who hath unlocked the door of knowledge before the faces of Thy servants that they may recognize Him Who is the Day-Star of Thy Revelation, the Dawning-Place of Thy signs, the Heaven of Thy manifestation and the Sun of Thy divine beauty. In Thy holy Books, in Thy Scriptures and Thy Scrolls Thou hast promised all the peoples of the world that Thou Thyself shalt appear and shalt remove the veils of glory from Thy face, even as Thou didst announce in Thy words unto Thy Friend[234] through Whom the Day-Star of Revelation shone brightly above the horizon of Hijáz, and the dawning light of divine Truth shed its radiance among all men, proclaiming: 'The Day when mankind shall stand before the Lord of the worlds.'[235] And before Muhammad Thou didst impart this gladtiding unto Him Who conversed with Thee,[236] saying: 'Bring forth thy people from the darkness into the light and remind them of the days of God.'[237] Moreover Thou didst proclaim this truth unto the Spirit[238] and unto Thy Prophets and Thy Messengers, whether of the remote or more recent past. If all that which Thou hast sent down in glorification of this Most Great Remembrance, this Great Announcement, were to stream forth from the wellspring of Thy most august Pen, the inmates of the cities of knowledge and understanding would be dumbfounded, except such as Thou wouldst deliver through the potency of Thy might and wouldst protect as a token of Thy bountiful favour and Thy grace. I bear witness that Thou hast in truth fulfilled Thy pledge and hast made manifest the One Whose advent was foretold by Thy Prophets, Thy chosen ones and by them that serve Thee. He hath come from the heaven of glory and power, bearing the banners of Thy signs and the standards of Thy testimonies. Through the potency of Thine indomitable power and strength, He stood up before the faces of all men and summoned all mankind to the summit of transcendent glory and unto the all-highest Horizon, in such wise that neither the oppression of the ecclesiastics nor the onslaught of the rulers was able to deter Him. He arose with inflexible resolve and, unloosing His tongue, proclaimed in ringing tones: 'He Who is the All-Bountiful is come, riding aloft on the clouds. Advance, O people of the earth, with shining faces and radiant hearts!'.[239]

To the Jewish People

How many Manifestations of Holiness, how many Revealers of the light everlasting, have appeared since the time of Moses, and yet Israel, wrapt in the densest veils of satanic fancy and false imaginings, is still expectant that the idol of her own handiwork will appear with such signs as she herself hath conceived! Thus hath God laid hold of them for their sins, hath extinguished in them the spirit of faith, and tormented them with the flames of the nethermost fire. And this for no other reason except that Israel refused to apprehend the meaning of such words as have been revealed in the Bible concerning the signs of the coming Revelation. As she never grasped their true significance, and, to outward seeming, such events never came to pass, she, therefore, remained deprived of recognizing the beauty of Jesus and of beholding the face of God. And they still await His coming! From time immemorial even unto this day, all the kindreds and peoples of the earth have clung to such fanciful and unseemly thoughts, and thus have deprived themselves of the clear waters streaming from the springs of purity and holiness.[240]

The Most Great Law is come, and the Ancient Beauty ruleth upon the throne of David. Thus hath My Pen spoken that which the histories of bygone ages have related. At this time, however, David crieth aloud and saith: 'O my loving Lord! Do Thou number me with such as have stood steadfast in Thy Cause, O Thou through Whom the faces have been illumined, and the footsteps have slipped!'

The Breath hath been wafted, and the Breeze hath blown, and from Zion hath appeared that which was hidden, and from Jerusalem is heard the Voice of God, the One, the Incomparable, the Omniscient.[241]

To the Christians

Say, O followers of the Son![242] Have ye shut out yourselves from Me by reason of My Name? Wherefore ponder ye not in your hearts? Day and night ye have been calling upon your Lord, the Omnipotent, but when He came from the heaven of eternity in His great glory, ye turned aside from Him and remained sunk in heedlessness.

Consider those who rejected the Spirit[243] when He came unto them with manifest dominion. How numerous the Pharisees who had secluded themselves in synagogues in His name, lamenting over their separation from Him, and yet when the portals of reunion were flung open and the divine Luminary shone resplendent from the Dayspring of Beauty, they disbelieved in God, the Exalted, the Mighty. They failed to attain His presence, notwithstanding that His advent had been promised them in the Book of Isaiah as well as in the Books of the Prophets and the Messengers. No one from among them turned his face towards the Dayspring of divine bounty except such as were destitute of any power amongst men. And yet, today, every man endowed with power and invested with sovereignty prideth himself on His Name. Moreover, call thou to mind the one who sentenced Jesus to death. He was the most learned of his age in his own country, whilst he who was only a fisherman believed in Him. Take good heed and be of them that observe the warning.

Consider likewise, how numerous at this time are the monks who have secluded themselves in their churches, calling upon the Spirit, but when He appeared through the power of Truth, they failed to draw nigh unto Him and are numbered with those that have gone far astray. Happy are they that have abandoned them and set their faces towards Him Who is the Desire of all that are in the heavens and all that are on the earth.

They read the Evangel and yet refuse to acknowledge the All-Glorious Lord, notwithstanding that He hath come through the potency of His exalted, His mighty and gracious dominion. We, verily, have come for your sakes, and have borne the misfortunes of the world for your salvation. Flee ye the One Who hath sacrificed His life that ye may be quickened? Fear God, O followers of the Spirit, and walk not in the footsteps of every divine that hath gone far astray. Do ye imagine that He seeketh His own interests, when He hath, at all times, been threatened by the swords of the enemies; or that He seeketh the vanities of the world, after He hath been imprisoned in the most desolate of cities? Be fair in your judgement and follow not the footsteps of the unjust.

Open the doors of your hearts. He Who is the Spirit verily standeth before them. Wherefore keep ye afar from Him Who hath purposed to draw you nigh unto a Resplendent Spot? Say: We, in truth, have opened unto you the gates of the Kingdom. Will ye bar the doors of your houses in My face? This indeed is naught but a grievous error. He, verily, hath again come down from heaven, even as He came down from it the first time. Beware lest ye dispute that which He proclaimeth, even as the people before you disputed His utterances. Thus instructeth you the True One, could ye but perceive it.

The river Jordan is joined to the Most Great Ocean, and the Son, in the holy vale, crieth out: 'Here am I, here am I O Lord, my God!', whilst Sinai circleth round the House, and the Burning Bush calleth aloud: 'He Who is the Desired One is come in His transcendent majesty.' Say, Lo! The Father is come, and that which ye were promised in the Kingdom is fulfilled! This is the Word which the Son concealed, when to those around Him He said: 'Ye cannot bear it now.' And when the appointed time was fulfilled and the Hour had struck, the Word shone forth above the horizon of the Will of God. Beware, O followers of the Son, that ye cast it not behind your backs. Take ye fast hold of it. Better is this for you than all that ye possess. Verily He is nigh unto them that do good. The Hour which We had concealed from the knowledge of the peoples of the earth and of the favoured angels hath come to pass. Say, verily, He hath testified of Me, and I do testify of Him. Indeed, He hath purposed no one other than Me. Unto this beareth witness every fair-minded and understanding soul.

Though beset with countless afflictions, We summon the people unto God, the Lord of names. Say, strive ye to attain that which ye have been promised in the Books of God, and walk not in the way of the ignorant. My body hath endured imprisonment that ye may be released from the bondage of self. Set your faces then towards His countenance and follow not the footsteps of every hostile oppressor. Verily, He hath consented to be sorely abased that ye may attain unto glory, and yet, ye are disporting yourselves in the vale of heedlessness. He, in truth, liveth in the most desolate of abodes for your sakes, whilst ye dwell in your palaces.

Say, did ye not hearken to the Voice of the Crier, calling aloud in the wilderness of the Bayán, bearing unto you the glad-tidings of the coming of your Lord, the All-Merciful? Lo! He is come in the sheltering shadow of Testimony, invested with conclusive proof and evidence, and those who truly believe in Him regard His presence as the embodiment of the Kingdom of God. Blessed is the man who turneth towards Him, and woe betide such as deny or doubt Him.

Announce thou unto the priests: Lo! He Who is the Ruler is come. Step out from behind the veil in the name of thy Lord, He Who layeth low the necks of all men. Proclaim then unto all mankind the glad-tidings of this mighty, this glorious Revelation. Verily, He Who is the Spirit of Truth is come to guide you unto all truth. He speaketh not as prompted by His own self, but as bidden by Him Who is the All-Knowing, the All-Wise.

Say, this is the One Who hath glorified the Son and hath exalted His Cause. Cast away, O peoples of the earth, that which ye have and take fast hold of that which ye are bidden by the All-Powerful, He Who is the Bearer of the Trust of God. Purge ye your ears and set your hearts towards Him that ye may hearken to the most wondrous Call which hath been raised from Sinai, the habitation of your Lord, the Most Glorious. It will, in truth, draw you nigh unto the Spot wherein ye will perceive the splendour of the light of His countenance which shineth above this luminous Horizon.

O concourse of priests! Leave the bells, and come forth, then, from your churches. It behoveth you, in this day, to proclaim aloud the Most Great Name among the nations. Prefer ye to be silent, whilst every stone and every tree shouteth aloud: 'The Lord is come in His great glory!'? Well is it with the man who hasteneth unto Him. Verily, he is numbered among them whose names will be eternally recorded and who will be mentioned by the Concourse on High. Thus hath it been decreed by the Spirit in this wondrous Tablet. He that summoneth men in My name is, verily, of Me, and he will show forth that which is beyond the power of all that are on earth. Follow ye the Way of the Lord and walk not in the footsteps of them that are sunk in heedlessness. Well is it with the slumberer who is stirred by the Breeze of God and ariseth from amongst the dead, directing his steps towards the Way of the Lord. Verily, such a man is regarded, in the sight of God, the True One, as a jewel amongst men and is reckoned with the blissful.[244]

To the People of the Qur'án

O people of the Qur'án, Verily, the Prophet of God, Muhammad, sheddeth tears at the sight of your cruelty. Ye have assuredly followed your evil and corrupt desires, and turned away your face from the light of guidance. Erelong will ye witness the result of your deeds; for the Lord, My God, lieth in wait and is watchful of your behavior. [245]

Happy is the man who will arise to serve My Cause, and glorify My beauteous Name. Take hold of My Book with the power of My might, and cleave tenaciously to whatsoever commandment thy Lord, the Ordainer, the All-Wise, hath prescribed therein. Behold, O Muhammad, how the sayings and doings of the followers of Shí'ih Islám have dulled the joy and fervor of its early days, and tarnished the pristine brilliancy of its light. In its primitive days, whilst they still adhered to the precepts associated with the name of their Prophet, the Lord of mankind, their career was marked by an unbroken chain of victories and triumphs. As they gradually strayed from the path of their Ideal Leader and Master, as they turned away from the Light of God and corrupted the principle of His Divine unity, and as they increasingly centered their attention upon them who were only the revealers of the potency of His Word, their power was turned into weakness, their glory into shame, their courage into fear. Thou dost witness to what a pass they have come. Behold, how they have joined partners with Him Who is the Focal-Point of Divine unity. Behold how their evil doings have hindered them from recognizing, in the Day of Resurrection, the Word of Truth, exalted be His glory. We cherish the hope that this people will henceforth shield themselves from vain hopes and idle fancies, and will attain to a true understanding of the meaning of Divine unity.[246]

Twelve hundred and eighty years have passed since the dawn of the Muhammadan Dispensation, and with every break of day, these blind and ignoble people have recited their Qur'án, and yet have failed to grasp one letter of that Book! Again and again they read those verses which clearly testify to the reality of these holy themes, and bear witness to the truth of the Manifestations of eternal Glory, and still apprehend not their purpose. They have even failed to realize, all this time, that, in every age, the reading of the scriptures and holy books is for no other purpose except to enable the reader to apprehend their meaning and unravel their innermost mysteries. Otherwise reading, without understanding, is of no abiding profit unto man.[247]

Likewise, it is clear, how in this day, the people of the Qur'án have perverted the text of God's holy Book, concerning the signs of the expected Manifestation, and interpreted it according to their inclination and desires.[248]

Furthermore, it is already evident and known unto thee that those things to which the Jews and the Christians have clung, and the cavilings which they heaped upon the Beauty of Muhammad, the same have in this day been upheld by the people of the Qur'án, and been witnessed in their denunciations of the 'Point of the Bayán', may the souls of all that dwell within the kingdom of divine Revelations be a sacrifice unto Him! [249]

Even as thou dost witness how the people of the Qur'án, like unto the people of old, have allowed the words 'Seal of the Prophets' to veil their eyes. And yet, they themselves testify to this verse: None knoweth the interpretation thereof but God and they that are well-grounded in knowledge. [250] And when He Who is well-grounded in all knowledge, He Who is the Mother, the Soul, the Secret, and the Essence thereof, revealeth that which is the least contrary to their desire, they bitterly oppose Him and shamelessly deny Him. These thou hast already heard and witnessed. Such deeds and words have been solely instigated by leaders of religion, they that worship no God but their own desire, who bear allegiance to naught but gold, who are wrapt in the densest veils of learning, and who, enmeshed by its obscurities, are lost in the wilds of error.[251]

O heedless one! Rely not on thy glory, and thy power. Thou art even as the last trace of sunlight upon the mountain-top. Soon will it fade away as decreed by God, the All-Possessing, the Most High. Thy glory and the glory of such as are like thee have been taken away, and this verily is what hath been ordained by the One with Whom is the Mother Tablet. Where is he to be found who contended with God, and whither is gone he that gainsaid His signs, and turned aside from His sovereignty? Where are they who have slain His chosen ones and spilt the blood of His holy ones? Reflect, that haply thou mayest perceive the breaths of thine acts, O foolish doubter! Because of you the Apostle (Muhammad) lamented, and the Chaste One (Fátimih) cried out, and the countries were laid waste, and darkness fell upon all regions. O concourse of divines! Because of you the people were abased, and the banner of Islám was hauled down, and its mighty throne subverted.[252]

To the Followers of the Bayán

O followers of the Bayán! Fear ye the All-Merciful. This is the One Who hath been glorified by Muhammad, the Apostle of God, and before Him by the Spirit[253] and yet before Him by the One Who discoursed with God.[254] This is the Point of the Bayán calling aloud before the Throne, saying: By the righteousness of God, ye have been created to glorify this Most Great Announcement, this Perfect Way which lay hid within the souls of the Prophets, which was treasured in the hearts of the chosen ones of God and was written down by the glorious Pen of your Lord, the Possessor of Names.

Fear ye the All-Merciful, O people of the Bayán, and commit not that which the followers of the Qur'án have committed—they who in the daytime and in the night season professed belief in the Faith of God, yet when the Lord of all men did appear, turned aside from Him and pronounced so cruel a sentence against Him that, on the Day of Return, the Mother Book sorely bewailed His plight.

O people of the Bayán! Abandon your idle fancies and vain imaginings, then with the eye of fairness look at the Dayspring of His Revelation and consider the things He hath manifested, the words He hath divinely revealed and the sufferings that have befallen Him at the hands of His enemies. He is the One Who hath willingly accepted every manner of tribulation for the proclamation of His Cause and the exaltation of His Word. At one time He suffered imprisonment in the land of Tá (Tihrán), at another in the land of Mím (Mázindarán), then once again in the former land, for the sake of the Cause of God, the Maker of the heavens. In His love for the Cause of God, the Almighty, the All-Bountiful, He was subjected there to chains and fetters.

O people of the Bayán! Have ye forgotten My exhortations, which My Pen hath revealed and My tongue hath uttered? Have ye bartered away My certitude in exchange for your idle fancies and My Way for your selfish desires? Have ye cast away the precepts of God and His remembrance and have ye forsaken His laws and ordinances? Fear ye God and abandon vain imaginings to the begetters thereof and leave superstitions to the devisers thereof and misgivings to the breeders thereof. Advance ye then with radiant faces and stainless hearts towards the horizon above which the Day-Star of certitude shineth resplendent at the bidding of God, the Lord of Revelations.[255]

Behold how the people of the Bayán have utterly failed to recognize that the sole object of whatsoever My Previous Manifestation and Harbinger of My Beauty hath revealed hath been My Revelation and the proclamation of My Cause. Never—and to this He Who is the Sovereign Truth beareth Me witness—would He have, but for Me, pronounced what He did pronounce.[256]

Thou well knowest, O my God, that I was regarded as one of the people of the Bayán, and consorted with them with love and fellowship, and summoned them to Thee in the daytime and in the night season, through the wonders of Thy Revelation and Thine inspiration, and sustained at their hands what the inmates of the cities of Thine invention are powerless to recount. I swear by Thy might, O my Beloved! Every morning I waken to find that I am made a target for the darts of their envy, and every night, when I lie down to rest, I discover that I have fallen a victim to the spears of their hate. Though Thou hast made known unto me the secrets of their hearts, and hast set me above them, I have refused to uncover their deeds, and have dealt patiently with them, mindful of the time which Thou hast fixed. And when Thy promise came to pass, and the set time was fulfilled, Thou didst lift, to an imperceptible degree, the veil of concealment, and lo, all the inmates of the kingdoms of Thy Revelation and of Thy creation shook and trembled, except those who were created by Thee, through the fire of Thy love, and the breath of Thine eagerness, and the water of Thy loving-kindness, and the clay of Thy grace. These are they who are glorified by the Concourse on high and the denizens of the Cities of eternity.

I give praise to Thee, therefore, O my God, that Thou hast preserved them that have acknowledged Thy unity, and hast destroyed them that have joined partners with Thee, and hast divided the one from the other through yet another word that hath proceeded out of the mouth of Thy will, and flowed down from the pen of Thy purpose. Thereby have Thy servants, who were created through the word of Thy commandment, and were begotten by Thy will, caviled at me, and so fiercely opposed me that they repudiated Thee, and have rejected Thy signs, and have risen up against Thee.

Thy glory beareth me witness, O my Beloved! My pen is powerless to describe what their hands have wrought against Him Who is the Manifestation of Thy Cause, and the Day-Spring of Thy Revelation, and the Dawning-Place of Thine inspiration. For all this I give praise to Thee. I swear by Thy glory, O my God! My heart yearneth after the things ordained by Thee in the heaven of Thy decree and the kingdom of Thine appointment. For whatsoever befalleth me in Thy path is the beloved of my soul and the goal of my desire. This, verily, is to be ascribed to naught except Thy power and Thy might.[257]

To the Leaders of Religion

Say: O leaders of religion! Weigh not the Book of God with such standards and sciences as are current amongst you, for the Book itself is the unerring Balance established amongst men.

The eye of My loving-kindness weepeth sore over you, inasmuch as ye have failed to recognize the One upon Whom ye have been calling in the daytime and in the night season, at even and at morn.

O ye leaders of religion! Who is the man amongst you that can rival Me in vision or insight? Where is he to be found that dareth to claim to be My equal in utterance or wisdom? No, by My Lord, the All-Merciful! All on the earth shall pass away; and this is the face of your Lord, the Almighty, the Well-Beloved.

We have decreed, O people, that the highest and last end of all learning be the recognition of Him Who is the Object of all knowledge; and yet, behold how ye have allowed your learning to shut you out, as by a veil, from Him Who is the Dayspring of this Light, through Whom every hidden thing hath been revealed. Could ye but discover the source whence the splendour of this utterance is diffused, ye would cast away the peoples of the world and all that they possess, and would draw nigh unto this most blessed Seat of glory.

Say: This, verily, is the heaven in which the Mother Book is treasured, could ye but comprehend it. He it is Who hath caused the Rock to shout, and the Burning Bush to lift up its voice, upon the Mount rising above the Holy Land, and proclaim: "The Kingdom is God's, the sovereign Lord of all, the All-Powerful, the Loving!"

We have not entered any school, nor read any of your dissertations. Incline your ears to the words of this unlettered One, wherewith He summoneth you unto God, the Ever-Abiding. Better is this for you than all the treasures of the earth, could ye but comprehend it.[258]

O concourse of divines! When My verses were sent down, and My clear tokens were revealed, We found you behind the veils. This, verily, is a strange thing. Ye glory in My Name, yet ye recognized Me not at the time your Lord, the All-Merciful, appeared amongst you with proof and testimony. We have rent the veils asunder. Beware lest ye shut out the people by yet another veil. Pluck asunder the chains of vain imaginings, in the name of the Lord of all men, and be not of the deceitful. Should ye turn unto God and embrace His Cause, spread not disorder within it, and measure not the Book of God with your selfish desires. This, verily, is the counsel of God aforetime and hereafter, and to this God's witnesses and chosen ones, yea, each and every one of Us, do solemnly attest. [259]

Beware lest any name debar you from Him Who is the Possessor of all names, or any word shut you out from this Remembrance of God, this Source of Wisdom amongst you. Turn unto God and seek His protection, O concourse of divines, and make not of yourselves a veil between Me and My creatures. Thus doth your Lord admonish you, and command you to be just, lest your works should come to naught and ye yourselves be oblivious of your plight. Shall he who denieth this Cause be able to vindicate the truth of any cause throughout creation? Nay, by Him Who is the Fashioner of the universe! Yet the people are wrapped in a palpable veil. Say: Through this Cause the day-star of testimony hath dawned, and the luminary of proof hath shed its radiance upon all that dwell on earth. Fear God, O men of insight, and be not of those who disbelieve in Me. Take heed lest the word "Prophet" withhold you from this Most Great Announcement, or any reference to "Vicegerency" debar you from the sovereignty of Him Who is the Vicegerent of God, which overshadoweth all the worlds. Every name hath been created by His Word, and every cause is dependent on His irresistible, His mighty and wondrous Cause. Say: This is the Day of God, the Day on which naught shall be mentioned save His own Self, the omnipotent Protector of all worlds. This is the Cause that hath made all your superstitions and idols to tremble.

We, verily, see amongst you him who taketh hold of the Book of God and citeth from it proofs and arguments wherewith to repudiate his Lord, even as the followers of every other Faith sought reasons in their Holy Books for refuting Him Who is the Help in Peril, the Self-Subsisting. Say: God, the True One, is My witness that neither the Scriptures of the world, nor all the books and writings in existence, shall, in this Day, avail you aught without this, the Living Book, Who proclaimeth in the midmost heart of creation: "Verily, there is none other God but Me, the All-Knowing, the All-Wise."

O concourse of divines! Beware lest ye be the cause of strife in the land, even as ye were the cause of the repudiation of the Faith in its early days. Gather the people around this Word that hath made the pebbles to cry out: "The Kingdom is God's, the Dawning-place of all signs!" Thus doth your Lord admonish you, as a bounty on His part; He, of a truth, is the Ever-Forgiving, the Most Generous.[260]

To the Kings and Rulers of the World

O kings of the earth! Give ear unto the Voice of God, calling from this sublime, this fruit-laden Tree, that hath sprung out of the Crimson Hill, upon the holy Plain, intoning the words: "There is none other God but He, the Mighty, the All-Powerful, the All-Wise."

Fear God, O concourse of kings, and suffer not yourselves to be deprived of this most sublime grace. Fling away, then, the things ye possess, and take fast hold on the Handle of God, the Exalted, the Great. Set your hearts towards the Face of God, and abandon that which your desires have bidden you to follow, and be not of those who perish.

Relate unto them, O Servant, the story of 'Alí,[261] when He came unto them with truth, bearing His glorious and weighty Book, and holding in His hands a testimony and proof from God, and holy and blessed tokens from Him. Ye, however, O kings, have failed to heed the Remembrance of God in His days and to be guided by the lights which arose and shone forth above the horizon of a resplendent Heaven. Ye examined not His Cause when so to do would have been better for you than all that the sun shineth upon, could ye but perceive it. Ye remained careless until the divines of Persia—those cruel ones—pronounced judgement against Him, and unjustly slew Him. His spirit ascended unto God, and the eyes of the inmates of Paradise and the angels that are nigh unto Him wept sore by reason of this cruelty. Beware that ye be not careless henceforth as ye have been careless aforetime. Return, then, unto God, your Maker, and be not of the heedless.

My face hath come forth from the veils, and shed its radiance upon all that is in heaven and on earth; and yet, ye turned not towards Him, notwithstanding that ye were created for Him, O concourse of kings! Follow, therefore, that which I speak unto you, and hearken unto it with your hearts, and be not of such as have turned aside. For your glory consisteth not in your sovereignty, but rather in your nearness unto God and your observance of His command as sent down in His holy and preserved Tablets. Should any one of you rule over the whole earth, and over all that lieth within it and upon it, its seas, its lands, its mountains, and its plains, and yet be not remembered by God, all these would profit him not, could ye but know it.

Arise, then, and make steadfast your feet, and make ye amends for that which hath escaped you, and set then yourselves towards His holy Court, on the shore of His mighty Ocean, so that the pearls of knowledge and wisdom, which God hath stored up within the shell of His radiant heart, may be revealed unto you..... Beware lest ye hinder the breeze of God from blowing over your hearts, the breeze through which the hearts of such as have turned unto Him can be quickened....[262]

O kings of the earth! He Who is the sovereign Lord of all is come. The Kingdom is God's, the omnipotent Protector, the Self-Subsisting. Worship none but God, and, with radiant hearts, lift up your faces unto your Lord, the Lord of all names. This is a Revelation to which whatever ye possess can never be compared, could ye but know it.

We see you rejoicing in that which ye have amassed for others and shutting out yourselves from the worlds which naught except My guarded Tablet can reckon. The treasures ye have laid up have drawn you far away from your ultimate objective. This ill beseemeth you, could ye but understand it. Wash from your hearts all earthly defilements, and hasten to enter the Kingdom of your Lord, the Creator of earth and heaven, Who caused the world to tremble and all its peoples to wail, except them that have renounced all things and clung to that which the Hidden Tablet hath ordained.[263]

O kings of the earth! The Most Great Law hath been revealed in this Spot, this scene of transcendent splendour. Every hidden thing hath been brought to light by virtue of the Will of the Supreme Ordainer, He Who hath ushered in the Last Hour, through Whom the Moon hath been cleft, and every irrevocable decree expounded.

Ye are but vassals, O kings of the earth! He Who is the King of Kings hath appeared, arrayed in His most wondrous glory, and is summoning you unto Himself, the Help in Peril, the Self-Subsisting. Take heed lest pride deter you from recognizing the Source of Revelation, lest the things of this world shut you out as by a veil from Him Who is the Creator of heaven. Arise, and serve Him Who is the Desire of all nations, Who hath created you through a word from Him, and ordained you to be, for all time, the emblems of His sovereignty.

By the righteousness of God! It is not Our wish to lay hands on your kingdoms. Our mission is to seize and possess the hearts of men. Upon them the eyes of Bahá are fastened. To this testifieth the Kingdom of Names, could ye but comprehend it. Whoso followeth his Lord will renounce the world and all that is therein; how much greater, then, must be the detachment of Him Who holdeth so august a station! Forsake your palaces, and haste ye to gain admittance into His Kingdom. This, indeed, will profit you both in this world and in the next. To this testifieth the Lord of the realm on high, did ye but know it.[264]

Lay not aside the fear of God, O kings of the earth, and beware that ye transgress not the bounds which the Almighty hath fixed. Observe the injunctions laid upon you in His Book, and take good heed not to overstep their limits. Be vigilant, that ye may not do injustice to anyone, be it to the extent of a grain of mustard seed. Tread ye the path of justice, for this, verily, is the straight path.

Compose your differences and reduce your armaments, that the burden of your expenditures may be lightened, and that your minds and hearts may be tranquillized. Heal the dissensions that divide you, and ye will no longer be in need of any armaments except what the protection of your cities and territories demandeth. Fear ye God, and take heed not to outstrip the bounds of moderation and be numbered among the extravagant.

We have learned that ye are increasing your outlay every year, and are laying the burden thereof on your subjects. This, verily, is more than they can bear, and is a grievous injustice. Decide ye justly between men, O kings, and be ye the emblems of justice amongst them. This, if ye judge fairly, is the thing that behoveth you, and beseemeth your station.

Beware not to deal unjustly with anyone that appealeth to you and entereth beneath your shadow. Walk ye in the fear of God, and be ye of them that lead a godly life. Rest not on your power, your armies, and treasures. Put your whole trust and confidence in God, Who hath created you, and seek ye His help in all your affairs. Succour cometh from Him alone. He succoureth whom He willeth with the hosts of the heavens and of the earth.

Know ye that the poor are the trust of God in your midst. Watch that ye betray not His trust, that ye deal not unjustly with them and that ye walk not in the ways of the treacherous. Ye will most certainly be called upon to answer for His trust on the day when the Balance of Justice shall be set, the day when unto everyone shall be rendered his due, when the doings of all men, be they rich or poor, shall be weighed.

If ye pay no heed unto the counsels which, in peerless and unequivocal language, We have revealed in this Tablet, Divine chastisement shall assail you from every direction, and the sentence of His justice shall be pronounced against you. On that day ye shall have no power to resist Him, and shall recognize your own impotence. Have mercy on yourselves and on those beneath you, and judge ye between them according to the precepts prescribed by God in His most holy and exalted Tablet, a Tablet wherein He hath assigned to each and every thing its settled measure, in which He hath given, with distinctness, an explanation of all things, and which is in itself a monition unto them that believe in Him.[265]

O ye the elected representatives of the people in every land! Take ye counsel together, and let your concern be only for that which profiteth mankind and bettereth the condition thereof, if ye be of them that scan heedfully. Regard the world as the human body which, though at its creation whole and perfect, hath been afflicted, through various causes, with grave disorders and maladies. Not for one day did it gain ease, nay its sickness waxed more severe, as it fell under the treatment of ignorant physicians, who gave full rein to their personal desires and have erred grievously. And if, at one time, through the care of an able physician, a member of that body was healed, the rest remained afflicted as before. Thus informeth you the All-Knowing, the All-Wise.

We behold it, in this day, at the mercy of rulers so drunk with pride that they cannot discern clearly their own best advantage, much less recognize a Revelation so bewildering and challenging as this. And whenever any one of them hath striven to improve its condition, his motive hath been his own gain, whether confessedly so or not; and the unworthiness of this motive hath limited his power to heal or cure.[266]

Hearken ye, O Rulers of America and the Presidents of the Republics therein, unto that which the Dove is warbling on the Branch of Eternity: "There is none other God but Me, the Ever-Abiding, the Forgiving, the All-Bountiful." Adorn ye the temple of dominion with the ornament of justice and of the fear of God, and its head with the crown of the remembrance of your Lord, the Creator of the heavens. Thus counselleth you He Who is the Dayspring of Names, as bidden by Him Who is the All-Knowing, the All-Wise. The Promised One hath appeared in this glorified Station, whereat all beings, both seen and unseen, have rejoiced. Take ye advantage of the Day of God. Verily, to meet Him is better for you than all that whereon the sun shineth, could ye but know it. O concourse of rulers! Give ear unto that which hath been raised from the Dayspring of Grandeur: "Verily, there is none other God but Me, the Lord of Utterance, the All-Knowing." Bind ye the broken with the hands of justice, and crush the oppressor who flourisheth with the rod of the commandments of your Lord, the Ordainer, the All-Wise.[267]

Blessed Are They

Say: Blessed the slumberer who is awakened by My Breeze. Blessed the lifeless one who is quickened through My reviving breaths. Blessed the eye that is solaced by gazing at My beauty. Blessed the wayfarer who directeth his steps towards the Tabernacle of My glory and majesty. Blessed the distressed one who seeketh refuge beneath the shadow of My canopy. Blessed the sore athirst who hasteneth to the soft-flowing waters of My loving-kindness. Blessed the insatiate soul who casteth away his selfish desires for love of Me and taketh his place at the banquet table which I have sent down from the heaven of divine bounty for My chosen ones. Blessed the abased one who layeth fast hold on the cord of My glory; and the needy one who entereth beneath the shadow of the Tabernacle of My wealth. Blessed the ignorant one who seeketh the fountain of My knowledge; and the heedless one who cleaveth to the cord of My remembrance. Blessed the soul that hath been raised to life through My quickening breath and hath gained admittance into My heavenly Kingdom. Blessed the man whom the sweet savours of reunion with Me have stirred and caused to draw nigh unto the Dayspring of My Revelation. Blessed the ear that hath heard and the tongue that hath borne witness and the eye that hath seen and recognized the Lord Himself, in His great glory and majesty, invested with grandeur and dominion. Blessed are they that have attained His presence. Blessed the man who hath sought enlightenment from the Day-Star of My Word. Blessed he who hath attired his head with the diadem of My love. Blessed is he who hath heard of My grief and hath arisen to aid Me among My people. Blessed is he who hath laid down his life in My path and hath borne manifold hardships for the sake of My Name. Blessed the man who, assured of My Word, hath arisen from among the dead to celebrate My praise. Blessed is he that hath been enraptured by My wondrous melodies and hath rent the veils asunder through the potency of My might. Blessed is he who hath remained faithful to My Covenant, and whom the things of the world have not kept back from attaining My Court of holiness. Blessed is the man who hath detached himself from all else but Me, hath soared in the atmosphere of My love, hath gained admittance into My Kingdom, gazed upon My realms of glory, quaffed the living waters of My bounty, hath drunk his fill from the heavenly river of My loving providence, acquainted himself with My Cause, apprehended that which I concealed within the treasury of My Words, and hath shone forth from the horizon of divine knowledge engaged in My praise and glorification. Verily, he is of Me. Upon him rest My mercy, My loving-kindness, My bounty and My glory.[268]

Glory of Bahá'u'lláh

And when this process of progressive Revelation culminated in the stage at which His peerless, His most sacred, and exalted Countenance was to be unveiled to men's eyes, He chose to hide His own Self behind a thousand veils, lest profane and mortal eyes discover His glory. This He did at a time when the signs and tokens of a divinely-appointed Revelation were being showered upon Him— signs and tokens which none can reckon except the Lord, your God, the Lord of all worlds. And when the set time of concealment was fulfilled, We sent forth, whilst still wrapt within a myriad veils, an infinitesimal glimmer of the effulgent Glory enveloping the Face of the Youth, and lo, the entire company of the dwellers of the Realms above were seized with violent commotion and the favored of God fell down in adoration before Him. He hath, verily, manifested a glory such as none in the whole creation hath witnessed, inasmuch as He hath arisen to proclaim in person His Cause unto all who are in the heavens and all who are on the earth.[269]

The everlasting Candle shineth in its naked glory. Behold how it hath consumed every mortal veil. O ye moth-like lovers of His light! Brave every danger, and consecrate your souls to its consuming flame. O ye that thirst after Him! Strip yourselves of every earthly affection, and hasten to embrace your Beloved. With a zest that none can equal make haste to attain unto Him. The Flower, thus far hidden from the sight of men, is unveiled to your eyes. In the open radiance of His glory He standeth before you. His voice summoneth all the holy and sanctified beings to come and be united with Him. Happy is he that turneth thereunto; well is it with him that hath attained, and gazed on the light of so wondrous a countenance.[270]

Know verily that the veil hiding Our countenance hath not been completely lifted. We have revealed Our Self to a degree corresponding to the capacity of the people of Our age. Should the Ancient Beauty be unveiled in the fullness of His glory mortal eyes would be blinded by the dazzling intensity of His revelation.[271]

Power of Bahá'u'lláh

Say, by the righteousness of God! The All-Merciful is come invested with power and sovereignty. Through His power the foundations of religions have quaked and the Nightingale of Utterance hath warbled its melody upon the highest branch of true understanding. Verily, He Who was hidden in the knowledge of God and is mentioned in the Holy Scriptures hath appeared. Say, this is the Day when the Speaker on Sinai hath mounted the throne of Revelation and the people have stood before the Lord of the worlds. This is the Day wherein the earth hath told out her tidings and hath laid bare her treasures; when the oceans have brought forth their pearls and the divine Lote-Tree its fruit; when the Sun hath shed its radiance and the Moons have diffused their lights, and the Heavens have revealed their stars, and the Hour its signs, and the Resurrection its dreadful majesty; when the pens have unloosed their outpourings and the spirits have laid bare their mysteries.[272]

Give heed to My warning, ye people of Persia! If I be slain at your hands, God will assuredly raise up one who will fill the seat made vacant through My death, for such is God's method carried into effect of old, and no change can ye find in God's method of dealing.[273]

By the righteousness of God! Should they cast Him into a fire kindled on the continent, He will assuredly rear His head in the midmost heart of the ocean and proclaim: "He is the Lord of all that are in heaven and all that are on earth!" And if they cast Him into a darksome pit, they will find Him seated on earth's loftiest heights calling aloud to all mankind: "Lo, the Desire of the World is come in His majesty, His sovereignty, His transcendent dominion!" And if He be buried beneath the depths of the earth, His Spirit soaring to the apex of heaven shall peal the summons: "Behold ye the coming of the Glory; witness ye the Kingdom of God, the Most Holy, the Gracious, the All-Powerful!" And if they shed His blood, every drop thereof shall cry out and invoke God in this Name through which the fragrance of His raiment hath been diffused in all directions.[274]

Within the throat of this Youth...there lie prisoned accents which, if revealed to mankind to an extent smaller than a needle's eye, would suffice to cause every mountain to crumble, the leaves of the trees to be discolored and their fruits to fall; would compel every head to bow down in worship and every face to turn in adoration towards this omnipotent Ruler Who, at sundry times and in diverse manners, appeareth as a devouring flame, as a billowing ocean, as a radiant light, as the tree which, rooted in the soil of holiness, lifteth its branches and spreadeth out its limbs as far as and beyond the throne of deathless glory." [275]

Through the movement of Our Pen of Glory We have, at the bidding of the Omnipotent Ordainer, breathed a new life into every human frame, and instilled into every word a fresh potency. All created things proclaim the evidences of this worldwide regeneration...Every single letter proceeding from Our mouth is endowed with such regenerative power as to enable it to bring into existence a new creation, a creation the magnitude of which is inscrutable to all save God. He verily hath knowledge of all things. It is in Our power, should We wish it, to enable a speck of floating dust to generate, in less than the twinkling of an eye, suns of infinite, of unimaginable splendor, to cause a dewdrop to develop into vast and numberless oceans, to infuse into every letter such a force as to empower it to unfold all the knowledge of past and future ages. We are possessed of such power which, if brought to light, will transmute the most deadly of poisons into a panacea of unfailing efficacy.[276]

Great is the blessedness of him who hath in this Day cast away the things current amongst men and hath clung unto that which is ordained by God, the Lord of Names and the Fashioner of all created things, He Who is come from the heaven of eternity through the power of the Most Great Name, invested with so invincible an authority that all the powers of the earth are unable to withstand Him.[277]

Knowledge of Bahá'u'lláh

Within the treasury of Our Wisdom there lieth unrevealed a knowledge, one word of which, if we chose to divulge it to mankind, would cause every human being to recognize the Manifestation of God and to acknowledge His omniscience, would enable every one to discover the secrets of all the sciences, and to attain so high a station as to find himself wholly independent of all past and future learning. Other knowledges We do as well possess, not a single letter of which We can disclose, nor do We find humanity able to hear even the barest reference to their meaning. Thus have We informed you of the knowledge of God, the All-Knowing, the All-Wise.[278]

Thou knowest full well that We perused not the books which men possess and We acquired not the learning current amongst them, and yet whenever We desire to quote the sayings of the learned and of the wise, presently there will appear before the face of thy Lord in the form of a tablet all that which hath appeared in the world and is revealed in the Holy Books and Scriptures. Thus do We set down in writing that which the eye perceiveth. Verily His knowledge encompasseth the earth and the heavens.

This is a Tablet wherein the Pen of the Unseen hath inscribed the knowledge of all that hath been and shall be—a knowledge that none other but My wondrous Tongue can interpret. Indeed My heart as it is in itself hath been purged by God from the concepts of the learned and is sanctified from the utterances of the wise. In truth naught doth it mirror forth but the revelations of God. Unto this beareth witness the Tongue of Grandeur in this perspicuous Book.[279]

Most Great Infallibility of Bahá'u'lláh

O thou who hast set thy face towards the Realm on High and hast quaffed My sealed wine from the hand of bounteousness! Know thou that the term 'Infallibility' hath numerous meanings and divers stations.... However, the Most Great Infallibility is confined to the One Whose station is immeasurably exalted beyond ordinances or prohibitions and is sanctified from errors and omissions. Indeed He is a Light which is not followed by darkness and a Truth not overtaken by error. Were He to pronounce water to be wine or heaven to be earth or light to be fire, He speaketh the truth and no doubt would there be about it; and unto no one is given the right to question His authority or to say why or wherefore. Whosoever raiseth objections will be numbered with the froward in the Book of God, the Lord of the worlds. 'Verily He shall not be asked of His doings but all others shall be asked of their doings.'[280] He is come from the invisible heaven, bearing the banner 'He doeth whatsoever He willeth' and is accompanied by hosts of power and authority while it is the duty of all besides Him to strictly observe whatever laws and ordinances have been enjoined upon them, and should anyone deviate therefrom, even to the extent of a hair's breadth, his work would be brought to naught.[281]

Revelation of Bahá'u'lláh

O My servants! My holy, My divinely ordained Revelation may be likened unto an ocean in whose depths are concealed innumerable pearls of great price, of surpassing luster. It is the duty of every seeker to bestir himself and strive to attain the shores of this ocean, so that he may, in proportion to the eagerness of his search and the efforts he hath exerted, partake of such benefits as have been pre-ordained in God's irrevocable and hidden Tablets. If no one be willing to direct his steps towards its shores, if every one should fail to arise and find Him, can such a failure be said to have robbed this ocean of its power or to have lessened, to any degree, its treasures? How vain, how contemptible, are the imaginations which your hearts have devised, and are still devising! O My servants! The one true God is My witness! This most great, this fathomless and surging Ocean is near, astonishingly near, unto you. Behold it is closer to you than your life-vein! Swift as the twinkling of an eye ye can, if ye but wish it, reach and partake of this imperishable favor, this God-given grace, this incorruptible gift, this most potent and unspeakably glorious bounty.[282]

I testify that no sooner had the First Word proceeded, through the potency of Thy will and purpose, out of His mouth, and the First Call gone forth from His lips than the whole creation was revolutionized, and all that are in the heavens and all that are on earth were stirred to the depths. Through that Word the realities of all created things were shaken, were divided, separated, scattered, combined and reunited, disclosing, in both the contingent world and the heavenly kingdom, entities of a new creation, and revealing, in the unseen realms, the signs and tokens of Thy unity and oneness. Through that Call Thou didst announce unto all Thy servants the advent of Thy most great Revelation and the appearance of Thy most perfect Cause.[283]

To demonstrate the truth of His Revelation He hath not been, nor is He, dependent upon any one. Well nigh a hundred volumes of luminous verses and perspicuous words have already been sent down from the heaven of the will of Him Who is the Revealer of signs, and are available unto all. It is for thee to direct thyself towards the Ultimate Goal, and the Supreme End, and the Most Sublime Pinnacle, that thou mayest hear and behold what hath been revealed by God, the Lord of the worlds.[284]

My God, my Well-Beloved! No place is there for any one to flee to when once Thy laws have been sent down, and no refuge can be found by any soul after the revelation of Thy commandments. Thou hast inspired the Pen with the mysteries of Thine eternity, and bidden it teach man that which he knoweth not, and caused him to partake of the living waters of truth from the cup of Thy Revelation and Thine inspiration.[285]

Were anyone to ponder in his heart that which hath, in this Revelation, streamed forth from the Pen of Glory, he would be assured that whatever this Wronged One hath affirmed He hath had no intention of establishing any position or distinction for Himself. The purpose hath rather been to attract the souls, through the sublimity of His words, unto the summit of transcendent glory and to endow them with the capacity of perceiving that which will purge and purify the peoples of the world from the strife and dissension which religious differences provoke. Unto this bear witness My heart, My Pen, My inner and My outer Being. God grant that all men may turn unto the treasuries latent within their own beings.[286]

GOD, the True One, testifieth and the Revealers of His names and attributes bear witness that Our sole purpose in raising the Call and in proclaiming His sublime Word is that the ear of the entire creation may, through the living waters of divine utterance, be purged from lying tales and become attuned to the holy, the glorious and exalted Word which hath issued forth from the repository of the knowledge of the Maker of the Heavens and the Creator of Names. Happy are they that judge with fairness.[287]

O ye that dwell on earth! The distinguishing feature that marketh the pre-eminent character of this Supreme Revelation consisteth in that We have, on the one hand, blotted out from the pages of God's holy Book whatsoever hath been the cause of strife, of malice and mischief amongst the children of men, and have, on the other, laid down the essential prerequisites of concord, of understanding, of complete and enduring unity. Well is it with them that keep My statutes.[288]

The Revelation of which I am the bearer ... is adapted to humanity's spiritual receptiveness and capacity; otherwise, the Light that shines within me can neither wax nor wane. Whatever I manifest is nothing more or less than the measure of the Divine glory which God has bidden me reveal.[289]

None among the Manifestations of old, except to a prescribed degree, hath ever completely apprehended the nature of this Revelation. I testify before God to the greatness, the inconceivable greatness of this Revelation. Again and again have We, in most of Our Tablets, borne witness to this truth, that mankind may be roused from its heedlessness. How great is the Cause, how staggering the weight of its Message! In this most mighty Revelation all the Dispensations of the past have attained their highest, their final consummation. That which hath been made manifest in this preeminent, this most exalted Revelation, stands unparalleled in the annals of the past, nor will future ages witness its like.[290]

In truth the station of this Revelation transcendeth the station of whatever hath been manifested in the past or will be made manifest in the future.[291]

Bahá'u'lláh: The Royal Falcon

The Tongue of Wisdom proclaimeth: He that hath Me not is bereft of all things. Turn ye away from all that is on earth and seek none else but Me. I am the Sun of Wisdom and the Ocean of Knowledge. I cheer the faint and revive the dead. I am the guiding Light that illumineth the way. I am the royal Falcon on the arm of the Almighty. I unfold the drooping wings of every broken bird and start it on its flight.[292]

The Spiritual Reality of Mankind

Lofty Station of Mankind

I bear witness, O my God, that Thou hast created me to know Thee and to worship Thee.[293]

Having created the world and all that liveth and moveth therein, He, through the direct operation of His unconstrained and sovereign Will, chose to confer upon man the unique distinction and capacity to know Him and to love Him—a capacity that must needs be regarded as the generating impulse and the primary purpose underlying the whole of creation.... Upon the inmost reality of each and every created thing He hath shed the light of one of His names, and made it a recipient of the glory of one of His attributes. Upon the reality of man, however, He hath focused the radiance of all of His names and attributes, and made it a mirror of His own Self. Alone of all created things man hath been singled out for so great a favor, so enduring a bounty.

These energies with which the Day Star of Divine bounty and Source of heavenly guidance hath endowed the reality of man lie, however, latent within him, even as the flame is hidden within the candle and the rays of light are potentially present in the lamp. The radiance of these energies may be obscured by worldly desires even as the light of the sun can be concealed beneath the dust and dross which cover the mirror. Neither the candle nor the lamp can be lighted through their own unaided efforts, nor can it ever be possible for the mirror to free itself from its dross. It is clear and evident that until a fire is kindled the lamp will never be ignited, and unless the dross is blotted out from the face of the mirror it can never represent the image of the sun nor reflect its light and glory.

And since there can be no tie of direct intercourse to bind the one true God with His creation ... He hath ordained that in every age and dispensation a pure and stainless Soul be made manifest in the kingdoms of earth and heaven.... These Essences of Detachment, these resplendent Realities are the channels of God's all-pervasive grace. Led by the light of unfailing guidance, and invested with supreme sovereignty, They are commissioned to use the inspiration of Their words, the effusions of Their infallible grace and the sanctifying breeze of Their Revelation for the cleansing of every longing heart and receptive spirit from the dross and dust of earthly cares and limitations. Then, and only then, will the Trust of God, latent in the reality of man, emerge, as resplendent as the rising Orb of Divine Revelation, from behind the veil of concealment, and implant the ensign of its revealed glory upon the summits of men's hearts.[294]

Whatever is in the heavens and whatever is on the earth is a direct evidence of the revelation within it of the attributes and names of God, inasmuch as within every atom are enshrined the signs that bear eloquent testimony to the revelation of that Most Great Light. Methinks, but for the potency of that revelation, no being could ever exist. How resplendent the luminaries of knowledge that shine in an atom, and how vast the oceans of wisdom that surge within a drop! To a supreme degree is this true of man, who, among all created things, hath been invested with the robe of such gifts, and hath been singled out for the glory of such distinction. For in him are potentially revealed all the attributes and names of God to a degree that no other created being hath excelled or surpassed. All these names and attributes are applicable to him. Even as He hath said: "Man is My mystery, and I am his mystery." Manifold are the verses that have been repeatedly revealed in all the Heavenly Books and the Holy Scriptures, expressive of this most subtle and lofty theme. Even as He hath revealed: "We will surely show them Our signs in the world and within themselves."[295]

All praise and glory be to God Who, through the power of His might, hath delivered His creation from the nakedness of non-existence, and clothed it with the mantle of life. From among all created things He hath singled out for His special favor the pure, the gem-like reality of man, and invested it with a unique capacity of knowing Him and of reflecting the greatness of His glory. This twofold distinction conferred upon him hath cleansed away from his heart the rust of every vain desire, and made him worthy of the vesture with which his Creator hath deigned to clothe him. It hath served to rescue his soul from the wretchedness of ignorance.

This robe with which the body and soul of man hath been adorned is the very foundation of his well-being and development. Oh, how blessed the day when, aided by the grace and might of the one true God, man will have freed himself from the bondage and corruption of the world and all that is therein, and will have attained unto true and abiding rest beneath the shadow of the Tree of Knowledge! [296]

O My servants! Could ye apprehend with what wonders of My munificence and bounty I have willed to entrust your souls, ye would, of a truth, rid yourselves of attachment to all created things, and would gain a true knowledge of your own selves—a knowledge which is the same as the comprehension of Mine own Being. Ye would find yourselves independent of all else but Me, and would perceive, with your inner and outer eye, and as manifest as the revelation of My effulgent Name, the seas of My loving-kindness and bounty moving within you.[297]

He Who is the eternal King—may the souls of all that dwell within the mystic Tabernacle be a sacrifice unto Him—hath spoken: "He hath known God who hath known himself."[298]

O SON OF BEING! With the hands of power I made thee and with the fingers of strength I created thee; and within thee have I placed the essence of My light. Be thou content with it and seek naught else, for My work is perfect and My command is binding. Question it not, nor have a doubt thereof.[299]

O SON OF SPIRIT! I created thee rich, why dost thou bring thyself down to poverty? Noble I made thee, wherewith dost thou abase thyself? Out of the essence of knowledge I gave thee being, why seekest thou enlightenment from anyone beside Me? Out of the clay of love I molded thee, how dost thou busy thyself with another? Turn thy sight unto thyself, that thou mayest find Me standing within thee, mighty, powerful and self-subsisting.[300]

By the sorrows which afflict the beauty of the All-Glorious! Such is the station ordained for the true believer that if to an extent smaller than a needle's eye the glory of that station were to be unveiled to mankind, every beholder would be consumed away in his longing to attain it. For this reason it hath been decreed that in this earthly life the full measure of the glory of his own station should remain concealed from the eyes of such a believer. If the veil be lifted, and the full glory of the station of those who have turned wholly towards God, and in their love for Him renounced the world, be made manifest, the entire creation would be dumbfounded.[301]

Far, far from Thy glory be what mortal man can affirm of Thee, or attribute unto Thee, or the praise with which he can glorify Thee! Whatever duty Thou hast prescribed unto Thy servants of extolling to the utmost Thy majesty and glory is but a token of Thy grace unto them, that they may be enabled to ascend unto the station conferred upon their own inmost being, the station of the knowledge of their own selves.[302]

Lofty is the station of man! Not long ago this exalted Word streamed forth from the treasury of Our Pen of Glory: Great and blessed is this Day—the Day in which all that lay latent in man hath been and will be made manifest. Lofty is the station of man, were he to hold fast to righteousness and truth and to remain firm and steadfast in the Cause. In the eyes of the All-Merciful a true man appeareth even as a firmament; its sun and moon are his sight and hearing, and his shining and resplendent character its stars. His is the loftiest station, and his influence educateth the world of being.[303]

The Soul

Thou hast asked Me concerning the nature of the soul. Know, verily, that the soul is a sign of God, a heavenly gem whose reality the most learned of men hath failed to grasp, and whose mystery no mind, however acute, can ever hope to unravel. It is the first among all created things to declare the excellence of its Creator, the first to recognize His glory, to cleave to His truth, and to bow down in adoration before Him. If it be faithful to God, it will reflect His light, and will, eventually, return unto Him. If it fail, however, in its allegiance to its Creator, it will become a victim to self and passion, and will, in the end, sink in their depths.

Whoso hath, in this Day, refused to allow the doubts and fancies of men to turn him away from Him Who is the Eternal Truth, and hath not suffered the tumult provoked by the ecclesiastical and secular authorities to deter him from recognizing His Message, such a man will be regarded by God, the Lord of all men, as one of His mighty signs, and will be numbered among them whose names have been inscribed by the Pen of the Most High in His Book. Blessed is he that hath recognized the true stature of such a soul, that hath acknowledged its station, and discovered its virtues.

Much hath been written in the books of old concerning the various stages in the development of the soul, such as concupiscence, irascibility, inspiration, benevolence, contentment, Divine good-pleasure, and the like; the Pen of the Most High, however, is disinclined to dwell upon them. Every soul that walketh humbly with its God, in this Day, and cleaveth unto Him, shall find itself invested with the honor and glory of all goodly names and stations.[304]

Verily I say, the human soul is, in its essence, one of the signs of God, a mystery among His mysteries. It is one of the mighty signs of the Almighty, the harbinger that proclaimeth the reality of all the worlds of God. Within it lieth concealed that which the world is now utterly incapable of apprehending. Ponder in thine heart the revelation of the Soul of God that pervadeth all His Laws, and contrast it with that base and appetitive nature that hath rebelled against Him, that forbiddeth men to turn unto the Lord of Names, and impelleth them to walk after their lusts and wickedness. Such a soul hath, in truth, wandered far in the path of error....[305]

It is clear and evident that when the veils that conceal the realities of the manifestations of the Names and Attributes of God, nay of all created things visible or invisible, have been rent asunder, nothing except the Sign of God will remain—a sign which He, Himself, hath placed within these realities. This sign will endure as long as is the wish of the Lord thy God, the Lord of the heavens and of the earth. If such be the blessings conferred on all created things, how superior must be the destiny of the true believer, whose existence and life are to be regarded as the originating purpose of all creation. Just as the conception of faith hath existed from the beginning that hath no beginning, and will endure till the end that hath no end, in like manner will the true believer eternally live and endure. His spirit will everlastingly circle round the Will of God. He will last as long as God, Himself, will last. He is revealed through the Revelation of God, and is hidden at His bidding. It is evident that the loftiest mansions in the Realm of Immortality have been ordained as the habitation of them that have truly believed in God and in His signs. Death can never invade that holy seat. Thus have We entrusted thee with the signs of thy Lord, that thou mayest persevere in thy love for Him, and be of them that comprehend this truth.[306]

Consider the rational faculty with which God hath endowed the essence of man. Examine thine own self, and behold how thy motion and stillness, thy will and purpose, thy sight and hearing, thy sense of smell and power of speech, and whatever else is related to, or transcendeth, thy physical senses or spiritual perceptions, all proceed from, and owe their existence to, this same faculty. So closely are they related unto it, that if in less than the twinkling of an eye its relationship to the human body be severed, each and every one of these senses will cease immediately to exercise its function, and will be deprived of the power to manifest the evidences of its activity. It is indubitably clear and evident that each of these afore-mentioned instruments has depended, and will ever continue to depend, for its proper functioning on this rational faculty, which should be regarded as a sign of the revelation of Him Who is the sovereign Lord of all. Through its manifestation all these names and attributes have been revealed, and by the suspension of its action they are all destroyed and perish.

It would be wholly untrue to maintain that this faculty is the same as the power of vision, inasmuch as the power of vision is derived from it and acteth in dependence upon it. It would, likewise, be idle to contend that this faculty can be identified with the sense of hearing, as the sense of hearing receiveth from the rational faculty the requisite energy for performing its functions.

This same relationship bindeth this faculty with whatsoever hath been the recipient of these names and attributes within the human temple. These diverse names and revealed attributes have been generated through the agency of this sign of God. Immeasurably exalted is this sign, in its essence and reality, above all such names and attributes. Nay, all else besides it will, when compared with its glory, fade into utter nothingness and become a thing forgotten.

Wert thou to ponder in thine heart, from now until the end that hath no end, and with all the concentrated intelligence and understanding which the greatest minds have attained in the past or will attain in the future, this divinely ordained and subtle Reality, this sign of the revelation of the All-Abiding, All-Glorious God, thou wilt fail to comprehend its mystery or to appraise its virtue. Having recognized thy powerlessness to attain to an adequate understanding of that Reality which abideth within thee, thou wilt readily admit the futility of such efforts as may be attempted by thee, or by any of the created things, to fathom the mystery of the Living God, the Day Star of unfading glory, the Ancient of everlasting days. This confession of helplessness which mature contemplation must eventually impel every mind to make is in itself the acme of human understanding, and marketh the culmination of man's development.[307]

O servants! Lifeless is the body that is bereft of a soul, and withered the heart that is devoid of the remembrance of its Lord. Commune with the remembrance of the Friend and shun the enemy. Your enemy is such things as ye have acquired of your own inclination, to which ye have firmly clung, and whereby ye have sullied your souls. The soul hath been created for the remembrance of the Friend; safeguard its purity.[308]

The Soul After Death

And now concerning thy question regarding the soul of man and its survival after death. Know thou of a truth that the soul, after its separation from the body, will continue to progress until it attaineth the presence of God, in a state and condition which neither the revolution of ages and centuries, nor the changes and chances of this world, can alter. It will endure as long as the Kingdom of God, His sovereignty, His dominion and power will endure. It will manifest the signs of God and His attributes, and will reveal His loving kindness and bounty. The movement of My Pen is stilled when it attempteth to befittingly describe the loftiness and glory of so exalted a station. The honor with which the Hand of Mercy will invest the soul is such as no tongue can adequately reveal, nor any other earthly agency describe. Blessed is the soul which, at the hour of its separation from the body, is sanctified from the vain imaginings of the peoples of the world. Such a soul liveth and moveth in accordance with the Will of its Creator, and entereth the all-highest Paradise. The Maids of Heaven, inmates of the loftiest mansions, will circle around it, and the Prophets of God and His chosen ones will seek its companionship. With them that soul will freely converse, and will recount unto them that which it hath been made to endure in the path of God, the Lord of all worlds. If any man be told that which hath been ordained for such a soul in the worlds of God, the Lord of the throne on high and of earth below, his whole being will instantly blaze out in his great longing to attain that most exalted, that sanctified and resplendent station.... The nature of the soul after death can never be described, nor is it meet and permissible to reveal its whole character to the eyes of men.... The world beyond is as different from this world as this world is different from that of the child while still in the womb of its mother. When the soul attaineth the Presence of God, it will assume the form that best befitteth its immortality and is worthy of its celestial habitation. Such an existence is a contingent and not an absolute existence, inasmuch as the former is preceded by a cause, whilst the latter is independent thereof. Absolute existence is strictly confined to God, exalted be His glory. Well is it with them that apprehend this truth.[309]

Thou hast, moreover, asked Me concerning the state of the soul after its separation from the body. Know thou, of a truth, that if the soul of man hath walked in the ways of God, it will, assuredly, return and be gathered to the glory of the Beloved. By the righteousness of God! It shall attain a station such as no pen can depict, or tongue describe. The soul that hath remained faithful to the Cause of God, and stood unwaveringly firm in His Path shall, after his ascension, be possessed of such power that all the worlds which the Almighty hath created can benefit through him. Such a soul provideth, at the bidding of the Ideal King and Divine Educator, the pure leaven that leaveneth the world of being, and furnisheth the power through which the arts and wonders of the world are made manifest. Consider how meal needeth leaven to be leavened with. Those souls that are the symbols of detachment are the leaven of the world. Meditate on this, and be of the thankful.

In several of Our Tablets We have referred to this theme, and have set forth the various stages in the development of the soul. Verily I say, the human soul is exalted above all egress and regress. It is still, and yet it soareth; it moveth, and yet it is still. It is, in itself, a testimony that beareth witness to the existence of a world that is contingent, as well as to the reality of a world that hath neither beginning nor end.[310]

Thou hast asked Me whether man, as apart from the Prophets of God and His chosen ones, will retain, after his physical death, the self-same individuality, personality, consciousness, and understanding that characterize his life in this world. If this should be the case, how is it, thou hast observed, that whereas such slight injuries to his mental faculties as fainting and severe illness deprive him of his understanding and consciousness, his death, which must involve the decomposition of his body and the dissolution of its elements, is powerless to destroy that understanding and extinguish that consciousness? How can any one imagine that man's consciousness and personality will be maintained, when the very instruments necessary to their existence and function will have completely disintegrated?

Know thou that the soul of man is exalted above, and is independent of all infirmities of body or mind. That a sick person showeth signs of weakness is due to the hindrances that interpose themselves between his soul and his body, for the soul itself remaineth unaffected by any bodily ailments. Consider the light of the lamp. Though an external object may interfere with its radiance, the light itself continueth to shine with undiminished power. In like manner, every malady afflicting the body of man is an impediment that preventeth the soul from manifesting its inherent might and power. When it leaveth the body, however, it will evince such ascendancy, and reveal such influence as no force on earth can equal. Every pure, every refined and sanctified soul will be endowed with tremendous power, and shall rejoice with exceeding gladness.

Consider the lamp which is hidden under a bushel. Though its light be shining, yet its radiance is concealed from men. Likewise, consider the sun which hath been obscured by the clouds. Observe how its splendor appeareth to have diminished, when in reality the source of that light hath remained unchanged. The soul of man should be likened unto this sun, and all things on earth should be regarded as his body. So long as no external impediment interveneth between them, the body will, in its entirety, continue to reflect the light of the soul, and to be sustained by its power. As soon as, however, a veil interposeth itself between them, the brightness of that light seemeth to lessen.

Consider again the sun when it is completely hidden behind the clouds. Though the earth is still illumined with its light, yet the measure of light which it receiveth is considerably reduced. Not until the clouds have dispersed, can the sun shine again in the plenitude of its glory. Neither the presence of the cloud nor its absence can, in any way, affect the inherent splendor of the sun. The soul of man is the sun by which his body is illumined, and from which it draweth its sustenance, and should be so regarded.[311]

And now concerning thy question whether human souls continue to be conscious one of another after their separation from the body. Know thou that the souls of the people of Bahá, who have entered and been established within the Crimson Ark, shall associate and commune intimately one with another, and shall be so closely associated in their lives, their aspirations, their aims and strivings as to be even as one soul. They are indeed the ones who are well-informed, who are keen-sighted, and who are endued with understanding. Thus hath it been decreed by Him Who is the All-Knowing, the All-Wise.

The people of Bahá, who are the inmates of the Ark of God, are, one and all, well aware of one another's state and condition, and are united in the bonds of intimacy and fellowship. Such a state, however, must depend upon their faith and their conduct. They that are of the same grade and station are fully aware of one another's capacity, character, accomplishments and merits. They that are of a lower grade, however, are incapable of comprehending adequately the station, or of estimating the merits, of those that rank above them. Each shall receive his share from thy Lord. Blessed is the man that hath turned his face towards God, and walked steadfastly in His love, until his soul hath winged its flight unto God, the Sovereign Lord of all, the Most Powerful, the Ever-Forgiving, the All-Merciful.[312]

A New World Order

Days of Divine Justice

The time for the destruction of the world and its people ... hath arrived. The hour is approaching ... when the most great convulsion will have appeared. The promised day is come, the day when tormenting trials will have surged above your heads, and beneath your feet, saying: "Taste ye what your hands have wrought!" Soon shall the blasts of His chastisement beat upon you, and the dust of hell enshroud you. And when the appointed hour is come, there shall suddenly appear that which shall cause the limbs of mankind to quake. The day is approaching when its [civilization's] flame will devour the cities, when the Tongue of Grandeur will proclaim: "The Kingdom is God's, the Almighty, the All-Praised!'" The day will soon come ... whereon they will cry out for help and receive no answer. The day is approaching ... when the wrathful anger of the Almighty will have taken hold of them. He, verily, is the Omnipotent, the All-Subduing, the Most Powerful. He shall cleanse the earth from the defilement of their corruption, and shall give it for an heritage unto such of His servants as are nigh unto Him.

Bestir yourselves, O people ... in anticipation of the days of Divine Justice, for the promised hour is now come. Abandon that which ye possess, and seize that which God, Who layeth low the necks of men, hath brought. Know ye of a certainty that if ye turn not back from that which ye have committed, chastisement will overtake you on every side, and ye shall behold things more grievous than that which ye beheld aforetime. We have fixed a time for you, O people! If ye fail, at the appointed hour, to turn towards God, He, verily, will lay violent hold on you, and will cause grievous afflictions to assail you from every direction. How severe indeed is the chastisement with which your Lord will then chastise you! God assuredly dominateth the lives of them that wronged Us, and is well aware of their doings. He will most certainly lay hold on them for their sins. He, verily, is the fiercest of Avengers. O ye peoples of the world! Know verily that an unforeseen calamity is following you and that grievous retribution awaiteth you. Think not the deeds ye have committed have been blotted from My sight. By My Beauty! All your doings hath My pen graven with open characters upon tablets of chrysolite.[313]

O ye that are lying as dead on the couch of heedlessness! Ages have passed and your precious lives are well-nigh ended, yet not a single breath of purity hath reached Our court of holiness from you. Though immersed in the ocean of misbelief, yet with your lips ye profess the one true faith of God. Him whom I abhor ye have loved, and of My foe ye have made a friend. Notwithstanding, ye walk on My earth complacent and self-satisfied, heedless that My earth is weary of you and everything within it shunneth you. Were ye but to open your eyes, ye would, in truth, prefer a myriad griefs unto this joy, and would count death itself better than this life.[314]

The world is in travail, and its agitation waxeth day by day. Its face is turned towards waywardness and unbelief. Such shall be its plight, that to disclose it now would not be meet and seemly. Its perversity will long continue. And when the appointed hour is come, there shall suddenly appear that which shall cause the limbs of mankind to quake. Then, and only then, will the Divine Standard be unfurled, and the Nightingale of Paradise warble its melody.[315]

Say: There is no place of refuge for you, no asylum to which ye can flee, no one to defend or to protect you in this Day from the fury of the wrath of God and from His vehement power, unless and until ye seek the shadow of His Revelation.[316]

Purpose of God's Religion

The Great Being saith: O ye children of men! The fundamental purpose animating the Faith of God and His Religion is to safeguard the interests and promote the unity of the human race, and to foster the spirit of love and fellowship amongst men. Suffer it not to become a source of dissension and discord, of hate and enmity. This is the straight Path, the fixed and immovable foundation. Whatsoever is raised on this foundation, the changes and chances of the world can never impair its strength, nor will the revolution of countless centuries undermine its structure.[317]

The purpose of religion as revealed from the heaven of God's holy Will is to establish unity and concord amongst the peoples of the world; make it not the cause of dissension and strife. The religion of God and His divine law are the most potent instruments and the surest of all means for the dawning of the light of unity amongst men. The progress of the world, the development of nations, the tranquillity of peoples, and the peace of all who dwell on earth are among the principles and ordinances of God. Religion bestoweth upon man the most precious of all gifts, offereth the cup of prosperity, imparteth eternal life, and showereth imperishable benefits upon mankind. It behoveth the chiefs and rulers of the world, and in particular the Trustees of God's House of Justice, to endeavour to the utmost of their power to safeguard its position, promote its interests and exalt its station in the eyes of the world.[318]

The first Ishráq

When the Day-Star of Wisdom rose above the horizon of God's Holy Dispensation it voiced this all-glorious utterance: They that are possessed of wealth and invested with authority and power must show the profoundest regard for religion. In truth, religion is a radiant light and an impregnable stronghold for the protection and welfare of the peoples of the world, for the fear of God impelleth man to hold fast to that which is good, and shun all evil. Should the lamp of religion be obscured, chaos and confusion will ensue, and the lights of fairness and justice, of tranquillity and peace cease to shine. Unto this will bear witness every man of true understanding.[319]

And yet, is not the object of every Revelation to effect a transformation in the whole character of mankind, a transformation that shall manifest itself both outwardly and inwardly, that shall affect both its inner life and external conditions? For if the character of mankind be not changed, the futility of God's universal Manifestations would be apparent.[320]

If any man were to meditate on that which the Scriptures, sent down from the heaven of God's holy Will, have revealed, he would readily recognize that their purpose is that all men shall be regarded as one soul, so that the seal bearing the words "The Kingdom shall be God's" may be stamped on every heart...[321]

Every man of insight will, in this day, readily admit that the counsels which the Pen of this Wronged One hath revealed constitute the supreme animating power for the advancement of the world and the exaltation of its peoples. Arise, O people, and, by the power of God's might, resolve to gain the victory over your own selves, that haply the whole earth may be freed and sanctified from its servitude to the gods of its idle fancies—gods that have inflicted such loss upon, and are responsible for the misery of their wretched worshippers. These idols form the obstacle that impedeth man in his efforts to advance in the path of perfection. We cherish the hope that the Hand of divine power may lend its assistance to mankind and deliver it from its state of grievous abasement.[322]

Love for Mankind

It is incumbent upon every man, in this Day, to hold fast unto whatsoever will promote the interests, and exalt the station, of all nations and just governments. Through each and every one of the verses which the Pen of the Most High hath revealed, the doors of love and unity have been unlocked and flung open to the face of men. We have erewhile declared—and Our Word is the truth—: 'Consort with the followers of all religions in a spirit of friendliness and fellowship.' Whatsoever hath led the children of men to shun one another, and hath caused dissensions and divisions amongst them, hath, through the revelation of these words, been nullified and abolished. From the heaven of God's Will, and for the purpose of ennobling the world of being and of elevating the minds and souls of men, hath been sent down that which is the most effective instrument for the education of the whole human race. The highest essence and most perfect expression of whatsoever the peoples of old have either said or written hath, through this most potent Revelation, been sent down from the heaven of the Will of the All-Possessing, the Ever-Abiding God. Of old it hath been revealed: 'Love of one's country is an element of the Faith of God.' The Tongue of Grandeur hath, however, in the day of His manifestation proclaimed: 'It is not his to boast who loveth his country, but it is his who loveth the world.' Through the power released by these exalted words He hath lent a fresh impulse and set a new direction to the birds of men's hearts, and hath obliterated every trace of restriction and limitation from God's holy Book.[323]

The Great Being saith: Blessed and happy is he that ariseth to promote the best interests of the peoples and kindreds of the earth. In another passage He hath proclaimed: It is not for him to pride himself who loveth his own country, but rather for him who loveth the whole world. The earth is but one country, and mankind its citizens.[324]

O ye beloved of the Lord! Commit not that which defileth the limpid stream of love or destroyeth the sweet fragrance of friendship. By the righteousness of the Lord! Ye were created to show love one to another and not perversity and rancour. Take pride not in love for yourselves but in love for your fellow-creatures. Glory not in love for your country, but in love for all mankind.[325]

Unity of Mankind

The first utterance of Him Who is the All-Wise is this: O children of dust! Turn your faces from the darkness of estrangement to the effulgent light of the daystar of unity. This is that which above all else will benefit the peoples of the earth. O friend! Upon the tree of utterance there hath never been, nor shall there ever be, a fairer leaf, and beneath the ocean of knowledge no pearl more wondrous can ever be found.[326]

That which the Lord hath ordained as the sovereign remedy and mightiest instrument for the healing of all the world is the union of all its peoples in one universal Cause, one common Faith. This can in no wise be achieved except through the power of a skilled, an all-powerful and inspired Physician. This, verily, is the truth, and all else naught but error.[327]

The incomparable Friend saith: The path to freedom hath been outstretched; hasten ye thereunto. The wellspring of wisdom is overflowing; quaff ye therefrom. Say: O well-beloved ones! The tabernacle of unity hath been raised; regard ye not one another as strangers. Ye are the fruits of one tree, and the leaves of one branch. Verily I say, whatsoever leadeth to the decline of ignorance and the increase of knowledge hath been, and will ever remain, approved in the sight of the Lord of creation. Say: O people! Walk ye neath the shadow of justice and truthfulness and seek ye shelter within the tabernacle of unity.[328]

O CONTENDING peoples and kindreds of the earth! Set your faces towards unity, and let the radiance of its light shine upon you. Gather ye together, and for the sake of God resolve to root out whatever is the source of contention amongst you. Then will the effulgence of the world's great Luminary envelop the whole earth, and its inhabitants become the citizens of one city, and the occupants of one and the same throne. This wronged One hath, ever since the early days of His life, cherished none other desire but this, and will continue to entertain no wish except this wish. There can be no doubt whatever that the peoples of the world, of whatever race or religion, derive their inspiration from one heavenly Source, and are the subjects of one God.[329]

My object is none other than the betterment of the world and the tranquillity of its peoples. The well-being of mankind, its peace and security, are unattainable unless and until its unity is firmly established. This unity can never be achieved so long as the counsels which the Pen of the Most High hath revealed are suffered to pass unheeded.[330]

Through the power of the words He hath uttered the whole of the human race can be illumined with the light of unity, and the remembrance of His Name is able to set on fire the hearts of all men, and burn away the veils that intervene between them and His glory.[331]

The utterance of God is a lamp, whose light is these words: Ye are the fruits of one tree, and the leaves of one branch. Deal ye one with another with the utmost love and harmony, with friendliness and fellowship. He Who is the Daystar of Truth beareth Me witness! So powerful is the light of unity that it can illuminate the whole earth.[332]

O CHILDREN OF MEN! Know ye not why We created you all from the same dust? That no one should exalt himself over the other. Ponder at all times in your hearts how ye were created. Since We have created you all from one same substance it is incumbent on you to be even as one soul, to walk with the same feet, eat with the same mouth and dwell in the same land, that from your inmost being, by your deeds and actions, the signs of oneness and the essence of detachment may be made manifest. Such is My counsel to you, O concourse of light! Heed ye this counsel that ye may obtain the fruit of holiness from the tree of wondrous glory.[333]

They that are endued with sincerity and faithfulness should associate with all the peoples and kindreds of the earth with joy and radiance, inasmuch as consorting with people hath promoted and will continue to promote unity and concord, which in turn are conducive to the maintenance of order in the world and to the regeneration of nations. Blessed are such as hold fast to the cord of kindliness and tender mercy and are free from animosity and hatred.

This Wronged One exhorteth the peoples of the world to observe tolerance and righteousness, which are two lights amidst the darkness of the world and two educators for the edification of mankind. Happy are they who have attained thereto and woe betide the heedless.[334]

The word of God which the Supreme Pen hath recorded on the

seventh leaf

of the Most Exalted Paradise is this: O ye men of wisdom among nations! Shut your eyes to estrangement, then fix your gaze upon unity. Cleave tenaciously unto that which will lead to the well-being and tranquillity of all mankind. This span of earth is but one homeland and one habitation. It behoveth you to abandon vainglory which causeth alienation and to set your hearts on whatever will ensure harmony. In the estimation of the people of Bahá man's glory lieth in his knowledge, his upright conduct, his praiseworthy character, his wisdom, and not in his nationality or rank.[335]

Say: O servants! Let not the means of order be made the cause of confusion and the instrument of union an occasion for discord. We fain would hope that the people of Bahá may be guided by the blessed words: Say: all things are of God. This exalted utterance is like unto water for quenching the fire of hate and enmity which smouldereth within the hearts and breasts of men. By this single utterance contending peoples and kindreds will attain the light of true unity. Verily He speaketh the truth and leadeth the way. He is the All-Powerful, the Exalted, the Gracious.[336]

It beseemeth all men, in this Day, to take firm hold on the Most Great Name, and to establish the unity of all mankind. There is no place to flee to, no refuge that any one can seek, except Him.[337]

He Who is the Eternal Truth hath, from the Day Spring of Glory, directed His eyes towards the people of Bahá, and is addressing them in these words: Address yourselves to the promotion of the well-being and tranquillity of the children of men. Bend your minds and wills to the education of the peoples and kindreds of the earth, that haply the dissensions that divide it may, through the power of the Most Great Name, be blotted out from its face, and all mankind become the upholders of one Order, and the inhabitants of one City. Illumine and hallow your hearts; let them not be profaned by the thorns of hate or the thistles of malice. Ye dwell in one world, and have been created through the operation of one Will. Blessed is he who mingleth with all men in a spirit of utmost kindliness and love."[338]

At a time when darkness had encompassed the world, the ocean of divine favour surged and His Light was made manifest, that the doings of men might be laid bare. This, verily, is that Light which hath been foretold in the heavenly scriptures. Should the Almighty so please, the hearts of all men will be purged and purified through His goodly utterance, and the light of unity will shed its radiance upon every soul and revive the whole earth.[339]

New World Order

The world's equilibrium hath been upset through the vibrating influence of this most great, this new World Order. Mankind's ordered life hath been revolutionized through the agency of this unique, this wondrous System—the like of which mortal eyes have never witnessed.[340]

Beseech ye the one true God to grant that all men may be graciously assisted to fulfil that which is acceptable in Our sight. Soon will the present-day order be rolled up, and a new one spread out in its stead. Verily, thy Lord speaketh the truth, and is the Knower of things unseen.[341]

By My Self! The day is approaching when We will have rolled up the world and all that is therein, and spread out a new order in its stead. He, verily, is powerful over all things.[342]

The whole earth ... is now in a state of pregnancy. The day is approaching when it will have yielded its noblest fruits, when from it will have sprung forth the loftiest trees, the most enchanting blossoms, the most heavenly blessings.[343]

Today, this Servant has assuredly come to vivify the world and to bring into unity all who are on the face of the earth. That which God willeth shall come to pass and thou shalt see the earth even as the Abhá (Most Glorious) Paradise.[344]

The Kitáb-i-Aqdas

While in prison We have revealed a Book which We have entitled 'The Most Holy Book'. We have enacted laws therein and adorned it with the commandments of thy Lord, Who exerciseth authority over all that are in the heavens and on the earth. Say: Take hold of it, O people, and observe that which hath been sent down in it of the wondrous precepts of your Lord, the Forgiving, the Bountiful. It will truly prosper you both in this world and in the next and will purge you of whatsoever ill beseemeth you. He is indeed the Ordainer, the Expounder, the Giver, the Generous, the Gracious, the All-Praised.[345]

They whom God hath endued with insight will readily recognize that the precepts laid down by God constitute the highest means for the maintenance of order in the world and the security of its peoples. He that turneth away from them is accounted among the abject and foolish.[346]

We school you with the rod of wisdom and laws, like unto the father who educateth his son, and this for naught but the protection of your own selves and the elevation of your stations. By My life, were ye to discover what We have desired for you in revealing Our holy laws, ye would offer up your very souls for this sacred, this mighty, and most exalted Faith.[347]

This Book...is a heaven which We have adorned with the stars of Our commandments and prohibitions.[348]

Whenever My laws appear like the sun in the heaven of Mine utterance, they must be faithfully obeyed by all, though My decree be such as to cause the heaven of every religion to be cleft asunder. He doeth what He pleaseth. He chooseth, and none may question His choice. Whatsoever He, the Well-Beloved, ordaineth, the same is, verily, beloved. To this He Who is the Lord of all creation beareth Me witness.[349]

The third Ishráq

It is incumbent upon everyone to observe God's holy commandments, inasmuch as they are the wellspring of life unto the world. The heaven of divine wisdom is illumined with the two luminaries of consultation and compassion and the canopy of world order is upraised upon the two pillars of reward and punishment.[350]

The ordinances of God have been sent down from the heaven of His most august Revelation. All must diligently observe them. Man's supreme distinction, his real advancement, his final victory, have always depended, and will continue to depend, upon them. Whoso keepeth the commandments of God shall attain everlasting felicity.

A twofold obligation resteth upon him who hath recognized the Day Spring of the Unity of God, and acknowledged the truth of Him Who is the Manifestation of His oneness. The first is steadfastness in His love, such steadfastness that neither the clamor of the enemy nor the claims of the idle pretender can deter him from cleaving unto Him Who is the Eternal Truth, a steadfastness that taketh no account of them whatever. The second is strict observance of the laws He hath prescribed—laws which He hath always ordained, and will continue to ordain, unto men, and through which the truth may be distinguished and separated from falsehood.[351]

Indeed, the laws of God are like unto the ocean and the children of men as fish, did they but know it. However, in observing them one must exercise tact and wisdom☐ Since most people are feeble and far-removed from the purpose of God, therefore one must observe tact and prudence under all conditions, so that nothing might happen that could cause disturbance and dissension or raise clamour among the heedless. Verily, His bounty hath surpassed the whole universe and His bestowals encompassed all that dwell on earth. One must guide mankind to the ocean of true understanding in a spirit of love and tolerance. The Kitáb-i-Aqdas itself beareth eloquent testimony to the loving providence of God.[352]

Our Exalted Herald, may the life of all else besides Him be offered up for His sake, hath revealed certain laws. However, in the realm of His Revelation these laws were made subject to Our sanction, hence this Wronged One hath put some of them into effect by embodying them in the Kitáb-i-Aqdas in different words. Others We set aside. He holdeth in His hand the authority. He doeth what He willeth and He ordaineth whatsoever He pleaseth. He is the Almighty, the All-Praised. There are also ordinances newly revealed. Blessed are they that attain. Blessed are they that observe His precepts.[353]

Say: From My laws the sweet-smelling savour of My garment can be smelled, and by their aid the standards of Victory will be planted upon the highest peaks. The Tongue of My power hath, from the heaven of My omnipotent glory, addressed to My creation these words: "Observe My commandments, for the love of My beauty." Happy is the lover that hath inhaled the divine fragrance of his Best-Beloved from these words, laden with the perfume of a grace which no tongue can describe. By My life! He who hath drunk the choice wine of fairness from the hands of My bountiful favour will circle around My commandments that shine above the Dayspring of My creation.

Think not that We have revealed unto you a mere code of laws. Nay, rather, We have unsealed the choice Wine with the fingers of might and power. To this beareth witness that which the Pen of Revelation hath revealed. Meditate upon this, O men of insight! [354]

In such manner hath the Kitáb-i-Aqdas been revealed that it attracteth and embraceth all the divinely appointed Dispensations. Blessed those who peruse it. Blessed those who apprehend it. Blessed those who meditate upon it. Blessed those who ponder its meaning. So vast is its range that it hath encompassed all men ere their recognition of it. Ere long will its sovereign power, its pervasive influence and the greatness of its might be manifested on earth. Verily, thy God is the All-Knowing, the All-Informed.[355]

Houses of Worship

O people of the world! Build ye houses of worship throughout the lands in the name of Him Who is the Lord of all religions. Make them as perfect as is possible in the world of being, and adorn them with that which befitteth them, not with images and effigies. Then, with radiance and joy, celebrate therein the praise of your Lord, the Most Compassionate. Verily, by His remembrance the eye is cheered and the heart is filled with light.[356]

Blessed is he who, at the hour of dawn, centring his thoughts on God, occupied with His remembrance, and supplicating His forgiveness, directeth his steps to the Mashriqu'l-Adhkár and, entering therein, seateth himself in silence to listen to the verses of God, the Sovereign, the Mighty, the All-Praised. Say: The Mashriqu'l-Adhkár is each and every building which hath been erected in cities and villages for the celebration of My praise. Such is the name by which it hath been designated before the throne of glory, were ye of those who understand.[357]

Local and Universal Houses of Justice

The Lord hath ordained that in every city a House of Justice be established wherein shall gather counsellors to the number of Bahá, and should it exceed this number it doth not matter. They should consider themselves as entering the Court of the presence of God, the Exalted, the Most High, and as beholding Him Who is the Unseen. It behoveth them to be the trusted ones of the Merciful among men and to regard themselves as the guardians appointed of God for all that dwell on earth. It is incumbent upon them to take counsel together and to have regard for the interests of the servants of God, for His sake, even as they regard their own interests, and to choose that which is meet and seemly. Thus hath the Lord your God commanded you. Beware lest ye put away that which is clearly revealed in His Tablet. Fear God, O ye that perceive.[358]

This passage, now written by the Pen of Glory, is accounted as part of the Most Holy Book: The men of God's House of Justice have been charged with the affairs of the people. They, in truth, are the Trustees of God among His servants and the daysprings of authority in His countries.

O people of God! That which traineth the world is Justice, for it is upheld by two pillars, reward and punishment. These two pillars are the sources of life to the world. Inasmuch as for each day there is a new problem and for every problem an expedient solution, such affairs should be referred to the House of Justice that the members thereof may act according to the needs and requirements of the time. They that, for the sake of God, arise to serve His Cause, are the recipients of divine inspiration from the unseen Kingdom. It is incumbent upon all to be obedient unto them. All matters of State should be referred to the House of Justice, but acts of worship must be observed according to that which God hath revealed in His Book.[359]

It is incumbent upon the Trustees of the House of Justice to take counsel together regarding those things which have not outwardly been revealed in the Book, and to enforce that which is agreeable to them. God will verily inspire them with whatsoever He willeth, and He, verily, is the Provider, the Omniscient.[360]

Justice

O SON OF SPIRIT! The best beloved of all things in My sight is Justice; turn not away therefrom if thou desirest Me, and neglect it not that I may confide in thee. By its aid thou shalt see with thine own eyes and not through the eyes of others, and shalt know of thine own knowledge and not through the knowledge of thy neighbor. Ponder this in thy heart; how it behooveth thee to be. Verily justice is My gift to thee and the sign of My loving-kindness. Set it then before thine eyes.[361]

This servant beseecheth the one True God—exalted be His glory—to graciously adorn the world of humanity with justice and fair-mindedness, although in truth the latter is but one of the expressions of the former. Verily, justice is a lamp that guideth man aright amidst the darkness of the world and shieldeth him from every danger. It is indeed a shining lamp. God grant that the rulers of the earth may be illumined by its light. This servant further imploreth God to graciously aid all men to do His will and pleasure. He, in truth, is the Lord of this world and of the world to come. No God is there but Him, the Almighty, the Most-Powerful.[362]

Know verily that the essence of justice and the source thereof are both embodied in the ordinances prescribed by Him Who is the Manifestation of the Self of God amongst men, if ye be of them that recognize this truth. He doth verily incarnate the highest, the infallible standard of justice unto all creation. Were His law to be such as to strike terror into the hearts of all that are in heaven and on earth, that law is naught but manifest justice.[363]

The word of God which the Supreme Pen hath recorded on the

sixth leaf

of the Most Exalted Paradise is the following: The light of men is Justice. Quench it not with the contrary winds of oppression and tyranny. The purpose of justice is the appearance of unity among men. The ocean of divine wisdom surgeth within this exalted word, while the books of the world cannot contain its inner significance. Were mankind to be adorned with this raiment, they would behold the day-star of the utterance, 'On that day God will satisfy everyone out of His abundance,'[364] shining resplendent above the horizon of the world.[365]

The Great Being saith: The structure of world stability and order hath been reared upon, and will continue to be sustained by, the twin pillars of reward and punishment. And in another connection He hath uttered the following in the eloquent tongue: Justice hath a mighty force at its command. It is none other than reward and punishment for the deeds of men. By the power of this force the tabernacle of order is established throughout the world, causing the wicked to restrain their natures for fear of punishment.[366]

O OPPRESSORS ON EARTH! Withdraw your hands from tyranny, for I have pledged Myself not to forgive any man's injustice. This is My covenant which I have irrevocably decreed in the preserved tablet and sealed with My seal.[367]

Blessed is the one who discovereth the fragrance of inner meanings from the traces of this Pen through whose movement the breezes of God are wafted over the entire creation, and through whose stillness the very essence of tranquillity appeareth in the realm of being. Glorified be the All-Merciful, the Revealer of so inestimable a bounty. Say: Because He bore injustice, justice hath appeared on earth, and because He accepted abasement, the majesty of God hath shone forth amidst mankind.[368]

The Great Being saith: O well-beloved ones! The tabernacle of unity hath been raised; regard ye not one another as strangers. Ye are the fruits of one tree, and the leaves of one branch. We cherish the hope that the light of justice may shine upon the world and sanctify it from tyranny. If the rulers and kings of the earth, the symbols of the power of God, exalted be His glory, arise and resolve to dedicate themselves to whatever will promote the highest interests of the whole of humanity, the reign of justice will assuredly be established amongst the children of men, and the effulgence of its light will envelop the whole earth.[369]

We entreat God to deliver the light of equity and the sun of justice from the thick clouds of waywardness, and cause them to shine forth upon men. No light can compare with the light of justice. The establishment of order in the world and the tranquillity of the nations depend upon it.[370]

Justice is a powerful force. It is, above all else, the conqueror of the citadels of the hearts and souls of men, and the revealer of the secrets of the world of being, and the standard-bearer of love and bounty.[371]

Say: "O God, my God! Attire mine head with the crown of justice, and my temple with the ornament of equity. Thou, verily, art the Possessor of all gifts and bounties."

Justice and equity are twin Guardians that watch over men. From them are revealed such blessed and perspicuous words as are the cause of the well-being of the world and the protection of the nations.[372]

Universal Language

The sixth Ishráq

is union and concord amongst the children of men. From the beginning of time the light of unity hath shed its divine radiance upon the world, and the greatest means for the promotion of that unity is for the peoples of the world to understand one another's writing and speech. In former Epistles We have enjoined upon the Trustees of the House of Justice either to choose one language from among those now existing or to adopt a new one, and in like manner to select a common script, both of which should be taught in all the schools of the world. Thus will the earth be regarded as one country and one home. The most glorious fruit of the tree of knowledge is this exalted word: Of one tree are all ye the fruit, and of one bough the leaves. Let not man glory in this that he loveth his country, let him rather glory in this that he loveth his kind.[373]

The day is approaching when all the peoples of the world will have adopted one universal language and one common script. When this is achieved, to whatsoever city a man may journey, it shall be as if he were entering his own home. These things are obligatory and absolutely essential.[374]

O members of parliaments throughout the world! Select ye a single language for the use of all on earth, and adopt ye likewise a common script. God, verily, maketh plain for you that which shall profit you and enable you to be independent of others. He, of a truth, is the Most Bountiful, the All-Knowing, the All-Informed. This will be the cause of unity, could ye but comprehend it, and the greatest instrument for promoting harmony and civilization, would that ye might understand! [375]

Universal Education

Man is the supreme Talisman. Lack of a proper education hath, however, deprived him of that which he doth inherently possess. Through a word proceeding out of the mouth of God he was called into being; by one word more he was guided to recognize the Source of his education; by yet another word his station and destiny were safeguarded. The Great Being saith: Regard man as a mine rich in gems of inestimable value. Education can, alone, cause it to reveal its treasures, and enable mankind to benefit therefrom.[376]

Consider, for instance, the revelation of the light of the Name of God, the Educator. Behold, how in all things the evidences of such a revelation are manifest, how the betterment of all beings dependeth upon it. This education is of two kinds. The one is universal. Its influence pervadeth all things and sustaineth them. It is for this reason that God hath assumed the title, "Lord of all worlds." The other is confined to them that have come under the shadow of this Name, and sought the shelter of this most mighty Revelation. They, however, that have failed to seek this shelter, have deprived themselves of this privilege, and are powerless to benefit from the spiritual sustenance that hath been sent down through the heavenly grace of this Most Great Name.[377]

We prescribe unto all men that which will lead to the exaltation of the Word of God amongst His servants, and likewise, to the advancement of the world of being and the uplift of souls. To this end, the greatest means is education of the child. To this must each and all hold fast. We have verily laid this charge upon you in manifold Tablets as well as in My Most Holy Book. Well is it with him who deferreth thereto.

We ask of God that He will assist each and every one to obey this inescapable command that hath appeared and been caused to descend through the Pen of the Ancient of Days.[378]

That which is of paramount importance for the children, that which must precede all else, is to teach them the oneness of God and the laws of God. For lacking this, the fear of God cannot be inculcated, and lacking the fear of God an infinity of odious and abominable actions will spring up, and sentiments will be uttered that transgress all bounds...

The parents must exert every effort to rear their offspring to be religious, for should the children not attain this greatest of adornments, they will not obey their parents, which in a certain sense means that they will not obey God. Indeed, such children will show no consideration to anyone, and will do exactly as they please.[379]

The word of God which the Supreme Pen hath recorded on the

eighth leaf

of the Most Exalted Paradise is the following: Schools must first train the children in the principles of religion, so that the Promise and the Threat recorded in the Books of God may prevent them from the things forbidden and adorn them with the mantle of the commandments; but this in such a measure that it may not injure the children by resulting in ignorant fanaticism and bigotry.[380]

It is incumbent upon the children to exert themselves to the utmost in acquiring the art of reading and writing.... Writing skills that will provide for urgent needs will be enough for some; and then it is better and more fitting that they should spend their time in studying those branches of knowledge which are of use.

As for what the Supreme Pen hath previously set down, the reason is that in every art and skill, God loveth the highest perfection.[381]

At the outset of every endeavour, it is incumbent to look to the end of it. Of all the arts and sciences, set the children to studying those which will result in advantage to man, will ensure his progress and elevate his rank.[382]

As to the children: We have directed that in the beginning they should be trained in the observances and laws of religion; and thereafter, in such branches of knowledge as are of benefit, and in commercial pursuits that are distinguished for integrity, and in deeds that will further the victory of God's Cause or will attract some outcome which will draw the believer closer to his Lord.

We beg of God to assist the children of His loved ones and adorn them with wisdom, good conduct, integrity and righteousness.

Blessed is that teacher who shall arise to instruct the children, and to guide the people into the pathways of God, the Bestower, the Well-Beloved.

Blessed is that teacher who remaineth faithful to the Covenant of God, and occupieth himself with the education of children. For him hath the Supreme Pen inscribed that reward which is revealed in the Most Holy Book.

Blessed, blessed is he! [383]

The seventh Ishráq

The Pen of Glory counselleth everyone regarding the instruction and education of children. Behold that which the Will of God hath revealed upon Our arrival in the Prison City and recorded in the Most Holy Book.[384] Unto every father hath been enjoined the instruction of his son and daughter in the art of reading and writing and in all that hath been laid down in the Holy Tablet. He that putteth away that which is commanded unto him, the Trustees are then to take from him that which is required for their instruction, if he be wealthy, and if not the matter devolveth upon the House of Justice. Verily, have We made it a shelter for the poor and needy.

He that bringeth up his son or the son of another, it is as though he hath brought up a son of Mine; upon him rest My Glory, My Loving-Kindness, My Mercy, that have compassed the world.[385]

Bend your minds and wills to the education of the peoples and kindreds of the earth, that haply the dissensions that divide it may, through the power of the Most Great Name, be blotted out from its face, and all mankind become the upholders of one Order, and the inhabitants of one City.[386]

Wealth and Poverty

The first Taráz

and the first effulgence which hath dawned from the horizon of the Mother Book is that man should know his own self and recognize that which leadeth unto loftiness or lowliness, glory or abasement, wealth or poverty. Having attained the stage of fulfilment and reached his maturity, man standeth in need of wealth, and such wealth as he acquireth through crafts or professions is commendable and praiseworthy in the estimation of men of wisdom, and especially in the eyes of servants who dedicate themselves to the education of the world and to the edification of its peoples.[387]

They who are possessed of riches, however, must have the utmost regard for the poor ... who are steadfast in patience. By My life! There is no honor, except what God may please to bestow, that can compare to this honor. Great is the blessedness awaiting the poor that endure patiently and conceal their sufferings, and well is it with the rich who bestow their riches on the needy and prefer them before themselves.

Please God, the poor may exert themselves and strive to earn the means of livelihood. This is a duty which, in this most great Revelation, hath been prescribed unto every one, and is accounted in the sight of God as a goodly deed. Whoso observeth this duty, the help of the invisible One shall most certainly aid him. He can enrich, through His grace, whomsoever He pleaseth. He, verily, hath power over all things....[388]

If ye meet the abased or the down-trodden, turn not away disdainfully from them, for the King of Glory ever watcheth over them and surroundeth them with such tenderness as none can fathom except them that have suffered their wishes and desires to be merged in the Will of your Lord, the Gracious, the All-Wise. O ye rich ones of the earth! Flee not from the face of the poor that lieth in the dust, nay rather befriend him and suffer him to recount the tale of the woes with which God's inscrutable Decree hath caused him to be afflicted. By the righteousness of God! Whilst ye consort with him, the Concourse on high will be looking upon you, will be interceding for you, will be extolling your names and glorifying your action.[389]

All have been enjoined to earn a living, and as for those who are incapable of doing so, it is incumbent on the Deputies of God and on the wealthy to make adequate provision for them.[390]

O YE RICH ONES ON EARTH! The poor in your midst are My trust; guard ye My trust, and be not intent only on your own ease.[391]

O SON OF MAN! Bestow My wealth upon My poor, that in heaven thou mayest draw from stores of unfading splendor and treasures of imperishable glory. But by My life! To offer up thy soul is a more glorious thing couldst thou but see with Mine eye.[392]

O SON OF MAN! Thou dost wish for gold and I desire thy freedom from it. Thou thinkest thyself rich in its possession, and I recognize thy wealth in thy sanctity therefrom. By My life! This is My knowledge, and that is thy fancy; how can My way accord with thine? [393]

O SON OF MY HANDMAID! Be not troubled in poverty nor confident in riches, for poverty is followed by riches, and riches are followed by poverty. Yet to be poor in all save God is a wondrous gift, belittle not the value thereof, for in the end it will make thee rich in God, and thus thou shalt know the meaning of the utterance, "In truth ye are the poor," and the holy words, "God is the all-possessing," shall even as the true morn break forth gloriously resplendent upon the horizon of the lover's heart, and abide secure on the throne of wealth.[394]

O YE THAT PRIDE YOURSELVES ON MORTAL RICHES! Know ye in truth that wealth is a mighty barrier between the seeker and his desire, the lover and his beloved. The rich, but for a few, shall in no wise attain the court of His presence nor enter the city of content and resignation. Well is it then with him, who, being rich, is not hindered by his riches from the eternal kingdom, nor deprived by them of imperishable dominion. By the Most Great Name! The splendor of such a wealthy man shall illuminate the dwellers of heaven even as the sun enlightens the people of the earth! [395]

O SON OF PASSION! Cleanse thyself from the defilement of riches and in perfect peace advance into the realm of poverty; that from the well-spring of detachment thou mayest quaff the wine of immortal life.[396]

The essence of wealth is love for Me; whoso loveth Me is the possessor of all things, and he that loveth Me not is indeed of the poor and needy. This is that which the Finger of Glory and Splendour hath revealed.[397]

Equality of Men and Women

All should know, and in this regard attain the splendours of the sun of certitude, and be illumined thereby: Women and men have been and will always be equal in the sight of God. The Dawning-Place of the Light of God sheddeth its radiance upon all with the same effulgence. Verily God created women for men, and men for women. The most beloved of people before God are the most steadfast and those who have surpassed others in their love for God, exalted be His glory....[398]

In this Day the Hand of divine grace hath removed all distinctions. The servants of God and His handmaidens are regarded on the same plane. Blessed is the servant who hath attained unto that which God hath decreed, and likewise the leaf moving in accordance with the breezes of His will. This favour is great and this station lofty. His bounties and bestowals are ever present and manifest. Who is able to offer befitting gratitude for His successive bestowals and continuous favours? [399]

Exalted, immensely exalted is He Who hath removed differences and established harmony. Glorified, infinitely glorified is He Who hath caused discord to cease, and decreed solidarity and unity. Praised be God, the Pen of the Most High hath lifted distinctions from between His servants and handmaidens, and, through His consummate favours and all-encompassing mercy, hath conferred upon all a station and rank of the same plane. He hath broken the back of vain imaginings with the sword of utterance and hath obliterated the perils of idle fancies through the pervasive power of His might.[400]

Racial Unity

O ye discerning ones! ... Verily, the words which have descended from the heaven of the Will of God are the source of unity and harmony for the world. Close your eyes to racial differences, and welcome all with the light of oneness.[401]

O humankind! Verily, ye are all the leaves and fruits of one tree; ye are all one. Therefore, associate in friendship; love one another; abandon prejudices of race; dispel forever this gloomy darkness of human ignorance, for the century of light, the Sun of Reality hath appeared. Now is the time for affiliation, and now is the period of unity and concord.[402]

Loyalty and Obedience to Government

The fifth Glad-Tidings

In every country where any of this people reside, they must behave towards the government of that country with loyalty, honesty and truthfulness. This is that which hath been revealed at the behest of Him Who is the Ordainer, the Ancient of Days.[403]

The one true God, exalted be His glory, hath bestowed the government of the earth upon the kings. To none is given the right to act in any manner that would run counter to the considered views of them who are in authority.[404]

Give a hearing ear, O people, to that which I, in truth, say unto you. The one true God, exalted be His glory, hath ever regarded, and will continue to regard, the hearts of men as His own, His exclusive possession. All else, whether pertaining to land or sea, whether riches or glory, He hath bequeathed unto the Kings and rulers of the earth. From the beginning that hath no beginning the ensign proclaiming the words "He doeth whatsoever He willeth" hath been unfurled in all its splendor before His Manifestation. What mankind needeth in this day is obedience unto them that are in authority, and a faithful adherence to the cord of wisdom. The instruments which are essential to the immediate protection, the security and assurance of the human race have been entrusted to the hands, and lie in the grasp, of the governors of human society. This is the wish of God and His decree....[405]

World Peace

The Great Being, wishing to reveal the prerequisites of the peace and tranquillity of the world and the advancement of its peoples, hath written: The time must come when the imperative necessity for the holding of a vast, an all-embracing assemblage of men will be universally realized. The rulers and kings of the earth must needs attend it, and, participating in its deliberations, must consider such ways and means as will lay the foundations of the world's Great Peace amongst men. Such a peace demandeth that the Great Powers should resolve, for the sake of the tranquillity of the peoples of the earth, to be fully reconciled among themselves. Should any king take up arms against another, all should unitedly arise and prevent him. If this be done, the nations of the world will no longer require any armaments, except for the purpose of preserving the security of their realms and of maintaining internal order within their territories. This will ensure the peace and composure of every people, government and nation.[406]

We pray God—exalted be His glory—and cherish the hope that He may graciously assist the manifestations of affluence and power and the daysprings of sovereignty and glory, the kings of the earth—may God aid them through His strengthening grace—to establish the Lesser Peace. This, indeed, is the greatest means for insuring the tranquillity of the nations. It is incumbent upon the Sovereigns of the world—may God assist them—unitedly to hold fast unto this Peace, which is the chief instrument for the protection of all mankind. It is Our hope that they will arise to achieve what will be conducive to the well-being of man. It is their duty to convene an all-inclusive assembly, which either they themselves or their ministers will attend, and to enforce whatever measures are required to establish unity and concord amongst men. They must put away the weapons of war, and turn to the instruments of universal reconstruction. Should one king rise up against another, all the other kings must arise to deter him. Arms and armaments will, then, be no more needed beyond that which is necessary to insure the internal security of their respective countries. If they attain unto this all-surpassing blessing, the people of each nation will pursue, with tranquillity and contentment, their own occupations, and the groanings and lamentations of most men would be silenced. We beseech God to aid them to do His will and pleasure. He, verily, is the Lord of the throne on high and of earth below, and the Lord of this world and of the world to come.[407]

The second I<u>sh</u>ráq

We have enjoined upon all mankind to establish the Most Great Peace—the surest of all means for the protection of humanity. The sovereigns of the world should, with one accord, hold fast thereunto, for this is the supreme instrument that can ensure the security and welfare of all peoples and nations. They, verily, are the manifestations of the power of God and the dayprings of His authority. We beseech the Almighty that He may graciously assist them in that which is conducive to the well-being of their subjects. A full explanation regarding this matter hath been previously set forth by the Pen of Glory; well is it with them that act accordingly.[408]

O ye rulers of the earth! Wherefore have ye clouded the radiance of the Sun, and caused it to cease from shining? Hearken unto the counsel given you by the Pen of the Most High, that haply both ye and the poor may attain unto tranquillity and peace. We beseech God to assist the kings of the earth to establish peace on earth. He, verily, doth what He willeth.

O kings of the earth! We see you increasing every year your expenditures, and laying the burden thereof on your subjects. This, verily, is wholly and grossly unjust. Fear the sighs and tears of this Wronged One, and lay not excessive burdens on your peoples. Do not rob them to rear palaces for yourselves; nay rather choose for them that which ye choose for yourselves. Thus We unfold to your eyes that which profiteth you, if ye but perceive. Your people are your treasures. Beware lest your rule violate the commandments of God, and ye deliver your wards to the hands of the robber. By them ye rule, by their means ye subsist, by their aid ye conquer. Yet, how disdainfully ye look upon them! How strange, how very strange!

Now that ye have refused the Most Great Peace, hold ye fast unto this, the Lesser Peace, that haply ye may in some degree better your own condition and that of your dependents.

O rulers of the earth! Be reconciled among yourselves, that ye may need no more armaments save in a measure to safeguard your territories and dominions. Beware lest ye disregard the counsel of the All-Knowing, the Faithful.

Be united, O kings of the earth, for thereby will the tempest of discord be stilled amongst you, and your peoples find rest, if ye be of them that comprehend. Should any one among you take up arms against another, rise ye all against him, for this is naught but manifest justice.[409]   .

We cherish the hope that through the earnest endeavours of such as are the exponents of the power of God—exalted be His glory—the weapons of war throughout the world may be converted into instruments of reconstruction and that strife and conflict may be removed from the midst of men.[410]

We desire but the good of the world and the happiness of the nations; yet they deem Us a stirrer up of strife and sedition worthy of bondage and banishment.... That all nations should become one in faith and all men as brothers; that the bonds of affection and unity between the sons of men should be strengthened; that diversity of religion should cease, and differences of race be annulled—what harm is there in this?... Yet so it shall be; these fruitless strifes, these ruinous wars shall pass away, and the 'Most Great Peace' shall come.... Yet do We see your kings and rulers lavishing their treasures more freely on means for the destruction of the human race than on that which would conduce to the happiness of mankind.... These strifes and this bloodshed and discord must cease, and all men be as one kindred and one family.... Let not a man glory in this, that he loves his country; let him rather glory in this, that he loves his kind....[411]

Personal Character,
Conduct and Spiritual
Transformation

Detachment From the Material World

The generations that have gone on before you—whither are they fled? And those round whom in life circled the fairest and the loveliest of the land, where now are they? Profit by their example, O people, and be not of them that are gone astray.

Others ere long will lay hands on what ye possess, and enter into your habitations. Incline your ears to My words, and be not numbered among the foolish.[412]

Exultest thou over the treasures thou dost possess, knowing they shall perish? Rejoicest thou in that thou rulest a span of earth, when the whole world, in the estimation of the people of Bahá, is worth as much as the black in the eye of a dead ant? Abandon it unto such as have set their affections upon it, and turn thou unto Him Who is the Desire of the world. Whither are gone the proud and their palaces? Gaze thou into their tombs, that thou mayest profit by this example, inasmuch as We made it a lesson unto every beholder. Were the breezes of Revelation to seize thee, thou wouldst flee the world, and turn unto the Kingdom, and wouldst expend all thou possessest, that thou mayest draw nigh unto this sublime Vision.[413]

The world is but a show, vain and empty, a mere nothing, bearing the semblance of reality. Set not your affections upon it. Break not the bond that uniteth you with your Creator, and be not of those that have erred and strayed from His ways. Verily I say, the world is like the vapor in a desert, which the thirsty dreameth to be water and striveth after it with all his might, until when he cometh unto it, he findeth it to be mere illusion.[414]

Say: O people! Let not this life and its deceits deceive you, for the world and all that is therein is held firmly in the grasp of His Will. He bestoweth His favor on whom He willeth, and from whom He willeth He taketh it away. He doth whatsoever He chooseth. Had the world been of any worth in His sight, He surely would never have allowed His enemies to possess it, even to the extent of a grain of mustard seed. He hath, however, caused you to be entangled with its affairs, in return for what your hands have wrought in His Cause. This, indeed, is a chastisement which ye, of your own will, have inflicted upon yourselves, could ye but perceive it. Are ye rejoicing in the things which, according to the estimate of God, are contemptible and worthless, things wherewith He proveth the hearts of the doubtful? [415]

Ye are even as the bird which soareth, with the full force of its mighty wings and with complete and joyous confidence, through the immensity of the heavens, until, impelled to satisfy its hunger, it turneth longingly to the water and clay of the earth below it, and, having been entrapped in the mesh of its desire, findeth itself impotent to resume its flight to the realms whence it came. Powerless to shake off the burden weighing on its sullied wings, that bird, hitherto an inmate of the heavens, is now forced to seek a dwelling-place upon the dust. Wherefore, O My servants, defile not your wings with the clay of waywardness and vain desires, and suffer them not to be stained with the dust of envy and hate, that ye may not be hindered from soaring in the heavens of My divine knowledge. [416]

Say: Rejoice not in the things ye possess; tonight they are yours, tomorrow others will possess them. Thus warneth you He Who is the All-Knowing, the All-Informed. Say: Can ye claim that what ye own is lasting or secure? Nay! By Myself, the All-Merciful, ye cannot, if ye be of them who judge fairly. The days of your life flee away as a breath of wind, and all your pomp and glory shall be folded up as were the pomp and glory of those gone before you. Reflect, O people! What hath become of your bygone days, your lost centuries? Happy the days that have been consecrated to the remembrance of God, and blessed the hours which have been spent in praise of Him Who is the All-Wise. By My life! Neither the pomp of the mighty, nor the wealth of the rich, nor even the ascendancy of the ungodly will endure. All will perish, at a word from Him. He, verily, is the All-Powerful, the All-Compelling, the Almighty. What advantage is there in the earthly things which men possess? That which shall profit them, they have utterly neglected. Erelong, they will awake from their slumber, and find themselves unable to obtain that which hath escaped them in the days of their Lord, the Almighty, the All-Praised. Did they but know it, they would renounce their all, that their names may be mentioned before His throne. They, verily, are accounted among the dead.[417]

O MAN OF TWO VISIONS! Close one eye and open the other. Close one to the world and all that is therein, and open the other to the hallowed beauty of the Beloved.[418]

O FRIENDS! Abandon not the everlasting beauty for a beauty that must die, and set not your affections on this mortal world of dust.[419]

O SON OF DUST! Blind thine eyes, that thou mayest behold My beauty; stop thine ears, that thou mayest hearken unto the sweet melody of My voice; empty thyself of all learning, that thou mayest partake of My knowledge; and sanctify thyself from riches, that thou mayest obtain a lasting share from the ocean of My eternal wealth. Blind thine eyes, that is, to all save My beauty; stop thine ears to all save My word; empty thyself of all learning save the knowledge of Me; that with a clear vision, a pure heart and an attentive ear thou mayest enter the court of My holiness.[420]

O SON OF DUST! All that is in heaven and earth I have ordained for thee, except the human heart, which I have made the habitation of My beauty and glory; yet thou didst give My home and dwelling to another than Me; and whenever the manifestation of My holiness sought His own abode, a stranger found He there, and, homeless, hastened unto the sanctuary of the Beloved. Notwithstanding I have concealed thy secret and desired not thy shame.[421]

O MY FRIEND! Thou art the daystar of the heavens of My holiness, let not the defilement of the world eclipse thy splendor. Rend asunder the veil of heedlessness, that from behind the clouds thou mayest emerge resplendent and array all things with the apparel of life.[422]

Night hath succeeded day, and day hath succeeded night, and the hours and moments of your lives have come and gone, and yet none of you hath, for one instant, consented to detach himself from that which perisheth. Bestir yourselves, that the brief moments that are still yours may not be dissipated and lost. Even as the swiftness of lightning your days shall pass, and your bodies shall be laid to rest beneath a canopy of dust. What can ye then achieve? How can ye atone for your past failure? [423]

The days of your life are far spent, O people, and your end is fast approaching. Put away, therefore, the things ye have devised and to which ye cleave, and take firm hold on the precepts of God, that haply ye may attain that which He hath purposed for you, and be of them that pursue a right course. Delight not yourselves in the things of the world and its vain ornaments, neither set your hopes on them. Let your reliance be on the remembrance of God, the Most Exalted, the Most Great. He will, erelong, bring to naught all the things ye possess. Let Him be your fear, and forget not His covenant with you, and be not of them that are shut out as by a veil from Him.[424]

Know ye that by "the world" is meant your unawareness of Him Who is your Maker, and your absorption in aught else but Him. The "life to come," on the other hand, signifieth the things that give you a safe approach to God, the All-Glorious, the Incomparable. Whatsoever deterreth you, in this Day, from loving God is nothing but the world. Flee it, that ye may be numbered with the blest. Should a man wish to adorn himself with the ornaments of the earth, to wear its apparels, or partake of the benefits it can bestow, no harm can befall him, if he alloweth nothing whatever to intervene between him and God, for God hath ordained every good thing, whether created in the heavens or in the earth, for such of His servants as truly believe in Him. Eat ye, O people, of the good things which God hath allowed you, and deprive not yourselves from His wondrous bounties. Render thanks and praise unto Him, and be of them that are truly thankful.[425]

Thine eye is My trust, suffer not the dust of vain desires to becloud its luster. Thine ear is a sign of My bounty, let not the tumult of unseemly motives turn it away from My Word that encompasseth all creation. Thine heart is My treasury, allow not the treacherous hand of self to rob thee of the pearls which I have treasured therein. Thine hand is a symbol of My loving-kindness, hinder it not from holding fast unto My guarded and hidden Tablets....[426]

O servants! The springs of divine bestowal are streaming forth. Quaff ye therefrom, that by the aid of the incomparable Friend ye may be sanctified from this darksome world of dust and enter His abode. Renounce the world and direct your steps toward the city of the Beloved.[427]

Life of the Spirit

Wert thou to attain to but a dewdrop of the crystal waters of divine knowledge, thou wouldst readily realize that true life is not the life of the flesh but the life of the spirit. For the life of the flesh is common to both men and animals, whereas the life of the spirit is possessed only by the pure in heart who have quaffed from the ocean of faith and partaken of the fruit of certitude. This life knoweth no death, and this existence is crowned by immortality. Even as it hath been said: "He who is a true believer liveth both in this world and in the world to come."[428]

O My friend, listen with heart and soul to the songs of the spirit, and treasure them as thine own eyes. For the heavenly wisdoms, like the clouds of spring, will not rain down on the earth of men's hearts forever; and though the grace of the All-Bounteous One is never stilled and never ceasing, yet to each time and era a portion is allotted and a bounty set apart, this in a given measure. "And no one thing is there, but with Us are its storehouses; and We send it not down but in settled measure."[429] The cloud of the Loved One's mercy raineth only on the garden of the spirit, and bestoweth this bounty only in the season of spring. The other seasons have no share in this greatest grace, and barren lands no portion of this favor.

O Brother! Not every sea hath pearls; not every branch will flower, nor will the nightingale sing thereon. Then, ere the nightingale of the mystic paradise repair to the garden of God, and the rays of the heavenly morning return to the Sun of Truth—make thou an effort, that haply in this dustheap of the mortal world thou mayest catch a fragrance from the everlasting garden, and live forever in the shadow of the peoples of this city. And when thou hast attained this highest station and come to this mightiest plane, then shalt thou gaze on the Beloved, and forget all else.[430]

From the sweet-scented streams of Thine eternity give me to drink, O my God, and of the fruits of the tree of Thy being enable me to taste, O my Hope! From the crystal springs of Thy love suffer me to quaff, O my Glory, and beneath the shadow of Thine everlasting providence let me abide, O my Light! Within the meadows of Thy nearness, before Thy presence, make me able to roam, O my Beloved, and at the right hand of the throne of Thy mercy, seat me, O my Desire! From the fragrant breezes of Thy joy let a breath pass over me, O my Goal, and into the heights of the paradise of Thy reality let me gain admission, O my Adored One! To the melodies of the dove of Thy oneness suffer me to hearken, O Resplendent One, and through the spirit of Thy power and Thy might quicken me, O my Provider! In the spirit of Thy love keep me steadfast, O my Succorer, and in the path of Thy good-pleasure set firm my steps, O my Maker! Within the garden of Thine immortality, before Thy countenance, let me abide for ever, O Thou Who art merciful unto me, and upon the seat of Thy glory stablish me, O Thou Who art my Possessor! To the heaven of Thy loving-kindness lift me up, O my Quickener, and unto the Day-Star of Thy guidance lead me, O Thou my Attractor! Before the revelations of Thine invisible spirit summon me to be present, O Thou Who art my Origin and my Highest Wish, and unto the essence of the fragrance of Thy beauty, which Thou wilt manifest, cause me to return, O Thou Who art my God!

Potent art Thou to do what pleaseth Thee. Thou art, verily, the Most Exalted, the All-Glorious, the All-Highest.[431]

True Seeker

The true seeker hunteth naught but the object of his quest, and the lover hath no desire save union with his beloved. Nor shall the seeker reach his goal unless he sacrifice all things. That is, whatever he hath seen, and heard, and understood, all must he set at naught, that he may enter the realm of the spirit, which is the City of God. Labor is needed, if we are to seek Him; ardor is needed, if we are to drink of the honey of reunion with Him; and if we taste of this cup, we shall cast away the world.

On this journey the traveler abideth in every land and dwelleth in every region. In every face, he seeketh the beauty of the Friend; in every country he looketh for the Beloved. He joineth every company, and seeketh fellowship with every soul, that haply in some mind he may uncover the secret of the Friend, or in some face he may behold the beauty of the Loved One.[432]

...O my brother, when a true seeker determineth to take the step of search in the path leading to the knowledge of the Ancient of Days, he must, before all else, cleanse and purify his heart, which is the seat of the revelation of the inner mysteries of God, from the obscuring dust of all acquired knowledge, and the allusions of the embodiments of satanic fancy. He must purge his breast, which is the sanctuary of the abiding love of the Beloved, of every defilement, and sanctify his soul from all that pertaineth to water and clay, from all shadowy and ephemeral attachments. He must so cleanse his heart that no remnant of either love or hate may linger therein, lest that love blindly incline him to error, or that hate repel him away from the truth. Even as thou dost witness in this day how most of the people, because of such love and hate, are bereft of the immortal Face, have strayed far from the Embodiments of the divine mysteries, and, shepherdless, are roaming through the wilderness of oblivion and error. That seeker must at all times put his trust in God, must renounce the peoples of the earth, detach himself from the world of dust, and cleave unto Him Who is the

Lord of Lords. He must never seek to exalt himself above any one, must wash away from the tablet of his heart every trace of pride and vainglory, must cling unto patience and resignation, observe silence, and refrain from idle talk. For the tongue is a smouldering fire, and excess of speech a deadly poison. Material fire consumeth the body, whereas the fire of the tongue devoureth both heart and soul. The force of the former lasteth but for a time, whilst the effects of the latter endure a century.

That seeker should also regard backbiting as grievous error, and keep himself aloof from its dominion, inasmuch as backbiting quencheth the light of the heart, and extinguisheth the life of the soul. He should be content with little, and be freed from all inordinate desire. He should treasure the companionship of those that have renounced the world, and regard avoidance of boastful and worldly people a precious benefit. At the dawn of every day he should commune with God, and with all his soul persevere in the quest of his Beloved. He should consume every wayward thought with the flame of His loving mention, and, with the swiftness of lightning, pass by all else save Him. He should succour the dispossessed, and never withhold his favour from the destitute. He should show kindness to animals, how much more unto his fellow-man, to him who is endowed with the power of utterance. He should not hesitate to offer up his life for his Beloved, nor allow the censure of the people to turn him away from the Truth. He should not wish for others that which he doth not wish for himself, nor promise that which he doth not fulfil. With all his heart should the seeker avoid fellowship with evil doers, and pray for the remission of their sins. He should forgive the sinful, and never despise his low estate, for none knoweth what his own end shall be. How often hath a sinner, at the hour of death, attained to the essence of faith, and, quaffing the immortal draught, hath taken his flight unto the celestial Concourse. And how often hath a devout believer, at the hour of his soul's ascension, been so changed as to fall into the nethermost fire. Our purpose in revealing these convincing and weighty utterances is to impress upon the seeker that he should regard all else beside God as transient, and count all things save Him, Who is the Object of all adoration, as utter nothingness.

These are among the attributes of the exalted, and constitute the hall-mark of the spiritually-minded. They have already been mentioned in connection with the requirements of the wayfarers that tread the Path of Positive Knowledge. When the detached wayfarer and sincere seeker hath fulfilled these essential conditions, then and only then can he be called a true seeker. Whensoever he hath fulfilled the conditions implied in the verse: "Whoso maketh efforts for Us,"[433] he shall enjoy the blessing conferred by the words: "In Our ways shall We assuredly guide him."[434] [435]

O friend! We came upon a pure soil and sowed therein the seeds of true understanding. Let it now be seen what the rays of the sun will do—whether they will cause these seeds to wither or to grow. Say: Through the ascendancy of God, the All-Knowing, the Incomparable, the Luminary of divine understanding hath, in this day, risen from behind the veil of the spirit, and the birds of every meadow are intoxicated with the wine of knowledge and exhilarated with the remembrance of the Friend. Well is it with them that discover and hasten unto Him.[436]

Surrender to Will of God

O <u>Sh</u>ay<u>kh</u>, O thou who hast surrendered thy will to God! By self-surrender and perpetual union with God is meant that men should merge their will wholly in the Will of God, and regard their desires as utter nothingness beside His Purpose. Whatsoever the Creator commandeth His creatures to observe, the same must they diligently, and with the utmost joy and eagerness, arise and fulfil. They should in no wise allow their fancy to obscure their judgment, neither should they regard their own imaginings as the voice of the Eternal. In the Prayer of Fasting We have revealed: "Should Thy Will decree that out of Thy mouth these words proceed and be addressed unto them, 'Observe, for My Beauty's sake, the fast, O people, and set no limit to its duration,' I swear by the majesty of Thy glory, that every one of them will faithfully observe it, will abstain from whatsoever will violate Thy law, and will continue to do so until they yield up their souls unto Thee." In this consisteth the complete surrender of one's will to the Will of God. Meditate on this, that thou mayest drink in the waters of everlasting life which flow through the words of the Lord of all mankind, and mayest testify that the one true God hath ever been immeasurably exalted above His creatures. He, verily, is the Incomparable, the Ever-Abiding, the Omniscient, the All-Wise. The station of absolute self-surrender transcendeth, and will ever remain exalted above, every other station.

It behoveth thee to consecrate thyself to the Will of God. Whatsoever hath been revealed in His Tablets is but a reflection of His Will. So complete must be thy consecration, that every trace of worldly desire will be washed from thine heart. This is the meaning of true unity.[437]

Blessed is the man that hath acknowledged his belief in God and in His signs, and recognized that "He shall not be asked of His doings". Such a recognition hath been made by God the ornament of every belief and its very foundation. Upon it must depend the acceptance of every goodly deed. Fasten your eyes upon it, that haply the whisperings of the rebellious may not cause you to slip.

Were He to decree as lawful the thing which from time immemorial had been forbidden, and forbid that which had, at all times, been regarded as lawful, to none is given the right to question His authority. Whoso will hesitate, though it be for less than a moment, should be regarded as a transgressor.[438]

O thou who hast fixed thy gaze upon the Dawning-Place of the Cause of God! Know thou for a certainty that the Will of God is not limited by the standards of the people, and God doth not tread in their ways. Rather is it incumbent upon everyone to firmly adhere to God's straight Path. Were He to pronounce the right to be the left or the south to be the north, He speaketh the truth and there is no doubt of it. Verily He is to be praised in His acts and to be obeyed in His behests. He hath no associate in His judgement nor any helper in His sovereignty. He doeth whatsoever He willeth and ordaineth whatsoever He pleaseth. Know thou moreover that all else besides Him have been created through the potency of a word from His presence, while of themselves they have no motion nor stillness, except at His bidding and by His leave.[439]

O My servants! Be as resigned and submissive as the earth, that from the soil of your being there may blossom the fragrant, the holy and multicolored hyacinths of My knowledge. Be ablaze as the fire, that ye may burn away the veils of heedlessness and set aglow, through the quickening energies of the love of God, the chilled and wayward heart. Be light and untrammeled as the breeze, that ye may obtain admittance into the precincts of My court, My inviolable Sanctuary.[440]

Know thou, O fruit of My Tree, that the decrees of the Sovereign Ordainer, as related to fate and predestination, are of two kinds. Both are to be obeyed and accepted. The one is irrevocable, the other is, as termed by men, impending. To the former all must unreservedly submit, inasmuch as it is fixed and settled. God, however, is able to alter or repeal it. As the harm that must result from such a change will be greater than if the decree had remained unaltered, all, therefore, should willingly acquiesce in what God hath willed and confidently abide by the same.

The decree that is impending, however, is such that prayer and entreaty can succeed in averting it.[441]

O SON OF SPIRIT! Ask not of Me that which We desire not for thee, then be content with what We have ordained for thy sake, for this is that which profiteth thee, if therewith thou dost content thyself.[442]

O SON OF MAN! Wert thou to speed through the immensity of space and traverse the expanse of heaven, yet thou wouldst find no rest save in submission to Our command and humbleness before Our Face.[443]

O MY FRIENDS! Have ye forgotten that true and radiant morn, when in those hallowed and blessed surroundings ye were all gathered in My presence beneath the shade of the tree of life, which is planted in the all-glorious paradise? Awe-struck ye listened as I gave utterance to these three most holy words: O friends! Prefer not your will to Mine, never desire that which I have not desired for you, and approach Me not with lifeless hearts, defiled with worldly desires and cravings. Would ye but sanctify your souls, ye would at this present hour recall that place and those surroundings, and the truth of My utterance should be made evident unto all of you.[444]

I beg of Thee by the Most Great Infallibility which Thou hast chosen to be the dayspring of Thy Revelation, and by Thy most sublime Word through whose potency Thou didst call the creation into being and didst reveal Thy Cause, and by this Name which hath caused all other names to groan aloud and the limbs of the sages to quake, I beg of Thee to make me detached from all else save Thee, in such wise that I may move not but in conformity with the good-pleasure of Thy Will, and speak not except at the bidding of Thy Purpose, and hear naught save the words of Thy praise and Thy glorification.[445]

I have no will but Thy will, O my Lord, and cherish no desire except Thy desire. From my pen floweth only the summons which Thine own exalted pen hath voiced, and my tongue uttereth naught save what the Most Great Spirit hath itself proclaimed in the kingdom of Thine eternity. I am stirred by nothing else except the winds of Thy will, and breathe no word except the words which, by Thy leave and Thine inspiration, I am led to pronounce.[446]

I implore Thee, O my Lord, by Thy name the splendors of which have encompassed the earth and the heavens, to enable me so to surrender my will to what Thou hast decreed in Thy Tablets, that I may cease to discover within me any desire except what Thou didst desire through the power of Thy sovereignty, and any will save what Thou didst destine for me by Thy will.[447]

Certitude

This is the Day wherein the divine Lote-Tree calleth aloud, saying: O people! Behold ye My fruits and My leaves, incline then your ears unto My rustling. Beware lest the doubts of men debar you from the light of certitude.[448]

Only when the lamp of search, of earnest striving, of longing desire, of passionate devotion, of fervid love, of rapture, and ecstasy, is kindled within the seeker's heart, and the breeze of His loving-kindness is wafted upon his soul, will the darkness of error be dispelled, the mists of doubts and misgivings be dissipated, and the lights of knowledge and certitude envelop his being. At that hour will the mystic Herald, bearing the joyful tidings of the Spirit, shine forth from the City of God resplendent as the morn, and, through the trumpet-blast of knowledge, will awaken the heart, the soul, and the spirit from the slumber of negligence. Then will the manifold favours and outpouring grace of the holy and everlasting Spirit confer such new life upon the seeker that he will find himself endowed with a new eye, a new ear, a new heart, and a new mind. He will contemplate the manifest signs of the universe, and will penetrate the hidden mysteries of the soul. Gazing with the eye of God, he will perceive within every atom a door that leadeth him to the stations of absolute certitude. He will discover in all things the mysteries of divine Revelation and the evidences of an everlasting manifestation.

I swear by God! Were he that treadeth the path of guidance and seeketh to scale the heights of righteousness to attain unto this glorious and supreme station, he would inhale at a distance of a thousand leagues the fragrance of God, and would perceive the resplendent morn of a divine Guidance rising above the dayspring of all things. Each and every thing, however small, would be to him a revelation, leading him to his Beloved, the Object of his quest. So great shall be the discernment of this seeker that he will discriminate between truth and falsehood even as he doth distinguish the sun from shadow. If in the uttermost corners of the East the sweet savours of God be wafted, he will assuredly recognize and inhale their fragrance, even though he be dwelling in the uttermost ends of the West. He will likewise clearly distinguish all the signs of God—His wondrous utterances, His great works, and mighty deeds—from the doings, words and ways of men, even as the jeweller who knoweth the gem from the stone, or the man who distinguisheth the spring from autumn and heat from cold. When the channel of the human soul is cleansed of all worldly and impeding attachments, it will unfailingly perceive the breath of the Beloved across immeasurable distances, and will, led by its perfume, attain and enter the City of Certitude. Therein he will discern the wonders of His ancient wisdom, and will perceive all the hidden teachings from the rustling leaves of the Tree—which flourisheth in that City. With both his inner and his outer ear he will hear from its dust the hymns of glory and praise ascending unto the Lord of Lords, and with his inner eye will he discover the mysteries of "return" and "revival." How unspeakably glorious are the signs, the tokens, the revelations, and splendours which He Who is the King of names and attributes hath destined for that City! The attainment of this City quencheth thirst without water, and kindleth the love of God without fire. Within every blade of grass are enshrined the mysteries of an inscrutable wisdom, and upon every rose-bush a myriad nightingales pour out, in blissful rapture, their melody. Its wondrous tulips unfold the mystery of the undying Fire in the Burning Bush, and its sweet savours of holiness breathe the perfume of the Messianic Spirit. It bestoweth wealth without gold, and conferreth immortality without death. In every leaf ineffable delights are treasured, and within every chamber unnumbered mysteries lie hidden.

They that valiantly labour in quest of God's will, when once they have renounced all else but Him, will be so attached and wedded to that City that a moment's separation from it would to them be unthinkable. They will hearken unto infallible proofs from the

Hyacinth of that assembly, and receive the surest testimonies from the beauty of its Rose and the melody of its Nightingale. Once in about a thousand years shall this City be renewed and re-adorned.[449]

Prayer and Meditation

O SON OF LIGHT! Forget all save Me and commune with My spirit. This is of the essence of My command, therefore turn unto it. [450]

...in every Dispensation the law concerning prayer hath been emphasized and universally enforced.[451]

Intone, O My servant, the verses of God that have been received by thee, as intoned by them who have drawn nigh unto Him, that the sweetness of thy melody may kindle thine own soul, and attract the hearts of all men. Whoso reciteth, in the privacy of his chamber, the verses revealed by God, the scattering angels of the Almighty shall scatter abroad the fragrance of the words uttered by his mouth, and shall cause the heart of every righteous man to throb. Though he may, at first, remain unaware of its effect, yet the virtue of the grace vouchsafed unto him must needs sooner or later exercise its influence upon his soul. Thus have the mysteries of the Revelation of God been decreed by virtue of the Will of Him Who is the Source of power and wisdom.[452]

Blessed is the spot, and the house, and the place, and the city, and the heart, and the mountain, and the refuge, and the cave, and the valley, and the land, and the sea, and the island, and the meadow where mention of God hath been made, and His praise glorified.[453]

He is the prayer-hearing, prayer-answering God!

By Thy glory, O Beloved One, Thou giver of light to the world! The flames of separation have consumed me, and my waywardness hath melted my heart within me. I ask of Thee, by Thy Most Great Name, O Thou the Desire of the world and the Well-Beloved of mankind, to grant that the breeze of Thine inspiration may sustain my soul, that Thy wondrous voice may reach my ear, that my eyes may behold Thy signs and Thy light as revealed in the manifestations of Thy names and Thine attributes, O Thou within Whose grasp are all things! [454]

Meditate upon that which hath streamed forth from the heaven of the Will of thy Lord, He Who is the Source of all grace, that thou mayest grasp the intended meaning which is enshrined in the sacred depths of the Holy Writings.[455]

...thou too shouldst, likewise, for the sake of God, meditate upon those things that have been sent down and manifested, that haply thou mayest, on this blessed Day, take thy portion of the liberal effusions of Him Who is truly the All-Bountiful, and mayest not remain deprived thereof.[456]

...One hour's reflection is preferable to seventy years of pious worship....[457]

Blessed is he that hath set himself towards Thee, and hasted to attain the Day-Spring of the lights of Thy face. Blessed is he who with all his affections hath turned to the Dawning-Place of Thy Revelation and the Fountain-Head of Thine inspiration. Blessed is he that hath expended in Thy path what Thou didst bestow upon him through Thy bounty and favor. Blessed is he who, in his sore longing after Thee, hath cast away all else except Thyself. Blessed is he who hath enjoyed intimate communion with Thee, and rid himself of all attachment to any one save Thee.[458]

Fasting

We have commanded you to pray and fast from the beginning of maturity; this is ordained by God, your Lord and the Lord of your forefathers. He hath exempted from this those who are weak from illness or age, as a bounty from His Presence, and He is the Forgiving, the Generous.

O Pen of the Most High! Say: O people of the world! We have enjoined upon you fasting during a brief period, and at its close have designated for you Naw-Rúz as a feast...The traveller, the ailing, those who are with child or giving suck, are not bound by the Fast; they have been exempted by God as a token of His grace. He, verily, is the Almighty, the Most Generous.

Abstain from food and drink from sunrise to sundown, and beware lest desire deprive you of this grace that is appointed in the Book.[459]

Thou seest, O God of Mercy, Thou Whose power pervadeth all created things, these servants of Thine, Thy thralls, who, according to the good-pleasure of Thy Will, observe in the daytime the fast prescribed by Thee, who arise, at the earliest dawn of day, to make mention of Thy Name, and to celebrate Thy praise, in the hope of obtaining their share of the goodly things that are treasured up within the treasuries of Thy grace and bounty. I beseech Thee, O Thou that holdest in Thine hands the reins of the entire creation, in Whose grasp is the whole kingdom of Thy names and of Thine attributes, not to deprive, in Thy Day, Thy servants from the showers pouring from the clouds of Thy mercy, nor to hinder them from taking their portion of the ocean of Thy good-pleasure.[460]

Ḥuqúqu'lláh

Should anyone acquire one hundred mi<u>th</u>qáls of gold, nineteen mi<u>th</u>qáls thereof are God's and to be rendered unto Him, the Fashioner of earth and heaven. Take heed, O people, lest ye deprive yourselves of so great a bounty. This We have commanded you, though We are well able to dispense with you and with all who are in the heavens and on earth; in it there are benefits and wisdoms beyond the ken of anyone but God, the Omniscient, the All-Informed. Say: By this means He hath desired to purify what ye possess and to enable you to draw nigh unto such stations as none can comprehend save those whom God hath willed. He, in truth, is the Beneficent, the Gracious, the Bountiful. O people! Deal not faithlessly with the Right of God, nor, without His leave, make free with its disposal. Thus hath His commandment been established in the holy Tablets, and in this exalted Book. He who dealeth faithlessly with God shall in justice meet with faithlessness himself; he, however, who acteth in accordance with God's bidding shall receive a blessing from the heaven of the bounty of his Lord, the Gracious, the Bestower, the Generous, the Ancient of Days. He, verily, hath willed for you that which is yet beyond your knowledge, but which shall be known to you when, after this fleeting life, your souls soar heavenwards and the trappings of your earthly joys are folded up. Thus admonisheth you He in Whose possession is the Guarded Tablet.[461]

Nothing that existeth in the world of being hath ever been or will ever be worthy of mention. However, if a person be graciously favoured to offer a pennyworth—nay, even less—in the path of God, this would in His sight be preferable and superior to all the treasures of the earth. It is for this reason that the one true God—exalted be His glory—hath in all His heavenly Scriptures praised those who observe His precepts and bestow their wealth for His sake. Beseech ye God that He may enable everyone to discharge the obligation of Ḥuqúq, inasmuch as the progress and promotion of the Cause of God depend on material means. If His faithful servants could realize how meritorious are benevolent deeds in these days, they would all arise to do that which is meet and seemly. In His hand is the source of authority and He ordaineth as He willeth. He is the Supreme Ruler, the Bountiful, the Equitable, the Revealer, the All-Wise. [462]

It is clear and evident that the payment of the Right of God is conducive to prosperity, to blessing, and to honour and divine protection. Well is it with them that comprehend and recognize this truth and woe betide them that believe not. And this is on condition that the individual should observe the injunctions prescribed in the Book with the utmost radiance, gladness and willing acquiescence. It behoveth you to counsel the friends to do that which is right and praiseworthy. Whoso hearkeneth to this call, it is to his own behoof, and whoso faileth bringeth loss upon himself. Verily our Lord of Mercy is the All-Sufficing, the All-Praised. [463]

Ḥuqúqu'lláh is indeed a great law. It is incumbent upon all to make this offering, because it is the source of grace, abundance, and of all good. It is a bounty which shall remain with every soul in every world of the worlds of God, the All-Possessing, the All-Bountiful. [464]

Recite the Verses of God

Recite ye the verses of God every morn and eventide. Whoso faileth to recite them hath not been faithful to the Covenant of God and His Testament, and whoso turneth away from these holy verses in this Day is of those who throughout eternity have turned away from God. Fear ye God, O My servants, one and all. Pride not yourselves on much reading of the verses or on a multitude of pious acts by night and day; for were a man to read a single verse with joy and radiance it would be better for him than to read with lassitude all the Holy Books of God, the Help in Peril, the Self-Subsisting. Read ye the sacred verses in such measure that ye be not overcome by languor and despondency. Lay not upon your souls that which will weary them and weigh them down, but rather what will lighten and uplift them, so that they may soar on the wings of the Divine verses towards the Dawning-place of His manifest signs; this will draw you nearer to God, did ye but comprehend.[465]

They who recite the verses of the All-Merciful in the most melodious of tones will perceive in them that with which the sovereignty of earth and heaven can never be compared. From them they will inhale the divine fragrance of My worlds—worlds which today none can discern save those who have been endowed with vision through this sublime, this beauteous Revelation. Say: These verses draw hearts that are pure unto those spiritual worlds that can neither be expressed in words nor intimated by allusion. Blessed be those who hearken.[466]

Teach your children the verses revealed from the heaven of majesty and power, so that, in most melodious tones, they may recite the Tablets of the All-Merciful in the alcoves within the Mashriqu'l-Adhkárs. Whoever hath been transported by the rapture born of adoration for My Name, the Most Compassionate, will recite the verses of God in such wise as to captivate the hearts of those yet wrapped in slumber. Well is it with him who hath quaffed the Mystic Wine of everlasting life from the utterance of his merciful Lord in My Name—a Name through which every lofty and majestic mountain hath been reduced to dust.[467]

Deepen in the Cause of God

Immerse yourselves in the ocean of My words, that ye may unravel its secrets, and discover all the pearls of wisdom that lie hid in its depths. Take heed that ye do not vacillate in your determination to embrace the truth of this Cause—a Cause through which the potentialities of the might of God have been revealed, and His sovereignty established. With faces beaming with joy, hasten ye unto Him. This is the changeless Faith of God, eternal in the past, eternal in the future. Let him that seeketh, attain it; and as to him that hath refused to seek it—verily, God is Self-Sufficient, above any need of His creatures.[468]

O wayfarer in the path of God! Take thou thy portion of the ocean of His grace, and deprive not thyself of the things that lie hidden in its depths. Be thou of them that have partaken of its treasures. A dewdrop out of this ocean would, if shed upon all that are in the heavens and on the earth, suffice to enrich them with the bounty of God, the Almighty, the All-Knowing, the All-Wise. With the hands of renunciation draw forth from its life-giving waters, and sprinkle therewith all created things, that they may be cleansed from all man-made limitations and may approach the mighty seat of God, this hallowed and resplendent Spot.[469]

May the brightness of His glory shining above the horizon of bounty rest upon you, O people of Bahá, upon every one who standeth firm and steadfast and upon those that are well grounded in the Faith and are endued with true understanding.[470]

Teach the Cause of God

Say: Teach ye the Cause of God, O people of Bahá, for God hath prescribed unto every one the duty of proclaiming His Message, and regardeth it as the most meritorious of all deeds. Such a deed is acceptable only when he that teacheth the Cause is already a firm believer in God, the Supreme Protector, the Gracious, the Almighty. He hath, moreover, ordained that His Cause be taught through the power of men☐s utterance, and not through resort to violence. Thus hath His ordinance been sent down from the Kingdom of Him Who is the Most Exalted, the All-Wise. Beware lest ye contend with any one, nay, strive to make him aware of the truth with kindly manner and most convincing exhortation. If your hearer respond, he will have responded to his own behoof, and if not, turn ye away from him, and set your faces towards God's sacred Court, the seat of resplendent holiness.[471]

O ye beloved of God! Repose not yourselves on your couches, nay bestir yourselves as soon as ye recognize your Lord, the Creator, and hear of the things which have befallen Him, and hasten to His assistance. Unloose your tongues, and proclaim unceasingly His Cause. This shall be better for you than all the treasures of the past and of the future, if ye be of them that comprehend this truth.[472]

Center your energies in the propagation of the Faith of God. Whoso is worthy of so high a calling, let him arise and promote it. Whoso is unable, it is his duty to appoint him who will, in his stead, proclaim this Revelation, whose power hath caused the foundations of the mightiest structures to quake, every mountain to be crushed into dust, and every soul to be dumbfounded. Let your principal concern be to rescue the fallen from the slough of impending extinction, and to help him embrace the ancient Faith of God. Your behavior towards your neighbor should be such as to manifest clearly the signs of the one true God, for ye are the first among men to be re-created by His Spirit, the first to adore and bow the knee before Him, the first to circle round His throne of glory.[473]

God hath prescribed unto every one the duty of teaching His Cause. Whoever ariseth to discharge this duty, must needs, ere he proclaimeth His Message, adorn himself with the ornament of an upright and praiseworthy character, so that his words may attract the hearts of such as are receptive to his call. Without it, he can never hope to influence his hearers.[474]

Whoso ariseth among you to teach the Cause of his Lord, let him, before all else, teach his own self, that his speech may attract the hearts of them that hear him. Unless he teacheth his own self, the words of his mouth will not influence the heart of the seeker. Take heed, O people, lest ye be of them that give good counsel to others but forget to follow it themselves....

Should such a man ever succeed in influencing any one, this success should be attributed not to him, but rather to the influence of the words of God, as decreed by Him Who is the Almighty, the All-Wise. In the sight of God he is regarded as a lamp that imparteth its light, and yet is all the while being consumed within itself.[475]

They that have forsaken their country for the purpose of teaching Our Cause—these shall the Faithful Spirit strengthen through its power. A company of Our chosen angels shall go forth with them, as bidden by Him Who is the Almighty, the All-Wise. How great the blessedness that awaiteth him that hath attained the honor of serving the Almighty! By My life! No act, however great, can compare with it, except such deeds as have been ordained by God, the All-Powerful, the Most Mighty. Such a service is, indeed, the prince of all goodly deeds, and the ornament of every goodly act. Thus hath it been ordained by Him Who is the Sovereign Revealer, the Ancient of Days.

Whoso ariseth to teach Our Cause must needs detach himself from all earthly things, and regard, at all times, the triumph of Our Faith as his supreme objective. This hath, verily, been decreed in the Guarded Tablet. And when he determineth to leave his home, for the sake of the Cause of his Lord, let him put his whole trust in God, as the best provision for his journey, and array himself with the robe of virtue. Thus hath it been decreed by God, the Almighty, the All-Praised.

If he be kindled with the fire of His love, if he forgoeth all created things, the words he uttereth shall set on fire them that hear him. Verily, thy Lord is the Omniscient, the All-Informed....[476]

The sanctified souls should ponder and meditate in their hearts regarding the methods of teaching. From the texts of the wondrous, heavenly Scriptures they should memorize phrases and passages bearing on various instances, so that in the course of their speech they may recite divine verses whenever the occasion demandeth it, inasmuch as these holy verses are the most potent elixir, the greatest and mightiest talisman. So potent is their influence that the hearer will have no cause for vacillation. I swear by My life! This Revelation is endowed with such a power that it will act as the lodestone for all nations and kindreds of the earth....[477]

O My Name! Utterance must needs possess penetrating power. For if bereft of this quality it would fail to exert influence. And this penetrating influence dependeth on the spirit being pure and the heart stainless. Likewise it needeth moderation, without which the hearer would be unable to bear it, rather he would manifest opposition from the very outset. And moderation will be obtained by blending utterance with the tokens of divine wisdom which are recorded in the sacred Books and Tablets. Thus when the essence of one's utterance is endowed with these two requisites it will prove highly effective and will be the prime factor in transforming the souls of men. This is the station of supreme victory and celestial dominion. Whoso attaineth thereto is invested with the power to teach the Cause of God and to prevail over the hearts and minds of men.[478]

By the righteousness of God! Whoso openeth his lips in this Day and maketh mention of the name of his Lord, the hosts of

Divine inspiration shall descend upon him from the heaven of My name, the All-Knowing, the All-Wise. On him shall also descend the Concourse on high, each bearing aloft a chalice of pure light. Thus hath it been foreordained in the realm of God's Revelation, by the behest of Him Who is the All-Glorious, the Most Powerful.[479]

By the righteousness of God...should a man, all alone, arise in the name of Bahá and put on the armor of His love, him will the Almighty cause to be victorious, though the forces of earth and heaven be arrayed against him. By God besides Whom is none other God! Should any one arise for the triumph of our Cause, him will God render victorious though tens of thousands of enemies be leagued against him. And if his love for Me wax stronger, God will establish his ascendancy over all the powers of earth and heaven. Thus have We breathed the spirit of power into all regions.[480]

Purge thou thy heart that We may cause fountains of wisdom and utterance to gush out therefrom, thus enabling thee to raise thy voice among all mankind. Unloose thy tongue and proclaim the truth for the sake of the remembrance of thy merciful Lord. Be not afraid of anyone, place thy whole trust in God, the Almighty, the All-Knowing.[481]

Steadfastness in the Cause of God

The second Tajallí

is to remain steadfast in the Cause of God—exalted be His glory—and to be unswerving in His love. And this can in no wise be attained except through full recognition of Him; and full recognition cannot be obtained save by faith in the blessed words: 'He doeth whatsoever He willeth.' Whoso tenaciously cleaveth unto this sublime word and drinketh deep from the living waters of utterance which are inherent therein, will be imbued with such a constancy that all the books of the world will be powerless to deter him from the Mother Book. O how glorious is this sublime station, this exalted rank, this ultimate purpose! [482]

The supreme cause for creating the world and all that is therein is for man to know God. In this Day whosoever is guided by the fragrance of the raiment of His mercy to gain admittance into the pristine Abode, which is the station of recognizing the Source of divine commandments and the Dayspring of His Revelation, hath everlastingly attained unto all good. Having reached this lofty station a twofold obligation resteth upon every soul. One is to be steadfast in the Cause with such steadfastness that were all the peoples of the world to attempt to prevent him from turning to the Source of Revelation, they would be powerless to do so. The other is observance of the divine ordinances which have streamed forth from the wellspring of His heavenly-propelled Pen. For man's knowledge of God cannot develop fully and adequately save by observing whatsoever hath been ordained by Him and is set forth in His heavenly Book. [483]

A twofold obligation resteth upon him who hath recognized the Day Spring of the Unity of God, and acknowledged the truth of Him Who is the Manifestation of His oneness. The first is steadfastness in His love, such steadfastness that neither the clamor of the enemy nor the claims of the idle pretender can deter him from cleaving unto Him Who is the Eternal Truth, a steadfastness that taketh no account of them whatever. The second is strict observance of the laws He hath prescribed—laws which He hath always ordained, and will continue to ordain, unto men, and through which the truth may be distinguished and separated from falsehood.

The first and foremost duty prescribed unto men, next to the recognition of Him Who is the Eternal Truth, is the duty of steadfastness in His Cause. Cleave thou unto it, and be of them whose minds are firmly fixed and grounded in God. No act, however meritorious, did or can ever compare unto it. It is the king of all acts, and to this thy Lord, the All-Highest, the Most Powerful, will testify....[484]

Do thou beseech God to enable thee to remain steadfast in this path, and to aid thee to guide the peoples of the world to Him Who is the manifest and sovereign Ruler, Who hath revealed Himself in a distinct attire, Who giveth utterance to a Divine and specific Message. This is the essence of faith and certitude.[485]

Well is it with those who, in the face of the remembrance of the Lord of Eternity, regard the peoples of the world as utter nothingness, as a thing forgotten, and hold fast to the firm handle of God in such wise that neither doubts nor insinuations, nor swords, nor cannon could hold them back or deprive them of His presence. Blessed are the steadfast; blessed are they that stand firm in His Faith.[486]

I entreat Thee, O Lord of the Kingdom of eternity, by the shrill voice of the Pen of Glory, and by the Burning Fire which calleth aloud from the verdant Tree, and by the Ark which Thou hast specially chosen for the people of Bahá, to grant that I may remain steadfast in my love for Thee, be well pleased with whatsoever Thou hast prescribed for me in Thy Book and may stand firm in Thy service and in the service of Thy loved ones.[487]

Defend the Cause of God

Warn, O Salmán, the beloved of the one true God, not to view with too critical an eye the sayings and writings of men. Let them rather approach such sayings and writings in a spirit of open-mindedness and loving sympathy. Those men, however, who, in this Day, have been led to assail, in their inflammatory writings, the tenets of the Cause of God, are to be treated differently. It is incumbent upon all men, each according to his ability, to refute the arguments of those that have attacked the Faith of God. Thus hath it been decreed by Him Who is the All-Powerful, the Almighty. He that wisheth to promote the Cause of the one true God, let him promote it through his pen and tongue, rather than have recourse to sword or violence. We have, on a previous occasion, revealed this injunction, and We now confirm it, if ye be of them that comprehend. By the righteousness of Him Who, in this Day, crieth within the inmost heart of all created things: "God, there is none other God besides Me!" If any man were to arise to defend, in his writings, the Cause of God against its assailants, such a man, however inconsiderable his share, shall be so honored in the world to come that the Concourse on high would envy his glory. No pen can depict the loftiness of his station, neither can any tongue describe its splendor. For whosoever standeth firm and steadfast in this holy, this glorious, and exalted Revelation, such power shall be given him as to enable him to face and withstand all that is in heaven and on earth. Of this God is Himself a witness.[488]

Character and Conduct

All men have been created to carry forward an ever-advancing civilization. The Almighty beareth Me witness: To act like the beasts of the field is unworthy of man. Those virtues that befit his dignity are forbearance, mercy, compassion and loving-kindness towards all the peoples and kindreds of the earth.[489]

The purpose of the one true God in manifesting Himself is to summon all mankind to truthfulness and sincerity, to piety and trustworthiness, to resignation and submissiveness to the Will of God, to forbearance and kindliness, to uprightness and wisdom. His object is to array every man with the mantle of a saintly character, and to adorn him with the ornament of holy and goodly deeds.[490]

Were man to appreciate the greatness of his station and the loftiness of his destiny he would manifest naught save goodly character, pure deeds, and a seemly and praiseworthy conduct.[491]

A good character is, verily, the best mantle for men from God. With it He adorneth the temples of His loved ones. By My life! The light of a good character surpasseth the light of the sun and the radiance thereof.[492]

O peoples of the world! Forsake all evil, hold fast that which is good. Strive to be shining examples unto all mankind, and true reminders of the virtues of God amidst men. He that riseth to serve My Cause should manifest My wisdom, and bend every effort to banish ignorance from the earth. Be united in counsel, be one in thought. Let each morn be better than its eve and each morrow richer than its yesterday. Man's merit lieth in service and virtue and not in the pageantry of wealth and riches. Take heed that your words be purged from idle fancies and worldly desires and your deeds be cleansed from craftiness and suspicion. Dissipate not the wealth of your precious lives in the pursuit of evil and corrupt affection, nor let your endeavours be spent in promoting your personal interest. Be generous in your days of plenty, and be patient in the hour of loss. Adversity is followed by success and rejoicings follow woe. Guard against idleness and sloth, and cling unto that which profiteth mankind, whether young or old, whether high or low. Beware lest ye sow tares of dissension among men or plant thorns of doubt in pure and radiant hearts.

O ye beloved of the Lord! Commit not that which defileth the limpid stream of love or destroyeth the sweet fragrance of friendship. By the righteousness of the Lord! Ye were created to show love one to another and not perversity and rancour. Take pride not in love for yourselves but in love for your fellow-creatures. Glory not in love for your country, but in love for all mankind. Let your eye be chaste, your hand faithful, your tongue truthful and your heart enlightened. Abase not the station of the learned in Bahá and belittle not the rank of such rulers as administer justice amidst you. Set your reliance on the army of justice, put on the armour of wisdom, let your adorning be forgiveness and mercy and that which cheereth the hearts of the well-favoured of God.[493]

Be generous in prosperity, and thankful in adversity. Be worthy of the trust of thy neighbor, and look upon him with a bright and friendly face. Be a treasure to the poor, an admonisher to the rich, an answerer to the cry of the needy, a preserver of the sanctity of thy pledge. Be fair in thy judgment, and guarded in thy speech. Be unjust to no man, and show all meekness to all men. Be as a lamp unto them that walk in darkness, a joy to the sorrowful, a sea for the thirsty, a haven for the distressed, an upholder and defender of the victim of oppression. Let integrity and uprightness distinguish all thine acts. Be a home for the stranger, a balm to the suffering, a tower of strength for the fugitive. Be eyes to the blind, and a guiding light unto the feet of the erring. Be an ornament to the countenance of truth, a crown to the brow of fidelity, a pillar of the temple of righteousness, a breath of life to the body of mankind, an ensign of the hosts of justice, a luminary above the horizon of virtue, a dew to the soil of the human heart, an ark on the ocean of knowledge, a sun in the heaven of bounty, a gem on the diadem of wisdom, a shining light in the firmament of thy generation, a fruit upon the tree of humility.[494]

In one of the Tablets these words have been revealed: O people of God! Do not busy yourselves in your own concerns; let your thoughts be fixed upon that which will rehabilitate the fortunes of mankind and sanctify the hearts and souls of men. This can best be achieved through pure and holy deeds, through a virtuous life and a goodly behaviour. Valiant acts will ensure the triumph of this Cause, and a saintly character will reinforce its power. Cleave unto righteousness, O people of Bahá! This, verily, is the commandment which this Wronged One hath given unto you, and the first choice of His unrestrained Will for every one of you.[495]

Say: O people of God! That which can ensure the victory of Him Who is the Eternal Truth, His hosts and helpers on earth, have been set down in the sacred Books and Scriptures, and are as clear and manifest as the sun. These hosts are such righteous deeds, such conduct and character, as are acceptable in His sight. Whoso ariseth, in this Day, to aid Our Cause, and summoneth to his assistance the hosts of a praiseworthy character and upright conduct, the influence flowing from such an action will, most certainly, be diffused throughout the whole world.[496]

Man is like unto a tree. If he be adorned with fruit, he hath been and will ever be worthy of praise and commendation. Otherwise a fruitless tree is but fit for fire. The fruits of the human tree are exquisite, highly desired and dearly cherished. Among them are upright character, virtuous deeds and a goodly utterance. The springtime for earthly trees occurreth once every year, while the one for human trees appeareth in the Days of God—exalted be His glory. Were the trees of men's lives to be adorned in this divine Springtime with the fruits that have been mentioned, the effulgence of the light of Justice would, of a certainty, illumine all the dwellers of the earth and everyone would abide in tranquillity and contentment beneath the sheltering shadow of Him Who is the Object of all mankind. The Water for these trees is the living water of the sacred Words uttered by the Beloved of the world. In one instant are such trees planted and in the next their branches shall, through the outpourings of the showers of divine mercy, have reached the skies. A dried-up tree, however, hath never been nor will be worthy of any mention.[497]

The virtues and attributes pertaining unto God are all evident and manifest, and have been mentioned and described in all the heavenly Books. Among them are trustworthiness, truthfulness, purity of heart while communing with God, forbearance, resignation to whatever the Almighty hath decreed, contentment with the things His Will hath provided, patience, nay, thankfulness in the midst of tribulation, and complete reliance, in all circumstances, upon Him. These rank, according to the estimate of God, among the highest and most laudable of all acts. All other acts are, and will ever remain, secondary and subordinate unto them....[498]

The Day Star of Truth that shineth in its meridian splendor beareth Us witness! They who are the people of God have no ambition except to revive the world, to ennoble its life, and regenerate its peoples. Truthfulness and good-will have, at all times, marked their relations with all men. Their outward conduct is but a reflection of their inward life, and their inward life a mirror of their outward conduct.[499]

O SON OF MAN! Rejoice in the gladness of thine heart, that thou mayest be worthy to meet Me and to mirror forth My beauty.[500]

Selflessness

O MY SERVANT! Free thyself from the fetters of this world, and loose thy soul from the prison of self. Seize thy chance, for it will come to thee no more.[501]

O SON OF SPIRIT! There is no peace for thee save by renouncing thyself and turning unto Me; for it behooveth thee to glory in My name, not in thine own; to put thy trust in Me and not in thyself, since I desire to be loved alone and above all that is.[502]

O BEFRIENDED STRANGER! The candle of thine heart is lighted by the hand of My power, quench it not with the contrary winds of self and passion. The healer of all thine ills is remembrance of Me, forget it not. Make My love thy treasure and cherish it even as thy very sight and life.[503]

O SON OF SPIRIT! Burst thy cage asunder, and even as the phoenix of love soar into the firmament of holiness. Renounce thyself and, filled with the spirit of mercy, abide in the realm of celestial sanctity.[504]

O EMIGRANTS! The tongue I have designed for the mention of Me, defile it not with detraction. If the fire of self overcome you, remember your own faults and not the faults of My creatures, inasmuch as every one of you knoweth his own self better than he knoweth others.[505]

O SON OF DESIRE! The learned and the wise have for long years striven and failed to attain the presence of the All-Glorious; they have spent their lives in search of Him, yet did not behold the beauty of His countenance. Thou without the least effort didst attain thy goal, and without search hast obtained the object of thy quest. Yet, notwithstanding, thou didst remain so wrapt in the veil of self, that thine eyes beheld not the beauty of the Beloved, nor did thy hand touch the hem of His robe. Ye that have eyes, behold and wonder.[506]

Fear ye God, O concourse of the foolish, and do not inflict tribulations upon those who have willed naught but that which God hath willed. Moreover, if ye heed my call, follow not your selfish desires. The day is approaching when everything now discernible will have faded away and ye shall weep for having failed in your duty towards God. Unto this testifieth this inscribed Tablet.[507]

Say: O people! The Lamp of God is burning; take heed, lest the fierce winds of your disobedience extinguish its light. Now is the time to arise and magnify the Lord, your God. Strive not after bodily comforts, and keep your heart pure and stainless. The Evil One is lying in wait, ready to entrap you. Gird yourselves against his wicked devices, and, led by the light of the name of the one true God, deliver yourselves from the darkness that surroundeth you. Center your thoughts in the Well-Beloved, rather than in your own selves.[508]

Say: Deliver your souls, O people, from the bondage of self, and purify them from all attachment to anything besides Me. Remembrance of Me cleanseth all things from defilement, could ye but perceive it. Say: Were all created things to be entirely divested of the veil of worldly vanity and desire, the Hand of God would in this Day clothe them, one and all, with the robe "He doeth whatsoever He willeth in the kingdom of creation," that thereby the sign of His sovereignty might be manifested in all things. Exalted then be He, the Sovereign Lord of all, the Almighty, the Supreme Protector, the All-Glorious, the Most Powerful.[509]

I am the one who is in misery, O God! Behold me cleaving fast to Thy Name, the All-Possessing. I am the one who is sure to perish; behold me clinging to Thy Name, the Imperishable. I implore Thee, therefore, by Thy Self, the Exalted, the Most High, not to abandon me unto mine own self and unto the desires of a corrupt inclination. Hold Thou my hand with the hand of Thy power, and deliver me from the depths of my fancies and idle imaginings, and cleanse me of all that is abhorrent unto Thee.[510]

Purity and Chastity

O SON OF SPIRIT! My first counsel is this: Possess a pure, kindly and radiant heart, that thine may be a sovereignty ancient, imperishable and everlasting.[511]

We, verily, have decreed in Our Book a goodly and bountiful reward to whosoever will turn away from wickedness and lead a chaste and godly life. He, in truth, is the Great Giver, the All-Bountiful.[512]

They that follow their lusts and corrupt inclinations, have erred and dissipated their efforts. They, indeed, are of the lost.[513]

Purity and chastity ... have been, and still are, the most great ornaments for the handmaidens of God. God is My Witness! The brightness of the light of chastity sheddeth its illumination upon the worlds of the spirit, and its fragrance is wafted even unto the Most Exalted Paradise. God ... hath verily made chastity to be a crown for the heads of His handmaidens. Great is the blessedness of that handmaiden that hath attained unto this great station.[514]

He is not to be numbered with the people of Bahá who followeth his mundane desires, or fixeth his heart on things of the earth. He is My true follower who, if he come to a valley of pure gold, will pass straight through it aloof as a cloud, and will neither turn back, nor pause. Such a man is, assuredly, of Me. From his garment the Concourse on high can inhale the fragrance of sanctity□. And if he met the fairest and most comely of women, he would not feel his heart seduced by the least shadow of desire for her beauty.[515]

Let your eye be chaste, your hand faithful, your tongue truthful and your heart enlightened.[516]

I swear by Him Who is the Most Great Ocean! ... Within the very breath of such souls as are pure and sanctified far-reaching potentialities are hidden. So great are these potentialities that they exercise their influence upon all created things.[517]

We verily behold your actions. If We perceive from them the sweet smelling savor of purity and holiness, We will most certainly bless you. Then will the tongues of the inmates of Paradise utter your praise and magnify your names amidst them who have drawn nigh unto God.[518]

Wisdom

The word of God which the Supreme Pen hath recorded on the

fifth leaf

of the Most Exalted Paradise is this: Above all else, the greatest gift and the most wondrous blessing hath ever been and will continue to be Wisdom. It is man's unfailing Protector. It aideth him and strengtheneth him. Wisdom is God's Emissary and the Revealer of His Name the Omniscient. Through it the loftiness of man's station is made manifest and evident. It is all-knowing and the foremost Teacher in the school of existence. It is the Guide and is invested with high distinction. Thanks to its educating influence earthly beings have become imbued with a gem-like spirit which outshineth the heavens. In the city of justice it is the unrivalled Speaker Who, in the year nine, illumined the world with the joyful tidings of this Revelation. And it was this peerless Source of wisdom that at the beginning of the foundation of the world ascended the stair of inner meaning and when enthroned upon the pulpit of utterance, through the operation of the divine Will, proclaimed two words. The first heralded the promise of reward, while the second voiced the ominous warning of punishment. The promise gave rise to hope and the warning begat fear. Thus the basis of world order hath been firmly established upon these twin principles. Exalted is the Lord of Wisdom, the Possessor of Great Bounty.[519]

O people of Bahá! Subdue the citadels of men's hearts with the swords of wisdom and of utterance. They that dispute, as prompted by their desires, are indeed wrapped in a palpable veil. Say: The sword of wisdom is hotter than summer heat, and sharper than blades of steel, if ye do but understand. Draw it forth in My name and through the power of My might, and conquer then with it the cities of the hearts of them that have secluded themselves in the stronghold of their corrupt desires. Thus biddeth you the Pen of the All-Glorious, whilst seated beneath the swords of the wayward.[520]

O SON OF MY HANDMAID! Quaff from the tongue of the merciful the stream of divine mystery, and behold from the dayspring of divine utterance the unveiled splendor of the daystar of wisdom. Sow the seeds of My divine wisdom in the pure soil of the heart, and water them with the waters of certitude, that the hyacinths of knowledge and wisdom may spring up fresh and green from the holy city of the heart.[521]

Knowledge

The source of all learning is the knowledge of God, exalted be His Glory, and this cannot be attained save through the knowledge of His Divine Manifestation.[522]

We beseech God to strengthen thee with His power, and enable thee to recognize Him Who is the Source of all knowledge, that thou mayest detach thyself from all human learning, for, "what would it profit any man to strive after learning when he hath already found and recognized Him Who is the Object of all knowledge?" Cleave to the Root of Knowledge, and to Him Who is the Fountain thereof, that thou mayest find thyself independent of all who claim to be well versed in human learning, and whose claim no clear proof, nor the testimony of any enlightening book, can support.[523]

No man shall attain the shores of the ocean of true understanding except he be detached from all that is in heaven and on earth. Sanctify your souls, O ye peoples of the world, that haply ye may attain that station which God hath destined for you and enter thus the tabernacle which, according to the dispensations of Providence, hath been raised in the firmament of the Bayán.

The essence of these words is this: they that tread the path of faith, they that thirst for the wine of certitude, must cleanse themselves of all that is earthly—their ears from idle talk, their minds from vain imaginings, their hearts from worldly affections, their eyes from that which perisheth. They should put their trust in God, and, holding fast unto Him, follow in His way. Then will they be made worthy of the effulgent glories of the sun of divine knowledge and understanding, and become the recipients of a grace that is infinite and unseen, inasmuch as man can never hope to attain unto the knowledge of the All-Glorious, can never quaff from the stream of divine knowledge and wisdom, can never enter the abode of immortality, nor partake of the cup of divine nearness and favour, unless and until he ceases to regard the words and deeds of mortal men as a standard for the true understanding and recognition of God and His Prophets.[524]

Know verily that Knowledge is of two kinds: Divine and Satanic. The one welleth out from the fountain of divine inspiration; the other is but a reflection of vain and obscure thoughts. The source of the former is God Himself; the motive-force of the latter the whisperings of selfish desire. The one is guided by the principle: "Fear ye God; God will teach you;"[525] the other is but a confirmation of the truth: "Knowledge is the most grievous veil between man and his Creator." The former bringeth forth the fruit of patience, of longing desire, of true understanding, and love; whilst the latter can yield naught but arrogance, vainglory and conceit.[526]

The first Tajallí

which hath dawned from the Day-Star of Truth is the knowledge of God—exalted be His glory. And the knowledge of the King of everlasting days can in no wise be attained save by recognizing Him Who is the Bearer of the Most Great Name.[527]

The third Tajallí

is concerning arts, crafts and sciences. Knowledge is as wings to man's life, and a ladder for his ascent. Its acquisition is incumbent upon everyone. The knowledge of such sciences, however, should be acquired as can profit the peoples of the earth, and not those which begin with words and end with words. Great indeed is the claim of scientists and craftsmen on the peoples of the world. Unto this beareth witness the Mother Book on the day of His return. Happy are those possessed of a hearing ear. In truth, knowledge is a veritable treasure for man, and a source of glory, of bounty, of joy, of exaltation, of cheer and gladness unto him. Thus hath the Tongue of Grandeur spoken in this Most Great Prison.[528]

O people of God! Righteous men of learning who dedicate themselves to the guidance of others and are freed and well guarded from the promptings of a base and covetous nature are, in the sight of Him Who is the Desire of the world, stars of the heaven of true knowledge. It is essential to treat them with deference. They are indeed fountains of soft-flowing water, stars that shine resplendent, fruits of the blessed Tree, exponents of celestial power, and oceans of heavenly wisdom. Happy is he that followeth them. Verily such a soul is numbered in the Book of God, the Lord of the mighty Throne, among those with whom it shall be well.[529]

Unveiled and unconcealed, this Wronged One hath, at all times, proclaimed before the face of all the peoples of the world that which will serve as the key for unlocking the doors of sciences, of arts, of knowledge, of well-being, of prosperity and wealth. Neither have the wrongs inflicted by the oppressors succeeded in silencing the shrill voice of the Most Exalted Pen, nor have the doubts of the perverse or of the seditious been able to hinder Him from revealing the Most Sublime Word.[530]

Whatsoever runneth counter to the Teachings in this day is rejected, for the Sun of Truth is shining resplendent above the horizon of knowledge. Happy are they who, with the waters of divine utterance, have cleansed their hearts from all allusions, whisperings and suggestions, and who have fixed their gaze upon the Dayspring of Glory. This, indeed, is the most gracious favour and the purest bounty. Whosoever hath attained thereunto hath attained unto all good, for otherwise the knowledge of aught else but God hath never proven, nor shall it ever prove, profitable unto men.[531]

Human Words and Utterance

No man of wisdom can demonstrate his knowledge save by means of words. This showeth the significance of the Word as is affirmed in all the Scriptures, whether of former times or more recently. For it is through its potency and animating spirit that the people of the world have attained so eminent a position. Moreover words and utterances should be both impressive and penetrating. However, no word will be infused with these two qualities unless it be uttered wholly for the sake of God and with due regard unto the exigencies of the occasion and the people.

The Great Being saith: Human utterance is an essence which aspireth to exert its influence and needeth moderation. As to its influence, this is conditional upon refinement which in turn is dependent upon hearts which are detached and pure. As to its moderation, this hath to be combined with tact and wisdom as prescribed in the Holy Scriptures and Tablets.

Every word is endowed with a spirit, therefore the speaker or expounder should carefully deliver his words at the appropriate time and place, for the impression which each word maketh is clearly evident and perceptible. The Great Being saith: One word may be likened unto fire, another unto light, and the influence which both exert is manifest in the world. Therefore an enlightened man of wisdom should primarily speak with words as mild as milk, that the children of men may be nurtured and edified thereby and may attain the ultimate goal of human existence which is the station of true understanding and nobility. And likewise He saith: One word is like unto springtime causing the tender saplings of the rose-garden of knowledge to become verdant and flourishing, while another word is even as a deadly poison. It behoveth a prudent man of wisdom to speak with utmost leniency and forbearance so that the sweetness of his words may induce everyone to attain that which befitteth man's station.[532]

O people! Words must be supported by deeds, for deeds are the true test of words. Without the former, the latter can never quench the thirst of the yearning soul, nor unlock the portals of vision before the eyes of the blind. The Lord of celestial wisdom saith: A harsh word is even as a sword thrust; a gentle word as milk. The latter leadeth the children of men unto knowledge and conferreth upon them true distinction.[533]

O SON OF BEING! Make mention of Me on My earth, that in My heaven I may remember thee, thus shall Mine eyes and thine be solaced.[534]

Say: If it be Our pleasure We shall render the Cause victorious through the power of a single word from Our presence.... However, since Our loving providence surpasseth all things, We have ordained that complete victory should be achieved through speech and utterance, that Our servants throughout the earth may thereby become the recipients of divine good. This is but a token of God's bounty vouchsafed unto them. Verily thy Lord is the All-Sufficing, the Most Exalted.[535]

Words and Deeds

Say: Beware, O people of Bahá, lest ye walk in the ways of them whose words differ from their deeds. Strive that ye may be enabled to manifest to the peoples of the earth the signs of God, and to mirror forth His commandments. Let your acts be a guide unto all mankind, for the professions of most men, be they high or low, differ from their conduct. It is through your deeds that ye can distinguish yourselves from others. Through them the brightness of your light can be shed upon the whole earth. Happy is the man that heedeth My counsel, and keepeth the precepts prescribed by Him Who is the All-Knowing, the All-Wise.[536]

O CHILDREN OF ADAM! Holy words and pure and goodly deeds ascend unto the heaven of celestial glory. Strive that your deeds may be cleansed from the dust of self and hypocrisy and find favor at the court of glory; for ere long the assayers of mankind shall, in the holy presence of the Adored One, accept naught but absolute virtue and deeds of stainless purity. This is the daystar of wisdom and of divine mystery that hath shone above the horizon of the divine will. Blessed are they that turn thereunto.[537]

O SON OF MY HANDMAID! Guidance hath ever been given by words, and now it is given by deeds. Every one must show forth deeds that are pure and holy, for words are the property of all alike, whereas such deeds as these belong only to Our loved ones. Strive then with heart and soul to distinguish yourselves by your deeds. In this wise We counsel you in this holy and resplendent tablet.[538]

The essence of faith is fewness of words and abundance of deeds; he whose words exceed his deeds, know verily his death is better than his life.[539]

O servants! Ye are even as saplings in a garden, which are near to perishing for want of water. Wherefore, revive your souls with the heavenly water that is raining down from the clouds of divine bounty. Words must be followed by deeds. Whoso accepteth the words of the Friend is in truth a man of deeds; otherwise a dead carcass is verily of greater worth.[540]

O servant of God! The day of deeds hath come: Now is not the time for words. The Messenger of God hath appeared: Now is not the hour for hesitation. Open thou thine inner eye that thou mayest behold the face of the Beloved, and hearken thou with thine inner ear that thou mayest hear the sweet murmur of His celestial voice.[541]

Trustworthiness

O people! The goodliest vesture in the sight of God in this day is trustworthiness. All bounty and honour shall be the portion of the soul that arrayeth itself with this greatest of adornments.[542]

The fourth Taráz

concerneth trustworthiness. Verily it is the door of security for all that dwell on earth and a token of glory on the part of the All-Merciful. He who partaketh thereof hath indeed partaken of the treasures of wealth and prosperity. Trustworthiness is the greatest portal leading unto the tranquillity and security of the people. In truth the stability of every affair hath depended and doth depend upon it. All the domains of power, of grandeur and of wealth are illumined by its light.

Not long ago these sublime words were revealed from the Pen of the Most High:

'We will now mention unto thee Trustworthiness and the station thereof in the estimation of God, thy Lord, the Lord of the Mighty Throne. One day of days We repaired unto Our Green Island. Upon Our arrival, We beheld its streams flowing, and its trees luxuriant, and the sunlight playing in their midst. Turning Our face to the right, We beheld what the pen is powerless to describe; nor can it set forth that which the eye of the Lord of Mankind witnessed in that most sanctified, that most sublime, that blest, and most exalted Spot. Turning, then, to the left We gazed on one of the Beauties of the Most Sublime Paradise, standing on a pillar of light, and calling aloud saying: "O inmates of earth and heaven! Behold ye My beauty, and My radiance, and My revelation, and My effulgence. By God, the True One! I am Trustworthiness and the revelation thereof, and the beauty thereof. I will recompense whosoever will cleave unto Me, and recognize My rank and station, and hold fast unto My hem. I am the most great ornament of the people of Bahá, and the vesture of glory unto all who are in the kingdom of creation. I am the supreme instrument for the prosperity of the world, and the horizon of assurance unto all beings." Thus have We sent down for thee that which will draw men nigh unto the Lord of creation.'[543]

Were a man in this day to adorn himself with the raiment of trustworthiness it were better for him in the sight of God than that he should journey on foot towards the holy court and be blessed with meeting the Adored One and standing before His Seat of Glory. Trustworthiness is as a stronghold to the city of humanity, and as eyes to the human temple. Whosoever remaineth deprived thereof shall, before His Throne, be reckoned as one bereft of vision.[544]

O people of Bahá! Trustworthiness is in truth the best of vestures for your temples and the most glorious crown for your heads. Take ye fast hold of it at the behest of Him Who is the Ordainer, the All-Informed.[545]

Beautify your tongues, O people, with truthfulness, and adorn your souls with the ornament of honesty. Beware, O people, that ye deal not treacherously with any one.[546]

Trustworthiness, wisdom and honesty are, of a truth, God's beauteous adornments for His creatures. These fair garments are a befitting vesture for every temple. Happy are those that comprehend, and well is it with them that acquire such virtues.[547]

Know thou for a certainty that whoso disbelieveth in God is neither trustworthy nor truthful. This, indeed, is the truth, the undoubted truth. He that acteth treacherously towards God will, also, act treacherously towards his king. Nothing whatever can deter such a man from evil, nothing can hinder him from betraying his neighbour, nothing can induce him to walk uprightly.[548]

Cleave thou to the fear of God and to whatsoever hath been revealed in His Book: thus biddeth thee He Who is the Word of

Truth and the Knower of things unseen. Say: trustworthiness is the sun of the heaven of My commandments, truthfulness is its moon, and praiseworthy attributes are its stars.[549]

It behoveth ye all so to adorn your inner and outer beings that, robed in trustworthiness, girt with righteousness and arrayed in truthfulness and rectitude, ye may become a means for the exaltation of the Cause and the education of the human race. [550]

Humility

Humility exalteth man to the heaven of glory and power, whilst pride abaseth him to the depths of wretchedness and degradation.[551]

They who are the beloved of God, in whatever place they gather and whomsoever they may meet, must evince, in their attitude towards God, and in the manner of their celebration of His praise and glory, such humility and submissiveness that every atom of the dust beneath their feet may attest the depth of their devotion.[552]

Beware that ye swell not with pride before God, and disdainfully reject His loved ones. Defer ye humbly to the faithful, they that have believed in God and in His signs, whose hearts witness to His unity, whose tongues proclaim His oneness, and who speak not except by His leave. Thus do We exhort you with justice, and warn you with truth, that perchance ye may be awakened.[553]

By the righteousness of God! Idle fancies have debarred men from the Horizon of Certitude, and vain imaginings withheld them from the Choice Sealed Wine. In truth I say, and for the sake of God I declare: This Servant, this Wronged One, is abashed to claim for Himself any existence whatever, how much more those exalted grades of being! Every man of discernment, while walking upon the earth, feeleth indeed abashed, inasmuch as he is fully aware that the thing which is the source of his prosperity, his wealth, his might, his exaltation, his advancement and power is, as ordained by God, the very earth which is trodden beneath the feet of all men. There can be no doubt that whoever is cognizant of this truth, is cleansed and sanctified from all pride, arrogance, and vainglory. Whatever hath been said hath come from God. Unto this, He, verily, hath borne, and beareth now, witness, and He, in truth, is the All-Knowing, the All-Informed.[554]

Beseech ye the one true God to grant that ye may taste the savor of such deeds as are performed in His path, and partake of the sweetness of such humility and submissiveness as are shown for His sake.[555]

O SON OF MAN! Humble thyself before Me, that I may graciously visit thee. Arise for the triumph of My cause, that while yet on earth thou mayest obtain the victory.[556]

O CHILDREN OF DESIRE! Put away the garment of vainglory, and divest yourselves of the attire of haughtiness.[557]

O BRETHREN! Be forbearing one with another and set not your affections on things below. Pride not yourselves in your glory, and be not ashamed of abasement. By My beauty! I have created all things from dust, and to dust will I return them again.[558]

Courtesy

O people of God! I admonish you to observe courtesy, for above all else it is the prince of virtues. Well is it with him who is illumined with the light of courtesy and is attired with the vesture of uprightness. Whoso is endued with courtesy hath indeed attained a sublime station. It is hoped that this Wronged One and everyone else may be enabled to acquire it, hold fast unto it, observe it, and fix our gaze upon it. This is a binding command which hath streamed forth from the Pen of the Most Great Name.[559]

Charity

Charity is pleasing and praiseworthy in the sight of God and is regarded as a prince among goodly deeds. Consider ye and call to mind that which the All-Merciful hath revealed in the Qur'án: They prefer them before themselves, though poverty be their own lot. And with such as are preserved from their own covetousness shall it be well.[560] Viewed in this light, the blessed utterance above is, in truth, the day-star of utterances.[561]

Be fair to yourselves and to others, that the evidences of justice may be revealed, through your deeds, among Our faithful servants. Beware lest ye encroach upon the substance of your neighbor. Prove yourselves worthy of his trust and confidence in you, and withhold not from the poor the gifts which the grace of God hath bestowed upon you. He, verily, shall recompense the charitable, and doubly repay them for what they have bestowed. No God is there but Him. All creation and its empire are His. He bestoweth His gifts on whom He will, and from whom He will He withholdeth them. He is the Great Giver, the Most Generous, the Benevolent.[562]

O CHILDREN OF DUST! Tell the rich of the midnight sighing of the poor, lest heedlessness lead them into the path of destruction, and deprive them of the Tree of Wealth. To give and to be generous are attributes of Mine; well is it with him that adorneth himself with My virtues.[563]

The essence of charity is for the servant to recount the blessings of his Lord, and to render thanks unto Him at all times and under all conditions.[564]

Golden Rule

O SON OF BEING! Ascribe not to any soul that which thou wouldst not have ascribed to thee, and say not that which thou doest not. This is My command unto thee, do thou observe it.[565]

Lay not on any soul a load which ye would not wish to be laid upon you, and desire not for anyone the things ye would not desire for yourselves. This is My best counsel unto you, did ye but observe it.[566]

Blessed is he who preferreth his brother before himself. Verily, such a man is reckoned, by virtue of the Will of God, the All-Knowing, the All-Wise, with the people of Bahá who dwell in the Crimson Ark.[567]

O son of man! If thine eyes be turned towards mercy, forsake the things that profit thee and cleave unto that which will profit mankind. And if thine eyes be turned towards justice, choose thou for thy neighbour that which thou choosest for thyself.[568]

O COMPANION OF MY THRONE! Hear no evil, and see no evil, abase not thyself, neither sigh and weep. Speak no evil, that thou mayest not hear it spoken unto thee, and magnify not the faults of others that thine own faults may not appear great; and wish not the abasement of anyone, that thine own abasement be not exposed.[569]

I was, moreover, opposed by mine own kindred, although, as Thou knowest, they were dear to me and I had desired for them that which I had desired for mine own self.[570]

Loving Fellowship

It is Our wish and desire that every one of you may become a source of all goodness unto men, and an example of uprightness to mankind. Beware lest ye prefer yourselves above your neighbors. Fix your gaze upon Him Who is the Temple of God amongst men. He, in truth, hath offered up His life as a ransom for the redemption of the world. He, verily, is the All-Bountiful, the Gracious, the Most High. If any differences arise amongst you, behold Me standing before your face, and overlook the faults of one another for My name's sake and as a token of your love for My manifest and resplendent Cause. We love to see you at all times consorting in amity and concord within the paradise of My good-pleasure, and to inhale from your acts the fragrance of friendliness and unity, of loving-kindness and fellowship. Thus counselleth you the All-Knowing, the Faithful. We shall always be with you; if We inhale the perfume of your fellowship, Our heart will assuredly rejoice, for naught else can satisfy Us. To this beareth witness every man of true understanding.[571]

Verily, it is enjoined upon you to offer a feast, once in every month, though only water be served; for God hath purposed to bind hearts together, albeit through both earthly and heavenly means.[572]

Companionship with the Righteous

O FRIEND! In the garden of thy heart plant naught but the rose of love, and from the nightingale of affection and desire loosen not thy hold. Treasure the companionship of the righteous and eschew all fellowship with the ungodly.[573]

O MY SON! The company of the ungodly increaseth sorrow, whilst fellowship with the righteous cleanseth the rust from off the heart. He that seeketh to commune with God, let him betake himself to the companionship of His loved ones; and he that desireth to hearken unto the word of God, let him give ear to the words of His chosen ones.[574]

O SON OF DUST! Beware! Walk not with the ungodly and seek not fellowship with him, for such companionship turneth the radiance of the heart into infernal fire.[575]

O SON OF MY HANDMAID! Wouldst thou seek the grace of the Holy Spirit, enter into fellowship with the righteous, for he hath drunk the cup of eternal life at the hands of the immortal Cup-bearer and even as the true morn doth quicken and illumine the hearts of the dead.[576]

Consultation

The Great Being saith: The heaven of divine wisdom is illumined with the two luminaries of consultation and compassion. Take ye counsel together in all matters, inasmuch as consultation is the lamp of guidance which leadeth the way, and is the bestower of understanding.[577]

Consultation bestoweth greater awareness and transmuteth conjecture into certitude. It is a shining light which, in a dark world, leadeth the way and guideth. For everything there is and will continue to be a station of perfection and maturity. The maturity of the gift of understanding is made manifest through consultation.

In all things it is necessary to consult. This matter should be forcibly stressed by thee, so that consultation may be observed by all. The intent of what hath been revealed from the Pen of the Most High is that consultation may be fully carried out among the friends, inasmuch as it is and will always be a cause of awareness and of awakening and a source of good and well-being.[578]

Occupation

O people of Bahá! It is incumbent upon each one of you to engage in some occupation, such as a craft, a trade or the like. We have exalted your engagement in such work to the rank of worship of the one true God. Reflect, O people, on the grace and blessings of your Lord, and yield Him thanks at eventide and dawn. Waste not your hours in idleness and sloth, but occupy yourselves with what will profit you and others. Thus hath it been decreed in this Tablet from whose horizon hath shone the day-star of wisdom and utterance. The most despised of men in the sight of God are they who sit and beg. Hold ye fast unto the cord of means and place your trust in God, the Provider of all means.[579]

O MY SERVANTS! Ye are the trees of My garden; ye must give forth goodly and wondrous fruits, that ye yourselves and others may profit therefrom. Thus it is incumbent on every one to engage in crafts and professions, for therein lies the secret of wealth, O men of understanding! For results depend upon means, and the grace of God shall be all-sufficient unto you. Trees that yield no fruit have been and will ever be for the fire.[580]

O MY SERVANT! The best of men are they that earn a livelihood by their calling and spend upon themselves and upon their kindred for the love of God, the Lord of all worlds.[581]

Marriage

And when He desired to manifest grace and beneficence to men, and to set the world in order, He revealed observances and created laws; among them He established the law of marriage, made it as a fortress for well-being and salvation, and enjoined it upon us in that which was sent down out of the heaven of sanctity in His Most Holy Book. He saith, great is His glory: "Enter into wedlock, O people, that ye may bring forth one who will make mention of Me amid My servants. This is My bidding unto you; hold fast to it as an assistance to yourselves."[582]

It behoveth man to show forth that which will benefit mankind. He that bringeth forth no fruit is fit for the fire. Thus admonisheth you your Lord; He, verily, is the Mighty, the Bountiful. Enter ye into wedlock, that after you another may arise in your stead.... But for man, who, on My earth, would remember Me, and how could My attributes and My names be revealed? [583]

It hath been laid down in the Bayán that marriage is dependent upon the consent of both parties. Desiring to establish love, unity and harmony amidst Our servants, We have conditioned it, once the couple□s wish is known, upon the permission of their parents, lest enmity and rancour should arise amongst them. And in this We have yet other purposes. Thus hath Our commandment been ordained.[584]

Divorce

Truly, the Lord loveth union and harmony and abhorreth separation and divorce.[585]

Should resentment or antipathy arise between husband and wife, he is not to divorce her but to bide in patience throughout the course of one whole year, that perchance the fragrance of affection may be renewed between them. If, upon the completion of this period, their love hath not returned, it is permissible for divorce to take place. God's wisdom, verily, hath encompassed all things.[586]

Loving-Kindness Towards Parents

Well is it with him who in the Day of God hath laid fast hold upon His precepts and hath not deviated from His true and fundamental Law. The fruits that best befit the tree of human life are trustworthiness and godliness, truthfulness and sincerity; but greater than all, after recognition of the unity of God, praised and glorified be He, is regard for the rights that are due to one's parents. This teaching hath been mentioned in all the Books of God, and reaffirmed by the Most Exalted Pen. Consider that which the Merciful Lord hath revealed in the Qur'án, exalted are His words: Worship ye God, join with Him no peer or likeness; and show forth kindliness and charity towards your parents. Observe how loving-kindness to one's parents hath been linked to recognition of the one true God! Happy they who are endued with true wisdom and understanding, who see and perceive, who read and understand, and who observe that which God hath revealed in the Holy Books of old, and in this incomparable and wondrous Tablet.[587]

Say, O My people! Show honour to your parents and pay homage to them. This will cause blessings to descend upon you from the clouds of the bounty of your Lord, the Exalted, the Great.

Beware lest ye commit that which would sadden the hearts of your fathers and mothers. Follow ye the path of Truth which indeed is a straight path. Should anyone give you a choice between the opportunity to render a service to Me and a service to them, choose ye to serve them, and let such service be a path leading you to Me. This is My exhortation and command unto thee. Observe therefore that which thy Lord, the Mighty, the Gracious, hath prescribed unto thee.[588]

Cleanliness

Cleave ye unto the cord of refinement with such tenacity as to allow no trace of dirt to be seen upon your garments. Such is the injunction of One Who is sanctified above all refinement. Whoso falleth short of this standard with good reason shall incur no blame. God, verily, is the Forgiving, the Merciful. Wash ye every soiled thing with water that hath undergone no alteration in any one of the three respects; take heed not to use water that hath been altered through exposure to the air or to some other agent. Be ye the very essence of cleanliness amongst mankind. This, truly, is what your Lord, the Incomparable, the All-Wise, desireth for you.

God hath enjoined upon you to observe the utmost cleanliness, to the extent of washing what is soiled with dust, let alone with hardened dirt and similar defilement. Fear Him, and be of those who are pure. Should the garb of anyone be visibly sullied, his prayers shall not ascend to God, and the celestial Concourse will turn away from him. Make use of rose-water, and of pure perfume; this, indeed, is that which God hath loved from the beginning that hath no beginning, in order that there may be diffused from you what your Lord, the Incomparable, the All-Wise, desireth.[589]

It hath been enjoined upon you to pare your nails, to bathe yourselves each week in water that covereth your bodies, and to clean yourselves with whatsoever ye have formerly employed. Take heed lest through negligence ye fail to observe that which hath been prescribed unto you by Him Who is the Incomparable, the Gracious. Immerse yourselves in clean water; it is not permissible to bathe yourselves in water that hath already been used.... Truly, We desire to behold you as manifestations of paradise on earth, that there may be diffused from you such fragrance as shall rejoice the hearts of the favoured of God. If the bather, instead of entering the water, wash himself by pouring it upon his body, it shall be better for him and shall absolve him of the need for bodily immersion. The Lord, verily, hath willed, as a bounty from His presence, to make life easier for you that ye may be of those who are truly thankful.[590]

Wash your feet once every day in summer, and once every three days during winter.[591]

Ye have been enjoined to renew the furnishings of your homes after the passing of each nineteen years; thus hath it been ordained by One Who is Omniscient and All-Perceiving. He, verily, is desirous of refinement, both for you yourselves and for all that ye possess; lay not aside the fear of God and be not of the negligent. Whoso findeth that his means are insufficient to this purpose hath been excused by God, the Ever-Forgiving, the Most Bounteous.[592]

Music

We have made it lawful for you to listen to music and singing. Take heed, however, lest listening thereto should cause you to overstep the bounds of propriety and dignity. Let your joy be the joy born of My Most Great Name, a Name that bringeth rapture to the heart, and filleth with ecstasy the minds of all who have drawn nigh unto God. We, verily, have made music as a ladder for your souls, a means whereby they may be lifted up unto the realm on high; make it not, therefore, as wings to self and passion. Truly, We are loath to see you numbered with the foolish.[593]

Moderation

The word of God which the Supreme Pen hath recorded on the

ninth leaf

of the Most Exalted Paradise is this: In all matters moderation is desirable. If a thing is carried to excess, it will prove a source of evil.[594]

It is incumbent upon them who are in authority to exercise moderation in all things. Whatsoever passeth beyond the limits of moderation will cease to exert a beneficial influence.[595]

Whoso cleaveth to justice, can, under no circumstances, transgress the limits of moderation. He discerneth the truth in all things, through the guidance of Him Who is the All-Seeing. The civilization, so often vaunted by the learned exponents of arts and sciences, will, if allowed to overleap the bounds of moderation, bring great evil upon men. Thus warneth you He Who is the All-Knowing. If carried to excess, civilization will prove as prolific a source of evil as it had been of goodness when kept within the restraints of moderation.[596]

True Liberty

Liberty must, in the end, lead to sedition, whose flames none can quench. Thus warneth you He Who is the Reckoner, the All-Knowing. Know ye that the embodiment of liberty and its symbol is the animal. That which beseemeth man is submission unto such restraints as will protect him from his own ignorance, and guard him against the harm of the mischief-maker. Liberty causeth man to overstep the bounds of propriety, and to infringe on the dignity of his station. It debaseth him to the level of extreme depravity and wickedness.

Regard men as a flock of sheep that need a shepherd for their protection. This, verily, is the truth, the certain truth. We approve of liberty in certain circumstances, and refuse to sanction it in others. We, verily, are the All-Knowing.

Say: True liberty consisteth in man's submission unto My commandments, little as ye know it. Were men to observe that which We have sent down unto them from the Heaven of Revelation, they would, of a certainty, attain unto perfect liberty. Happy is the man that hath apprehended the Purpose of God in whatever He hath revealed from the Heaven of His Will that pervadeth all created things. Say: The liberty that profiteth you is to be found nowhere except in complete servitude unto God, the Eternal Truth. Whoso hath tasted of its sweetness will refuse to barter it for all the dominion of earth and heaven.[597]

Prohibited Behaviors

We have, under all circumstances, enjoined on men what is right, and forbidden what is wrong.[598]

These are the ordinances of God that have been set down in the Books and Tablets by His Most Exalted Pen. Hold ye fast unto His statutes and commandments, and be not of those who, following their idle fancies and vain imaginings, have clung to the standards fixed by their own selves, and cast behind their backs the standards laid down by God.[599]

Ye have been forbidden to commit murder or adultery, or to engage in backbiting or calumny; shun ye, then, what hath been prohibited in the holy Books and Tablets.[600]

Let none contend with another, and let no soul slay another; this, verily, is that which was forbidden you in a Book that hath lain concealed within the Tabernacle of glory. What! Would ye kill him whom God hath quickened, whom He hath endowed with spirit through a breath from Him? Grievous then would be your trespass before His throne! Fear God, and lift not the hand of injustice and oppression to destroy what He hath Himself raised up; nay, walk ye in the way of God, the True One.[601]

Ye have been forbidden in the Book of God to engage in contention and conflict, to strike another, or to commit similar acts whereby hearts and souls may be saddened.[602]

Should anyone wax angry with you, respond to him with gentleness; and should anyone upbraid you, forbear to upbraid him in return, but leave him to himself and put your trust in God, the omnipotent Avenger, the Lord of might and justice.[603]

It is forbidden you to trade in slaves, be they men or women. It is not for him who is himself a servant to buy another of God's servants, and this hath been prohibited in His Holy Tablet. Thus, by His mercy, hath the commandment been recorded by the Pen of justice. Let no man exalt himself above another; all are but bondslaves before the Lord, and all exemplify the truth that there is none other God but Him.[604]

It is inadmissible that man, who hath been endowed with reason, should consume that which stealeth it away. Nay, rather it behoveth him to comport himself in a manner worthy of the human station, and not in accordance with the misdeeds of every heedless and wavering soul.[605]

It is forbidden for an intelligent person to drink that which depriveth him of his intelligence; it behoveth him to engage in that which is worthy of man, not in the act of every heedless doubter.[606]

Become ye intoxicated with the wine of the love of God, and not with that which deadeneth your minds, O ye that adore Him! Verily, it hath been forbidden unto every believer, whether man or woman.[607]

Gambling and the use of opium have been forbidden unto you. Eschew them both, O people, and be not of those who transgress. Beware of using any substance that induceth sluggishness and torpor in the human temple and inflicteth harm upon the body. We, verily, desire for you naught save what shall profit you, and to this bear witness all created things, had ye but ears to hear.[608]

Living in seclusion or practising asceticism is not acceptable in the presence of God.[609]

The kissing of hands hath been forbidden in the Book. This practice is prohibited by God, the Lord of glory and command. To none is it permitted to seek absolution from another soul; let repentance be between yourselves and God. He, verily, is the Pardoner, the Bounteous, the Gracious, the One Who absolveth the repentant.[610]

Waste not your hours in idleness and sloth, but occupy yourselves with what will profit you and others. Thus hath it been decreed in this Tablet from whose horizon hath shone the day-star of wisdom and utterance. The most despised of men in the sight of God are they who sit and beg. Hold ye fast unto the cord of means and place your trust in God, the Provider of all means.[611]

It is unlawful to beg, and it is forbidden to give to him who beggeth. All have been enjoined to earn a living, and as for those who are incapable of doing so, it is incumbent on the Deputies of God and on the wealthy to make adequate provision for them.[612]

It hath been forbidden you to carry arms unless essential....[613]

Beware lest ye shed the blood of anyone. Unsheathe the sword of your tongue from the scabbard of utterance, for therewith ye can conquer the citadels of men's hearts. We have abolished the law to wage holy war against each other. God's mercy, hath, verily, encompassed all created things, if ye do but understand.[614]

Take heed that ye enter no house in the absence of its owner, except with his permission. Comport yourselves with propriety under all conditions, and be not numbered with the wayward.[615]

They who dwell within the tabernacle of God, and are established upon the seats of everlasting glory, will refuse, though they be dying of hunger, to stretch their hands and seize unlawfully the property of their neighbor, however vile and worthless he may be.[616]

Burden not an animal with more than it can bear. We, truly, have prohibited such treatment through a most binding interdiction in the Book. Be ye the embodiments of justice and fairness amidst all creation.[617]

It is forbidden you to transport the body of the deceased a greater distance than one hour's journey from the city; rather should it be interred, with radiance and serenity, in a nearby place.[618]

O SON OF MAN! Breathe not the sins of others so long as thou art thyself a sinner. Shouldst thou transgress this command, accursed wouldst thou be, and to this I bear witness.[619]

O people of the world! Follow not the promptings of the self, for it summoneth insistently to wickedness and lust; follow, rather, Him Who is the Possessor of all created things, Who biddeth you to show forth piety, and manifest the fear of God.[620]

Were He to decree as lawful the thing which from time immemorial had been forbidden, and forbid that which had, at all times, been regarded as lawful, to none is given the right to question His authority. Whoso will hesitate, though it be for less than a moment, should be regarded as a transgressor.

Whoso hath not recognized this sublime and fundamental verity, and hath failed to attain this most exalted station, the winds of doubt will agitate him, and the sayings of the infidels will distract his soul. He that hath acknowledged this principle will be endowed with the most perfect constancy. All honour to this all-glorious station, the remembrance of which adorneth every exalted Tablet.[621]

O SON OF MAN! Neglect not My commandments if thou lovest My beauty, and forget not My counsels if thou wouldst attain My good pleasure.[622]

Fear of God

The essence of wisdom is the fear of God, the dread of His scourge and punishment, and the apprehension of His justice and decree.[623]

The word of God which the Abhá Pen hath revealed and inscribed on the

first leaf

of the Most Exalted Paradise is this: Verily I say: The fear of God hath ever been a sure defence and a safe stronghold for all the peoples of the world. It is the chief cause of the protection of mankind, and the supreme instrument for its preservation.[624]

We have admonished Our loved ones to fear God, a fear which is the fountainhead of all goodly deeds and virtues. It is the commander of the hosts of justice in the city of Bahá. Happy the man that hath entered the shadow of its luminous standard, and laid fast hold thereon.[625]

Say: Fear ye God and commit not such deeds as would cause My loved ones on earth to lament.[626]

We enjoin the servants of God and His handmaidens to be pure and to fear God, that they may shake off the slumber of their corrupt desires, and turn toward God, the Maker of the heavens and of the earth.[627]

The fear of God hath ever been the prime factor in the education of His creatures. Well is it with them that have attained thereunto! [628]

The fourth Ishráq

In this Revelation the hosts that can render it victorious are the hosts of praiseworthy deeds and upright character. The leader and commander of these hosts hath ever been the fear of God, a fear that encompasseth all things and reigneth over all things.[629]

Know ye that I am afraid of none except God. In none but Him have I placed My trust; to none will I cleave but Him, and wish for naught except the thing He hath wished for Me. This, indeed, is My heart's desire, did ye but know it. I have offered up My soul and My body as a sacrifice for God, the Lord of all worlds. Whoso hath known God shall know none but Him, and he that feareth God shall be afraid of no one except Him, though the powers of the whole earth rise up and be arrayed against him. I speak naught except at His bidding, and follow naught, through the power of God and His might, except His truth. He, verily, shall recompense the truthful.[630]

In formulating the principles and laws a part hath been devoted to penalties which form an effective instrument for the security and protection of men. However, dread of the penalties maketh people desist only outwardly from committing vile and contemptible deeds, while that which guardeth and restraineth man both outwardly and inwardly hath been and still is the fear of God. It is man's true protector and his spiritual guardian. It behoveth him to cleave tenaciously unto that which will lead to the appearance of this supreme bounty. Well is it with him who giveth ear unto whatsoever My Pen of Glory hath proclaimed and observeth that whereunto he is bidden by the Ordainer, the Ancient of Days.[631]

Say: O people! Fear ye God, and turn not away disdainfully from His Revelation.[632]

Tests and Difficulties

O SON OF MAN! My calamity is My providence, outwardly it is fire and vengeance, but inwardly it is light and mercy. Hasten thereunto that thou mayest become an eternal light and an immortal spirit. This is My command unto thee, do thou observe it.[633]

... the Almighty hath tried, and will continue to try, His servants, so that light may be distinguished from darkness, truth from falsehood, right from wrong, guidance from error, happiness from misery, and roses from thorns. Even as He hath revealed: "Do men think when they say 'We believe' they shall be let alone and not be put to proof?" [634] [635]

Know ye that trials and tribulations have, from time immemorial, been the lot of the chosen Ones of God and His beloved, and such of His servants as are detached from all else but Him, they whom neither merchandise nor traffic beguile from the remembrance of the Almighty, they that speak not till He hath spoken, and act according to His commandment. Such is God's method carried into effect of old, and such will it remain in the future. Blessed are the steadfastly enduring, they that are patient under ills and hardships, who lament not over anything that befalleth them, and who tread the path of resignation.[636]

O SON OF MAN! If adversity befall thee not in My path, how canst thou walk in the ways of them that are content with My pleasure? If trials afflict thee not in thy longing to meet Me, how wilt thou attain the light in thy love for My beauty? [637]

O SON OF MAN! For everything there is a sign. The sign of love is fortitude under My decree and patience under My trials.[638]

O SON OF MAN! The true lover yearneth for tribulation even as doth the rebel for forgiveness and the sinful for mercy.[639]

O SON OF BEING! Busy not thyself with this world, for with fire We test the gold, and with gold We test Our servants.[640]

...such things as throw consternation into the hearts of all men come to pass only that each soul may be tested by the touchstone of God, that the true may be known and distinguished from the false.[641]

Glorified art Thou, O Lord my God! Every man of insight confesseth Thy sovereignty and Thy dominion, and every discerning eye perceiveth the greatness of Thy majesty and the compelling power of Thy might. The winds of tests are powerless to hold back them that enjoy near access to Thee from setting their faces towards the horizon of Thy glory, and the tempests of trials must fail to draw away and hinder such as are wholly devoted to Thy will from approaching Thy court.

Methinks, the lamp of Thy love is burning in their hearts, and the light of Thy tenderness is lit within their breasts. Adversities are incapable of estranging them from Thy Cause, and the vicissitudes of fortune can never cause them to stray from Thy pleasure.

I beseech Thee, O my God, by them and by the sighs which their hearts utter in their separation from Thee, to keep them safe from the mischief of Thine adversaries, and to nourish their souls with what Thou hast ordained for Thy loved ones on whom shall come no fear and who shall not be put to grief.[642]

All praise be to Thee...Armed with the power of Thy name nothing can ever hurt me, and with Thy love in my heart all the world's afflictions can in no wise alarm me.[643]

O My servants! Sorrow not if, in these days and on this earthly plane, things contrary to your wishes have been ordained and manifested by God, for days of blissful joy, of heavenly delight, are assuredly in store for you. Worlds, holy and spiritually glorious, will be unveiled to your eyes. You are destined by Him, in this world and hereafter, to partake of their benefits, to share in their joys, and to obtain a portion of their sustaining grace. To each and every one of them you will, no doubt, attain.[644]

Repentance and Divine Forgiveness

The ninth Glad-Tidings

When the sinner findeth himself wholly detached and freed from all save God, he should beg forgiveness and pardon from Him. Confession of sins and transgressions before human beings is not permissible, as it hath never been nor will ever be conducive to divine forgiveness. Moreover such confession before people results in one's humiliation and abasement, and God—exalted be His glory—wisheth not the humiliation of His servants. Verily He is the Compassionate, the Merciful. The sinner should, between himself and God, implore mercy from the Ocean of mercy, beg forgiveness from the Heaven of generosity and say:

O God, my God! I implore Thee by the blood of Thy true lovers who were so enraptured by Thy sweet utterance that they hastened unto the Pinnacle of Glory, the site of the most glorious martyrdom, and I beseech Thee by the mysteries which lie enshrined in Thy knowledge and by the pearls that are treasured in the ocean of Thy bounty to grant forgiveness unto me and unto my father and my mother. Of those who show forth mercy, Thou art in truth the Most Merciful. No God is there but Thee, the Ever-Forgiving, the All-Bountiful.[645]

Thus have We recounted unto you the tales of the one true God, and sent down unto you the things He had preordained, that haply ye may ask forgiveness of Him, may return unto Him, may truly repent, may realize your misdeeds, may shake off your slumber, may be roused from your heedlessness, may atone for the things that have escaped you, and be of them that do good. Let him who will, acknowledge the truth of My words; and as to him that willeth not, let him turn aside. My sole duty is to remind you of your failure in duty towards the Cause of God, if perchance ye may be of them that heed My warning. Wherefore, hearken ye unto My speech, and return ye to God and repent, that He, through His grace, may have mercy upon you, may wash away your sins, and forgive your trespasses. The greatness of His mercy surpasseth the fury of His wrath, and His grace encompasseth all who have been called into being and been clothed with the robe of life, be they of the past or of the future.[646]

I am a sinner, O my Lord, and Thou art the Ever-Forgiving. As soon as I recognized Thee, I hastened to attain the exalted court of Thy loving-kindness. Forgive me, O my Lord, my sins which have hindered me from walking in the ways of Thy good-pleasure, and from attaining the shores of the ocean of Thy oneness.

There is no one, O my Lord, who can deal bountifully with me to whom I can turn my face, and none who can have compassion on me that I may crave his mercy. Cast me not out, I implore Thee, of the presence of Thy grace, neither do Thou withhold from me the outpourings of Thy generosity and bounty. Ordain for me, O my Lord, what Thou hast ordained for them that love Thee, and write down for me what Thou hast written down for Thy chosen ones. My gaze hath, at all times, been fixed on the horizon of Thy gracious providence, and mine eyes bent upon the court of Thy tender mercies. Do with me as beseemeth Thee. No God is there but Thee, the God of power, the God of glory, Whose help is implored by all men.[647]

He Who is the Eternal Truth knoweth well what the breasts of men conceal. His long forbearance hath emboldened His creatures, for not until the appointed time is come will He rend any veil asunder. His surpassing mercy hath restrained the fury of His wrath, and caused most people to imagine that the one true God is unaware of the things they have privily committed. By Him Who is the All-Knowing, the All-Informed! The mirror of His knowledge reflecteth, with complete distinctness, precision and fidelity, the doings of all men. Say: Praise be to Thee, O Concealer of the sins of the weak and helpless! Magnified be Thy name, O Thou that forgivest the heedless ones that trespass against Thee! [648]

O Lord! Thou seest this essence of sinfulness turning unto the ocean of Thy favour and this feeble one seeking the kingdom of Thy divine power and this poor creature inclining himself towards the day-star of Thy wealth. By Thy mercy and Thy grace, disappoint him not, O Lord, nor debar him from the revelations of Thy bounty in Thy days, nor cast him away from Thy door which Thou hast opened wide to all that dwell in Thy heaven and on Thine earth.

Alas! Alas! My sins have prevented me from approaching the Court of Thy holiness and my trespasses have caused me to stray far from the Tabernacle of Thy majesty. I have committed that which Thou didst forbid me to do and have put away what Thou didst order me to observe.

I pray Thee by Him Who is the sovereign Lord of Names to write down for me with the Pen of Thy bounty that which will enable me to draw nigh unto Thee and will purge me from my trespasses which have intervened between me and Thy forgiveness and Thy pardon.

Verily, Thou art the Potent, the Bountiful. No God is there but Thee, the Mighty, the Gracious.[649]

Physical Death

O SON OF THE SUPREME! I have made death a messenger of joy to thee. Wherefore dost thou grieve? [650]

O SON OF MAN! Thou art My dominion and My dominion perisheth not; wherefore fearest thou thy perishing? Thou art My light and My light shall never be extinguished; why dost thou dread extinction? Thou art My glory and My glory fadeth not; thou art My robe and My robe shall never be outworn. Abide then in thy love for Me, that thou mayest find Me in the realm of glory.[651]

Know thou that every hearing ear, if kept pure and undefiled, must, at all times and from every direction, hearken to the voice that uttereth these holy words: "Verily, we are God's, and to Him shall we return." The mysteries of man's physical death and of his return have not been divulged, and still remain unread. By the righteousness of God! Were they to be revealed, they would evoke such fear and sorrow that some would perish, while others would be so filled with gladness as to wish for death, and beseech, with unceasing longing, the one true God—exalted be His glory—to hasten their end.

Death proffereth unto every confident believer the cup that is life indeed. It bestoweth joy, and is the bearer of gladness. It conferreth the gift of everlasting life.[652]

O COMPANION OF MY THRONE! ...Live then the days of thy life, that are less than a fleeting moment, with thy mind stainless, thy heart unsullied, thy thoughts pure, and thy nature sanctified, so that, free and content, thou mayest put away this mortal frame, and repair unto the mystic paradise and abide in the eternal kingdom for evermore.[653]

Ye are all created out of water, and unto dust shall ye return. Reflect upon the end that awaiteth you, and walk not in the ways of the oppressor. Give ear unto the verses of God which He Who is the sacred Lote-Tree reciteth unto you. They are assuredly the infallible balance, established by God, the Lord of this world and the next. Through them the soul of man is caused to wing its flight towards the Dayspring of Revelation, and the heart of every true believer is suffused with light. Such are the laws which God hath enjoined upon you, such His commandments prescribed unto you in His Holy Tablet; obey them with joy and gladness, for this is best for you, did ye but know.[654]

Called to an Accounting

It is clear and evident that all men shall, after their physical death, estimate the worth of their deeds, and realize all that their hands have wrought. I swear by the Day Star that shineth above the horizon of Divine power! They that are the followers of the one true God shall, the moment they depart out of this life, experience such joy and gladness as would be impossible to describe, while they that live in error shall be seized with such fear and trembling, and shall be filled with such consternation, as nothing can exceed. Well is it with him that hath quaffed the choice and incorruptible wine of faith through the gracious favor and the manifold bounties of Him Who is the Lord of all Faiths....[655]

Know ye that the world and its vanities and its embellishments shall pass away. Nothing will endure except God's Kingdom which pertaineth to none but Him, the Sovereign Lord of all, the Help in Peril, the All-Glorious, the Almighty. The days of your life shall roll away, and all the things with which ye are occupied and of which ye boast yourselves shall perish, and ye shall, most certainly, be summoned by a company of His angels to appear at the spot where the limbs of the entire creation shall be made to tremble, and the flesh of every oppressor to creep. Ye shall be asked of the things your hands have wrought in this, your vain life, and shall be repaid for your doings. This is the day that shall inevitably come upon you, the hour that none can put back. To this the Tongue of Him that speaketh the truth and is the Knower of all things hath testified.[656]

Thou shalt, after thy departure, discover what We have revealed unto thee, and shalt find all thy doings recorded in the Book wherein the works of all them that dwell on earth, be they greater or less than the weight of an atom, are noted down.[657]

Set before thine eyes God's unerring Balance and, as one standing in His Presence, weigh in that Balance thine actions every day, every moment of thy life. Bring thyself to account ere thou art summoned to a reckoning, on the Day when no man shall have strength to stand for fear of God, the Day when the hearts of the heedless ones shall be made to tremble.[658]

O SON OF BEING! Bring thyself to account each day ere thou art summoned to a reckoning; for death, unheralded, shall come upon thee and thou shalt be called to give account for thy deeds.[659]

...every man hath been, and will continue to be, able of himself to appreciate the Beauty of God, the Glorified. Had he not been endowed with such a capacity, how could he be called to account for his failure? If, in the Day when all the peoples of the earth will be gathered together, any man should, whilst standing in the presence of God, be asked: "Wherefore hast thou disbelieved in My Beauty and turned away from My Self," and if such a man should reply and say: "Inasmuch as all men have erred, and none hath been found willing to turn his face to the Truth, I, too, following their example, have grievously failed to recognize the Beauty of the Eternal," such a plea will, assuredly, be rejected. For the faith of no man can be conditioned by any one except himself.[660]

O MY FRIENDS! Quench ye the lamp of error, and kindle within your hearts the everlasting torch of divine guidance. For ere long the assayers of mankind shall, in the holy presence of the Adored, accept naught but purest virtue and deeds of stainless holiness.[661]

Paradise and Hell

The purpose of God in creating man hath been, and will ever be, to enable him to know his Creator and to attain His Presence. To this most excellent aim, this supreme objective, all the heavenly Books and the divinely-revealed and weighty Scriptures unequivocally bear witness. Whoso hath recognized the Day Spring of Divine guidance and entered His holy court hath drawn nigh unto God and attained His Presence, a Presence which is the real Paradise, and of which the loftiest mansions of heaven are but a symbol. Such a man hath attained the knowledge of the station of Him Who is at the distance of two bows, Who standeth beyond the Sadratu'l-Muntahá. Whoso hath failed to recognize Him will have condemned himself to the misery of remoteness, a remoteness which is naught but utter nothingness and the essence of the nethermost fire.[662]

Even as Jesus...saith: "Except a man be born of water and of the Spirit, he cannot enter into the Kingdom of God. That which is born of the flesh is flesh; and that which is born of the Spirit is spirit."[663] The purport of these words is that whosoever in every dispensation is born of the Spirit and is quickened by the breath of the Manifestation of Holiness, he verily is of those that have attained unto "life" and "resurrection" and have entered into the "paradise" of the love of God. And whosoever is not of them, is condemned to "death" and "deprivation," to the "fire" of unbelief, and to the "wrath" of God. In all the scriptures, the books and chronicles, the sentence of death, of fire, of blindness, of want of understanding and hearing, hath been pronounced against those whose lips have tasted not the ethereal cup of true knowledge, and whose hearts have been deprived of the grace of the holy Spirit in their day.[664]

Incline your ears to the sweet melody of this Prisoner. Arise, and lift up your voices, that haply they that are fast asleep may be awakened. Say: O ye who are as dead! The Hand of Divine bounty proffereth unto you the Water of Life. Hasten and drink your fill. Whoso hath been reborn in this Day, shall never die; whoso remaineth dead, shall never live.[665]

The most burning fire is to question the signs of God, to dispute idly that which He hath revealed, to deny Him and carry one's self proudly before Him.[666]

As to Paradise: It is a reality and there can be no doubt about it, and now in this world it is realized through love of Me and My good-pleasure. Whosoever attaineth unto it God will aid him in this world below, and after death He will enable him to gain admittance into Paradise whose vastness is as that of heaven and earth. Therein the Maids of glory and holiness will wait upon him in the daytime and in the night season, while the day-star of the unfading beauty of his Lord will at all times shed its radiance upon him and he will shine so brightly that no one shall bear to gaze at him. Such is the dispensation of Providence, yet the people are shut out by a grievous veil. Likewise apprehend thou the nature of hell-fire and be of them that truly believe. For every act performed there shall be a recompense according to the estimate of God, and unto this the very ordinances and prohibitions prescribed by the Almighty amply bear witness. For surely if deeds were not rewarded and yielded no fruit, then the Cause of God—exalted is He—would prove futile. Immeasurably high is He exalted above such blasphemies! However, unto them that are rid of all attachments a deed is, verily, its own reward. Were We to enlarge upon this theme numerous Tablets would need to be written.[667]

Is there any doubt concerning God? Behold how He hath come down from the heaven of His grace, girded with power and invested with sovereignty. Is there any doubt concerning His signs? Open ye your eyes, and consider His clear evidence. Paradise is on your right hand, and hath been brought nigh unto you, while Hell hath been made to blaze. Witness its devouring flame. Haste ye to enter into Paradise, as a token of Our mercy unto you, and drink ye from the hands of the All-Merciful the Wine that is life indeed.[668]

His glory be with thee, inasmuch as thou hast journeyed from God unto God, and entered within the borders of the Court of unfading splendor—the Spot which mortal man can never describe. Therein hath the breeze of holiness, laden with the love of thy Lord, stirred thy spirit within thee, and the waters of understanding have washed from thee the stains of remoteness and ungodliness. Thou hast gained admittance into the Paradise of God's Remembrance, through thy recognition of Him Who is the Embodiment of that Remembrance amongst men.[669]

Tear asunder, in My Name, the veils that have grievously blinded your vision, and, through the power born of your belief in the unity of God, scatter the idols of vain imitation. Enter, then, the holy paradise of the good-pleasure of the All-Merciful. Sanctify your souls from whatsoever is not of God, and taste ye the sweetness of rest within the pale of His vast and mighty Revelation, and beneath the shadow of His supreme and infallible authority. Suffer not yourselves to be wrapt in the dense veils of your selfish desires, inasmuch as I have perfected in every one of you My creation, so that the excellence of My handiwork may be fully revealed unto men.[670]

Wert thou to ponder in thine heart the behavior of the Prophets of God thou wouldst assuredly and readily testify that there must needs be other worlds besides this world. The majority of the truly wise and learned have, throughout the ages, as it hath been recorded by the Pen of Glory in the Tablet of Wisdom, borne witness to the truth of that which the holy Writ of God hath revealed. Even the materialists have testified in their writings to the wisdom of these divinely-appointed Messengers, and have regarded the references made by the Prophets to Paradise, to hell fire, to future reward and punishment, to have been actuated by a desire to educate and uplift the souls of men. Consider, therefore, how the generality of mankind, whatever their beliefs or theories, have recognized the excellence, and admitted the superiority, of these Prophets of God. These Gems of Detachment are acclaimed by some as the embodiments of wisdom, while others believe them to be the mouthpiece of God Himself. How could such Souls have consented to surrender themselves unto their enemies if they believed all the worlds of God to have been reduced to this earthly life? Would they have willingly suffered such afflictions and torments as no man hath ever experienced or witnessed? [671]

The Prophets of God have come in truth and have spoken the truth. Whatsoever the Messenger of God hath announced hath been and will be made manifest. The world is established upon the foundations of reward and punishment. Knowledge and understanding have ever affirmed and will continue to affirm the reality of Paradise and Hell, for reward and punishment require their existence. Paradise signifieth first and foremost the good-pleasure of God. Whosoever attaineth His good-pleasure is reckoned and recorded among the inhabitants of the most exalted paradise and will attain, after the ascension of his soul, that which pen and ink are powerless to describe. For them that are endued with insight and have fixed their gaze upon the Most Sublime Vision, the Bridge, the Balance, Paradise, Hellfire, and all that hath been mentioned and recorded in the Sacred Scriptures are clear and manifest. At the time of the appearance and manifestation of the rays of the Daystar of Truth, all occupy the same station. God then proclaimeth that which He willeth, and whoso heareth His call and acknowledgeth His truth is accounted among the inhabitants of Paradise. Such a soul hath traversed the Bridge, the Balance, and all that hath been recorded regarding the Day of Resurrection, and hath reached his destination. The Day of God's Revelation is the Day of the most great Resurrection.[672]

O SON OF BEING! Thy Paradise is My love; thy heavenly home, reunion with Me. Enter therein and tarry not. This is that which hath been destined for thee in Our kingdom above and Our exalted dominion.[673]

They say: "Where is Paradise, and where is Hell?" Say: "The one is reunion with Me; the other thine own self...."[674]

O People of Bahá

By the righteousness of God! The world and its vanities, and its glory, and whatever delights it can offer, are all, in the sight of God, as worthless as, nay, even more contemptible than, dust and ashes. Would that the hearts of men could comprehend it! Cleanse yourselves thoroughly, O people of Bahá, from the defilement of the world, and of all that pertaineth unto it. God Himself beareth Me witness. The things of the earth ill beseem you. Cast them away unto such as may desire them, and fasten your eyes upon this most holy and effulgent Vision.[675]

...O ye My loved ones! Suffer not the hem of My sacred vesture to be smirched and mired with the things of this world, and follow not the promptings of your evil and corrupt desires.[676]

...O ye the beloved of the one true God! Pass beyond the narrow retreats of your evil and corrupt desires, and advance into the vast immensity of the realm of God, and abide ye in the meads of sanctity and of detachment, that the fragrance of your deeds may lead the whole of mankind to the ocean of God's unfading glory.[677]

Disencumber yourselves of all attachment to this world and the vanities thereof. Beware that ye approach them not, inasmuch as they prompt you to walk after your own lusts and covetous desires, and hinder you from entering the straight and glorious Path.[678]

Eschew all manner of wickedness, for such things are forbidden unto you in the Book which none touch except such as God hath cleansed from every taint of guilt, and numbered among the purified.[679]

A race of men...incomparable in character, shall be raised up which, with the feet of detachment, will tread under all who are in heaven and on earth, and will cast the sleeve of holiness over all that hath been created from water and clay.[680]

O friends! Be not careless of the virtues with which ye have been endowed, neither be neglectful of your high destiny.... Ye are the stars of the heaven of understanding, the breeze that stirreth at the break of day, the soft-flowing waters upon which must depend the very life of all men, the letters inscribed upon His sacred scroll.

O people of Bahá! Ye are the breezes of spring that are wafted over the world. Through you We have adorned the world of being with the ornament of the knowledge of the Most Merciful. Through you the countenance of the world hath been wreathed in smiles, and the brightness of His light shone forth. Cling ye to the Cord of steadfastness, in such wise that all vain imaginings may utterly vanish. Speed ye forth from the horizon of power, in the name of your Lord, the Unconstrained, and announce unto His servants, with wisdom and eloquence, the tidings of this Cause, whose splendor hath been shed upon the world of being. Beware lest anything withhold you from observing the things prescribed unto you by the Pen of Glory, as it moved over His Tablet with sovereign majesty and might. Great is the blessedness of him that hath hearkened to its shrill voice, as it was raised, through the power of truth, before all who are in heaven and all who are on earth. O people of Bahá! The river that is Life indeed hath flowed for your sakes. Quaff ye in My name, despite them that have disbelieved in God, the Lord of Revelation. We have made you to be the hands of Our Cause. Render ye victorious this Wronged One, Who hath been sore-tried in the hands of the workers of iniquity. He, verily, will aid everyone that aideth Him, and will remember everyone that remembereth Him. To this beareth witness this Tablet that hath shed the splendor of the loving-kindness of your Lord, the All-Glorious, the All-Compelling.

Blessed are the people of Bahá! God beareth Me witness! They are the solace of the eye of creation. Through them the universes have been adorned, and the Preserved Tablet embellished. They are the ones who have sailed on the ark of complete independence, with their faces set towards the Dayspring of Beauty. How great is their blessedness that they have attained unto what their Lord, the Omniscient, the All-Wise, hath willed. Through their light the heavens have been adorned, and the faces of those that have drawn nigh unto Him made to shine.[681]

Adorn your heads with the garlands of trustworthiness and fidelity, your hearts with the attire of the fear of God, your tongues with absolute truthfulness, your bodies with the vesture of courtesy. These are in truth seemly adornings unto the temple of man, if ye be of them that reflect. Cling, O ye people of Bahá, to the cord of servitude unto God, the True One, for thereby your stations shall be made manifest, your names written and preserved, your ranks raised and your memory exalted in the Preserved Tablet. Beware lest the dwellers on earth hinder you from this glorious and exalted station. Thus have We exhorted you in most of Our Epistles and now in this, Our Holy Tablet, above which hath beamed the Day-Star of the Laws of the Lord, your God, the Powerful, the All-Wise.[682]

Essence of the Wisdom of Bahá'u'lláh

In the Name of God, the Exalted, the Most High

THE source of all good is trust in God, submission unto His command, and contentment with His holy will and pleasure.

The essence of wisdom is the fear of God, the dread of His scourge and punishment, and the apprehension of His justice and decree.

The essence of religion is to testify unto that which the Lord hath revealed, and follow that which He hath ordained in His mighty Book.

The source of all glory is acceptance of whatsoever the Lord hath bestowed, and contentment with that which God hath ordained.

The essence of love is for man to turn his heart to the Beloved One, and sever himself from all else but Him, and desire naught save that which is the desire of his Lord.

True remembrance is to make mention of the Lord, the All-Praised, and forget aught else beside Him.

True reliance is for the servant to pursue his profession and calling in this world, to hold fast unto the Lord, to seek naught but His grace, inasmuch as in His Hands is the destiny of all His servants.

The essence of detachment is for man to turn his face towards the courts of the Lord, to enter His Presence, behold His Countenance, and stand as witness before Him.

The essence of understanding is to testify to one's poverty, and submit to the Will of the Lord, the Sovereign, the Gracious, the All-Powerful.

The source of courage and power is the promotion of the Word of God, and steadfastness in His Love.

The essence of charity is for the servant to recount the blessings of his Lord, and to render thanks unto Him at all times and under all conditions.

The essence of faith is fewness of words and abundance of deeds; he whose words exceed his deeds, know verily his death is better than his life.

The essence of true safety is to observe silence, to look at the end of things and to renounce the world.

The beginning of magnanimity is when man expendeth his wealth on himself, on his family and on the poor among his brethren in his Faith.

The essence of wealth is love for Me; whoso loveth Me is the possessor of all things, and he that loveth Me not is indeed of the poor and needy. This is that which the Finger of Glory and Splendour hath revealed.

The source of all evil is for man to turn away from his Lord and set his heart on things ungodly.

The most burning fire is to question the signs of God, to dispute idly that which He hath revealed, to deny Him and carry one's self proudly before Him.

The source of all learning is the knowledge of God, exalted be His Glory, and this cannot be attained save through the knowledge of His Divine Manifestation.

The essence of abasement is to pass out from under the shadow of the Merciful and seek the shelter of the Evil One.

The source of error is to disbelieve in the One true God, rely upon aught else but Him, and flee from His Decree.

True loss is for him whose days have been spent in utter ignorance of his self.

The essence of all that We have revealed for thee is Justice, is for man to free himself from idle fancy and imitation, discern with the eye of oneness His glorious handiwork, and look into all things with a searching eye.

Thus have We instructed thee, manifested unto thee Words of Wisdom, that thou mayest be thankful unto the Lord, thy God, and glory therein amidst all peoples.[683]

This is the Voice of God, if ye do but hearken. This is the Day Spring of the Revelation of God, did ye but know it. This is the Dawning-Place of the Cause of God, were ye to recognize it. This is the Source of the commandment of God, did ye but judge it fairly. This is the manifest and hidden Secret; would that ye might perceive it. O peoples of the world! Cast away, in My name that transcendeth all other names, the things ye possess, and immerse yourselves in this Ocean in whose depths lay hidden the pearls of wisdom and of utterance, an ocean that surgeth in My name, the All-Merciful.

Bahá'u'lláh

Notes

The abbreviated titles refer to the indicated publications:

Compilations	"The Compilation of Compilations"
Gems	"Gems of Divine Mysteries"
Gleanings	"Gleanings from the Writings of Bahá'u'lláh"
Hidden Words	"The Hidden Words of Bahá'u'lláh"
Kitáb-i-Aqdas	"The Kitáb-i-Aqdas"
Kitáb-i-Íqán	"The Kitáb-i-Íqán"
Prayers and Meditations	"Prayers and Meditations by Bahá'u'lláh"
Proclamation	"The Proclamation of Bahá'u'lláh"
Seven Valleys	"The Seven Valleys and The Four Valleys"
Summons	"The Summons of the Lord of Hosts"
Tabernacle	"Tabernacle of Unity"
Tablets of Bahá'u'lláh	"Tablets of Bahá'u'lláh Revealed after the Kitáb-i-Aqdas"

The symbol and abbreviations noted below are used in the citations:

#	number of an extract or selection in a compilation
p. [or] pp.	"page" [or] "pages"
par. [or] pars.	"paragraph" (number) [or] "paragraphs"
sec.	"section" (number)
vol.	"volume" (number)

Introduction

[1] Bahá'u'lláh, *Proclamation*, p. viii.

[2] See http://bahaitributes.wordpress.com.

[3] Ervin László; Hungarian philosopher of science and systems theorist. He has published more than 70 books and is editor of *World Futures: The Journal of General Evolution*.

[4] Dan Rather; CBS Evening News anchor from 1981-2005, and 60 Minutes correspondent from 1968-1981 and 1999-2006.

[5] Bahá'u'lláh, *Epistle to the Son of the Wolf*, p. 147.

[6] Shoghi Effendi, *The World Order of Bahá'u'lláh*, p. 100.

[7] 'Abdu'l-Bahá (23 May 1844 - 28 November 1921), was the eldest son of Bahá'u'lláh. In 1892, 'Abdu'l-Bahá was appointed in his father's will to be His successor and head of the Bahá'í Faith.

8 Bahá'u'lláh, *Gleanings*, CLI, p. 321.
9 'Abdu'l-Bahá, *The Promulgation of Universal Peace*, pp. 334-335.
10 Bahá'u'lláh, *Gleanings*, CXLVII, p. 317.
11 Bahá'í International Community, Statement on Baha'u'lláh, p. 8.
12 Bahá'u'lláh, *Summons*, pp. 64-65.
13 Bahá'u'lláh, *Epistle to the Son of the Wolf*, p. 44.
14 Bahá'u'lláh, *Tablets of Bahá'u'lláh*, p. 132.
15 Bahá'u'lláh, The *Kitáb-i-Íqán*, p. 134.
16 Bahá'u'lláh, cited in *The Promised Day is Come*, p. 6.
17 Bahá'u'lláh, *Gleanings*, CXVIII, p. 253.
18 Bahá'u'lláh, *Kitáb-i-Aqdas*, par. 149.
19 Bahá'u'lláh, *Hidden Words*, Persian #44.
20 Bahá'u'lláh, *Seven Valleys*, p. 35.
21 Bahá'u'lláh, *Hidden Words*, Arabic #59.
22 Bahá'u'lláh, *Gems*, p. 18.

Chapter 1 – God

God: The Unknowable Essence
1 Bahá'u'lláh, *Prayers and Meditations*, CLXXXIV, pp. 327-328.
2 Bahá'u'lláh, *Gleanings*, I, pp. 3-4.
3 Ibid., XXVI, pp. 60-61.
4 Bahá'u'lláh, *Kitáb-i-Íqán*, p. 98.
5 Bahá'u'lláh, *Gleanings*, XXVI, pp. 62-63.
6 Bahá'u'lláh, *Prayers and Meditations*, CLXXVI, p. 273.

Unity of God
7 Bahá'u'lláh, *Prayers and Meditations*, LVII, pp. 86-87.
8 Bahá'u'lláh, *Gleanings*, CXXIV, pp. 261-262.
9 Ibid., LXXXII, p. 162.
10 Ibid., LXXXIV, p. 166.
11 Ibid., LXXXIV, pp. 166-167.
12 Ibid., XCIV, pp. 192-193.

God: The Creator
13 Bahá'u'lláh, *Gleanings*, LXXVIII, p. 150.
14 Ibid., XXVII, pp. 64-65.
15 Ibid., XXVI, p. 61.
16 Ibid., XXVI, p. 62.
17 Bahá'u'lláh, *Tablets of Bahá'u'lláh*, pp. 187-188.
18 Ibid., p. 140.
19 Ibid., p. 141.

20 Ibid., p. 142.
21 Bahá'u'lláh, *Gleanings*, LXXVII, p. 149.
22 Ibid., XCV, p. 194.
23 Bahá'u'lláh, *Prayers and Meditations*, LVII, p. 87.

Word of God
24 Bahá'u'lláh, *Tablets of Bahá'u'lláh*, p. 173.
25 Bahá'u'lláh, *Tabernacle*, p. 47.
26 Bahá'u'lláh, *Tablets of Bahá'u'lláh*, pp. 140-141.
27 Bahá'u'lláh, *Gleanings*, LXXIV, pp. 141-142.
28 Ibid., XXXIII, pp. 76-77.
29 Bahá'u'lláh, *Tabernacle*, pp. 3-4.
30 Bahá'u'lláh, *Gleanings*, LXXXIX, p. 175.

Signs of God
31 Bahá'u'lláh, *Gleanings*, LXXXII, p. 160.
32 Ibid., XXVI, p. 62.
33 Bahá'u'lláh, *Prayers and Meditations*, CLXXVI, pp. 271-272.
34 Bahá'u'lláh, *Gleanings*, XCIII, p. 184.
35 Ibid., CXXIV, p. 262.
36 Ibid., LII, pp. 105-106.
37 Ibid., VCIII, p. 187.
38 Bahá'u'lláh, *Prayers and Meditations*, CLXXVIII, p. 295.

Love Between God and Mankind
39 Bahá'u'lláh, *Hidden Words*, Arabic #4.
40 Ibid., Arabic #3.
41 Ibid., Arabic #5.
42 Ibid., Arabic #9.
43 Ibid., Arabic #7.
44 Ibid., Arabic #10.
45 Ibid., Arabic #19.
46 Ibid., Arabic #20.
47 Ibid., Arabic #65.
48 Ibid., Arabic #66.
49 Ibid., Persian #4.
50 Ibid., Persian #7.
51 Ibid., Persian #34.
52 Ibid., Persian #52.
53 Bahá'u'lláh, *Tablets of Bahá'u'lláh*, p. 129.
54 Bahá'u'lláh, *Gleanings*, CXXIII, p. 261.
55 Ibid., CXXXIX, pp. 304-305.
56 Bahá'u'lláh, *Tablets of Bahá'u'lláh*, p. 155.
57 Bahá'u'lláh, *Gleanings*, XV, p. 36.

Chapter 2 – Manifestations of God

Manifestations of God
[58] Bahá'u'lláh, *Kitáb-i-Íqán*, pp. 99-103.
[59] Bahá'u'lláh, *Gleanings*, XXVII, p. 66.
[60] Ibid., XXVII, pp. 67-68.
[61] Bahá'u'lláh, *Kitáb-i-Íqán*, p. 67.
[62] Ibid., pp. 102-103.

Station of the Manifestation
[63] Bahá'u'lláh, *Kitáb-i-Aqdas*, note 160, p. 234.
[64] Bahá'u'lláh, *Gleanings*, XLIX, p. 102.
[65] Ibid., XXVII, pp. 66-67.
[66] Ibid., XXII, pp. 54-56.
[67] Ibid., XXII, pp. 50-53.

Divine Presence
[68] Bahá'u'lláh, *Epistle to the Son of the Wolf*, pp. 118-119.
[69] Qur'án 57:3.
[70] Bahá'u'lláh, *Kitáb-i-Íqán*, pp. 142-143.
[71] Bahá'u'lláh, *Summons*, pp. 23-24, par. 44.

Unity of God's Religion and His Prophets
[72] Bahá'u'lláh, *Gleanings*, CXXXII, pp. 287-88.
[73] Ibid., XXXIV, pp. 78-79.
[74] Ibid., XXIV, p. 59.

God's Purpose in Sending His Messengers
[75] Bahá'u'lláh, *Epistle to the Son of the Wolf*, p. 98.
[76] Bahá'u'lláh, *Gleanings*, XXXIV, pp. 79-80.
[77] Bahá'u'lláh, *Tablets of Bahá'u'lláh*, p. 161.
[78] Bahá'u'lláh, *Gleanings*, LXXXI, pp. 156-157.
[79] Bahá'u'lláh, cited in *The World Order of Bahá'u'lláh*, p. 116.

Divine Physicians
[80] Bahá'u'lláh, *Gleanings*, XXXIV, pp. 80-81.
[81] Bahá'u'lláh, *Tabernacle*, p. 5.
[82] Bahá'u'lláh, *Gleanings*, XVI, pp. 39-40.

Divine Revelation
[83] Bahá'u'lláh, *Gleanings*, XCV, p. 195.
[84] Ibid., XCIII, p. 186.
[85] Bahá'u'lláh, *Tablets of Bahá'u'lláh*, pp. 93-94.

Progressive Revelation
[86] Bahá'u'lláh, *Gleanings*, XXXVIII, pp. 87-88.
[87] Ibid., XXXIV, p. 81.
[88] Ibid., XXX, XXXI, pp. 73-75.
[89] Bahá'u'lláh, *Kitáb-i-Íqán*, pp. 199-200.

Language of the Messengers
[90] Bahá'u'lláh, *Kitáb-i-Íqán*, pp. 254-255.

Proofs of Prophethood
[91] Bahá'u'lláh, *Gleanings*, LII, p. 105.
[92] Ibid., XX, p. 49.
[93] Bahá'u'lláh, *Kitáb-i-Íqán*, p. 104.

Twin Duties Prescribed by God
[94] Bahá'u'lláh, *Kitáb-i-Aqdas*, par. 1.

Rejection and Persecution of God's Manifestations
[95] Bahá'u'lláh, *Kitáb-i-Íqán*, p. 4.
[96] Ibid., pp. 73-74.
[97] Bahá'u'lláh, *Gleanings*, XXIII, pp. 56-58.
[98] Ibid., XXXIX, pp. 88-90.

Forerunners of Manifestations
[99] Bahá'u'lláh, *Kitáb-i-Íqán*, p. 66.

Prophets Before Adam
[100] Bahá'u'lláh, *Gleanings*, LXXXVII, pp. 172-173.

Abraham
[101] Bahá'u'lláh, *Gleanings*, XXXII, pp. 75-76.
[102] Abraham.
[103] Bahá'u'lláh, *Kitáb-i-Íqán*, pp. 10-11.

Moses
[104] Bahá'u'lláh, *Kitáb-i-Íqán*, pp. 11-12.
[105] Bahá'u'lláh, *Tablets of Bahá'u'lláh*, p. 265.

Christ
[106] Bahá'u'lláh, *Kitáb-i-Íqán*, pp. 17-18.
[107] Ibid., pp. 130-131.
[108] Bahá'u'lláh, *Gleanings*, XXXVI, pp. 85-86.
[109] Bahá'u'lláh, *Kitáb-i-Íqán*, pp. 132-133.

[110] Bahá'u'lláh, *Epistle to the Son of the Wolf*, p. 148.
[111] Bahá'u'lláh, *Kitáb-i-Íqán*, p. 20.

Muhammad
[112] Bahá'u'lláh, *Gleanings*, XXXV, p. 83.
[113] Bahá'u'lláh, *Kitáb-i-Íqán*, pp. 108-109.
[114] Ibid., pp. 20-21.
[115] Bahá'u'lláh, *Gleanings*, XXXIII, p. 77.
[116] Bahá'u'lláh, *Kitáb-i-Íqán*, p. 162.
[117] Ibid., p. 40.
[118] Ibid., p. 201.
[119] Bahá'u'lláh, *Proclamation*, p. 98.
[120] The year 1260 A.H., the year of the Báb's Declaration.
[121] Bahá'u'lláh, *Kitáb-i-Íqán*, pp. 200-201.

The Báb
[122] Bahá'u'lláh, *Gleanings*, XXXIII, p. 77.
[123] Ibid., LXXVI, pp. 145-146.
[124] Bahá'u'lláh, cited in *The World Order of Bahá'u'lláh*, p. 125.
[125] Bahá'u'lláh, *Kitáb-i-Íqán*, pp. 234-235.
[126] Bahá'u'lláh, *Prayers and Meditations*, LVI, pp. 84-86.
[127] Bahá'u'lláh, *Tablets of Bahá'u'lláh*, p. 89.
[128] Bahá'u'lláh, cited in *The World Order of Bahá'u'lláh*, p. 124.

Bahá'u'lláh
[129] Bahá'u'lláh, *Tablets of Bahá'u'lláh*, pp. 47-48.
[130] Bahá'u'lláh, *Epistle to the Son of the Wolf*, pp. 1-2.
[131] Bahá'u'lláh, cited in *The World Order of Baha'u'llah*, pp. 103-107.
[132] Bahá'u'lláh, *Gleanings*, XLVII, pp. 101-102.
[133] Bahá'u'lláh, cited in *The World Order of Bahá'u'lláh*, p. 104.

Next Manifestation
[134] Bahá'u'lláh, *Kitáb-i-Aqdas*, par. 37.
[135] Bahá'u'lláh, cited in *The World Order of Bahá'u'lláh*, p. 117.

Chapter 3 – Bahá'u'lláh

Tihrán
[136] Tihrán
[137] Bahá'u'lláh, *Kitáb-i-Aqdas*, pars. 91-93.
[138] Bahá'u'lláh, *Gleanings*, LV, p. 109.

Imprisonment in the Siyáh-Chál
[139] Bahá'u'lláh, *Gleanings*, XXX, p. 73.
[140] Bahá'u'lláh, cited in *The Dawn-Breakers*, pp. 584-585.
[141] Bahá'u'lláh, *Epistle to the Son of the Wolf*, pp. 20-21.
[142] Ibid., pp. 76-77.

Dawning of Revelation
[143] Bahá'u'lláh, *Epistle to the Son of the Wolf*, p. 22.
[144] Bahá'u'lláh, *Summons*, pp. 5-6, pars. 6-7.
[145] Bahá'u'lláh, *Epistle to the Son of the Wolf*, p. 21.
[146] Bahá'u'lláh, *Summons*, p. 98, par. 192.
[147] Bahá'u'lláh, *Prayers and Meditations*, XVIII, pp. 20-21.
[148] Bahá'u'lláh, *Gleanings*, LXXVIII, p. 151.

Exiled to 'Iráq
[149] Bahá'u'lláh, cited in *God Passes By*, p. 109.
[150] Bahá'u'lláh, *Epistle to the Son of the Wolf*, pp. 21-22.
[151] Bahá'u'lláh, cited in *God Passes By*, p. 118.
[152] Bahá'u'lláh, *Tablets of Bahá'u'lláh*, p. 131.
[153] Bahá'u'lláh, *Epistle to the Son of the Wolf*, p. 23.
[154] Bahá'u'lláh, *Kitáb-i-Íqán*, pp. 249-250.

Withdrawal to the Wilderness of Kurdistán
[155] Bahá'u'lláh, *Kitáb-i-Íqán*, pp. 250-251.

Return to Baghdád
[156] Bahá'u'lláh, *Kitáb-i-Íqán*, pp. 251-252.
[157] Bahá'u'lláh, cited in *God Passes By*, p. 125.
[158] Ibid., p. 126.
[159] Bahá'u'lláh, cited in *The Dawn-Breakers*, p. 585.
[160] Bahá'u'lláh, *Gleanings*, LXVII, pp. 131-132.

Ridván
[161] Bahá'u'lláh, *Kitáb-i-Aqdas*, par. 75.
[162] Bahá'u'lláh, *Gleanings*, XIV, pp. 27-35.
[163] Ibid., CLI, pp. 319-322.

To Constantinople
[164] Bahá'u'lláh, *Epistle to the Son of the Wolf*, pp. 51-52.
[165] Bahá'u'lláh, cited in *God Passes By*, p. 149.
[166] Ibid., p. 155.
[167] Ibid., p. 145.
[168] Bahá'u'lláh, *Summons*, pp. 195-196, par. 25.

[169] Ibid., pp. 201-202, par. 39.
[170] Bahá'u'lláh, *Kitáb-i-Aqdas*, par. 89.
[171] Bahá'u'lláh, *Summons*, pp. 200-201, par. 37.

Exiled to Adrianople: The Remote Prison
[172] Bahá'u'lláh, cited in *God Passes By*, p. 161.
[173] Bahá'u'lláh, *Gleanings*, LXI, p. 125.
[174] Bahá'u'lláh, *Bahá'í Prayers*, p. 309.
[175] Bahá'u'lláh, cited in *God Passes By*, p. 171.
[176] Bahá'u'lláh, *Summons*, p. 143, par. 5.
[177] Ibid., p. 146, par. 14.

Days of Stress
[178] Mírzá Yahyá.
[179] Bahá'u'lláh, *Tablets of Bahá'u'lláh*, pp. 111-112.
[180] Bahá'u'lláh, cited in *God Passes By*, pp. 169-170.
[181] Bahá'u'lláh, *Epistle to the Son of the Wolf*, p. 70.
[182] Bahá'u'lláh, *Tablets of Bahá'u'lláh*, pp. 75-76.
[183] Bahá'u'lláh, cited in *God Passes By*, pp. 168-169.

Exiled to 'Akká: The Most Great Prison
[184] Bahá'u'lláh, *Epistle to the Son of the Wolf*, pp. 78-79.
[185] Bahá'u'lláh, *Summons*, pp. 73-74, par. 140.
[186] Bahá'u'lláh, cited in *God Passes By*, pp. 184-185.
[187] 'Akká.
[188] Bahá'u'lláh, *Summons*, pp. 81-82, par. 156.
[189] Bahá'u'lláh, cited in *God Passes By*, pp. 187-188.
[190] Bahá'u'lláh, *Tablets of Bahá'u'lláh*, p. 233.
[191] Bahá'u'lláh, *Gleanings*, LIX, p. 116.
[192] Bahá'u'lláh, *Prayers and Meditations*, XV, pp. 17-18.
[193] Ibid., CXVIII, pp. 200-201.

O Carmel
[194] Bahá'u'lláh, *Tablets of Bahá'u'lláh*, pp. 3-5.

Death of Mírzá Mihdí; The Purest Branch
[195] Bahá'u'lláh, *Prayers and Meditations*, XXX, pp. 34-35.
[196] Bahá'u'lláh, cited in *Messages to America*, pp. 33-34.
[197] Bahá'u'lláh, cited in *God Passes By*, p. 188.
[198] Bahá'u'lláh, cited in *Messages to America*, p. 34.

Life of Tribulations and Sorrows
[199] Bahá'u'lláh, cited in *The World Order of Bahá'u'lláh*, p. 174.

[200] Bahá'u'lláh, cited in *The Promised Day is Come*, p. 9.

[201] Bahá'u'lláh, *Gleanings*, XLV, XLVI, pp. 99-100.

[202] Bahá'u'lláh, *Summons*, p. 85, par. 162.

[203] Bahá'u'lláh, *Epistle to the Son of the Wolf*, p. 94.

[204] Bahá'u'lláh, *Gleanings*, XXXIX, pp. 89-90.

[205] Ibid., CXLII, pp. 308-309.

[206] Bahá'u'lláh, *Summons*, pp. 132-133, pars. 265-266, 268.

[207] Bahá'u'lláh, *Gleanings*, XVII, p. 42.

On His Ascension

[208] Bahá'u'lláh, *Kitáb-i-Aqdas*, par. 38.

[209] Ibid., par. 53.

[210] Bahá'u'lláh, *Tablets of Bahá'u'lláh*, p. 264.

'Abdu'l-Bahá: Appointed Successor

[211] Bahá'u'lláh, *Kitáb-i-Aqdas*, par. 121.

[212] Ibid., par. 174.

[213] Bahá'u'lláh, *Tablets of Bahá'u'lláh*, pp. 221-222.

[214] Bahá'u'lláh, cited in *The World Order of Bahá'u'lláh*, pp. 135-136.

Bahíyyih Khánum: The Greatest Holy Leaf

[215] Bahá'u'lláh, *Bahíyyih Khánum, The Greatest Holy Leaf*, pp. 3-4.

[216] Ibid., p. 4.

Greatness of This Day

[217] Bahá'u'lláh, cited in *The World Order of Bahá'u'lláh*, p. 106.

[218] Bahá'u'lláh, cited in *The Advent of Divine Justice*, pp. 78-80.

[219] Bahá'u'lláh, *Tablets of Bahá'u'lláh*, p. 3.

[220] Bahá'u'lláh, *Prayers and Meditations*, CLXXVI, p. 275.

[221] Bahá'u'lláh, *Proclamation*, p. 121.

[222] Bahá'u'lláh, *Gleanings*, CLXI, p. 340.

[223] Ibid., XXV, p. 60.

[224] Ibid., CLI, p. 320.

[225] Bahá'u'lláh, *Tabernacle*, p. 21.

[226] Ibid., pp. 25-26.

[227] Bahá'u'lláh, *Summons*, pp. 148-149, par. 18.

[228] Bahá'u'lláh, cited in *The World Order of Bahá'u'lláh*, p. 106.

Promised One of all Religions

[229] Bahá'u'lláh, *Gleanings*, CXLIV, p. 314.

[230] Bahá'u'lláh, cited in *God Passes By*, p. 100.

[231] Bahá'u'lláh, *Gleanings*, III, p. 5.

[232] Bahá'u'lláh, *Proclamation*, pp. 111-112.

[233] Ibid., p. 111.
[234] Muhammad.
[235] Qur'án 83:3.
[236] Moses.
[237] Qur'án 14:5.
[238] Jesus.
[239] Bahá'u'lláh, *Tablets of Bahá'u'lláh*, pp. 114-116.

To the Jewish People
[240] Bahá'u'lláh, *Kitáb-i-Íqán*, pp. 18-19.
[241] Bahá'u'lláh, *Proclamation*, pp. 89-90.

To the Christians
[242] Jesus.
[243] Ibid.
[244] Bahá'u'lláh, *Tablets of Bahá'u'lláh*, pp. 9-13.

To the People of the Qur'án
[245] Bahá'u'lláh, cited in *The World Order of Bahá'u'lláh*, p. 179.
[246] Bahá'u'lláh, *Gleanings*, XXVII, pp. 69-70.
[247] Bahá'u'lláh, *Kitáb-i-Íqán*, p. 172.
[248] Ibid., p. 87.
[249] Ibid., p. 135.
[250] Qur'án 3:7.
[251] Bahá'u'lláh, *Kitáb-i-Íqán*, pp. 213-214.
[252] Bahá'u'lláh, *Epistle to the Son of the Wolf*, pp. 99-100.

To the Followers of the Bayán
[253] Jesus.
[254] Moses.
[255] Bahá'u'lláh, *Tablets of Bahá'u'lláh*, pp. 103-105.
[256] Bahá'u'lláh, *Gleanings*, CXV, pp. 244-245.
[257] Bahá'u'lláh, *Prayers and Meditations*, CLXXIX, pp. 308-309.

To the Leaders of Religion
[258] Bahá'u'lláh, *Kitáb-i-Aqdas*, pars. 99-100, 102-104.
[259] Ibid., par. 165.
[260] Ibid., pars. 167-169.

To the Kings and Rulers of the World
[261] The Báb.
[262] Bahá'u'lláh, *Summons*, pp. 185-188, pars. 2-4, 6.
[263] Bahá'u'lláh, *Kitáb-i-Aqdas*, pars. 78-79.

264 Ibid., pars. 81-83.
265 Bahá'u'lláh, *Summons*, pp. 188-190, pars. 7, 10-12.
266 Ibid., pp. 90-91, pars. 174-175.
267 Bahá'u'lláh, *Kitáb-i-Aqdas*, par. 88.

Blessed Are They
268 Bahá'u'lláh, *Tablets of Bahá'u'lláh*, pp. 16-17.

Glory of Bahá'u'lláh
269 Bahá'u'lláh, *Gleanings*, XXXI, p. 75.
270 Ibid., CLI, pp. 321-322.
271 Bahá'u'lláh, cited in *The World Order of Bahá'u'lláh*, p. 116.

Power of Bahá'u'lláh
272 Bahá'u'lláh, *Tablets of Bahá'u'lláh*, p. 107.
273 Bahá'u'lláh, *Summons*, pp. 224-225, par. 96.
274 Ibid., pp. 60-61, par. 116.
275 Bahá'u'lláh, cited in *The World Order of Bahá'u'lláh*, pp. 108-109.
276 Bahá'u'lláh, cited in *The Advent of Divine Justice*, pp. 80-81.
277 Bahá'u'lláh, *Tablets of Bahá'u'lláh*, p. 48.

Knowledge of Bahá'u'lláh
278 Bahá'u'lláh, *Summons*, p. 35, par. 66.
279 Bahá'u'lláh, *Tablets of Bahá'u'lláh*, pp. 148-149.

Most Great Infallibility of Bahá'u'lláh
280 Qur'án 21:23.
281 Bahá'u'lláh, *Tablets of Bahá'u'lláh*, p. 108.

Revelation of Bahá'u'lláh
282 Bahá'u'lláh, *Gleanings*, CLIII, p. 326.
283 Bahá'u'lláh, *Prayers and Meditations*, CLXXVIII, pp. 295-296.
284 Bahá'u'lláh, *Epistle to the Son of the Wolf*, p. 115.
285 Bahá'u'lláh, *Prayers and Meditations*, CXVI, p. 197.
286 Bahá'u'lláh, *Tablets of Bahá'u'lláh*, p. 72.
287 Ibid., p. 21.
288 Ibid., p. 94.
289 Bahá'u'lláh, cited in *The World Order of Bahá'u'lláh*, p. 60.
290 Bahá'u'lláh, cited in *The Advent of Divine Justice*, p. 77.
291 Bahá'u'lláh, *Tablets of Bahá'u'lláh*, pp. 74-75.

Bahá'u'lláh: The Royal Falcon
292 Bahá'u'lláh, *Tabernacle*, p. 9.

Chapter 4 – The Spiritual Reality of Mankind

Lofty Station of Mankind
[293] Bahá'u'lláh, *Prayers and Meditations*, CLXXXI, p. 314.
[294] Bahá'u'lláh, *Gleanings*, XXVII, pp. 65-67.
[295] Ibid., XC, pp. 177-178.
[296] Ibid., XXXIV, pp. 77-78
[297] Ibid., CLIII, pp. 326-327.
[298] Bahá'u'lláh, *Kitáb-i-Íqán*, p. 101-102.
[299] Bahá'u'lláh, *Hidden Words*, Arabic #12.
[300] Ibid., Arabic #13.
[301] Bahá'u'lláh, cited in *The Advent of Divine Justice*, pp. 76-77.
[302] Bahá'u'lláh, *Gleanings*, I, pp. 4-5.
[303] Bahá'u'lláh, *Tablets of Bahá'u'lláh*, p. 220.

The Soul
[304] Bahá'u'lláh, *Gleanings*, LXXXII, pp. 158-159.
[305] Ibid., pp. 160-161.
[306] Bahá'u'lláh, *Gleanings*, LXXIII, pp. 140-141.
[307] Ibid., LXXXIII, pp. 164-166.
[308] Bahá'u'lláh, *Tabernacle*, p. 68.

The Soul After Death
[309] Bahá'u'lláh, *Gleanings*, LXXXI, pp. 155-157.
[310] Ibid., LXXXII, pp. 161-162.
[311] Ibid., LXXX, pp. 153-155.
[312] Ibid., LXXXVI, pp. 169-170.

Chapter 5 – A New World Order

Days of Divine Justice
[313] Bahá'u'lláh, cited in *The Promised Day is Come*, pp. 3-4.
[314] Bahá'u'lláh, *Hidden Words*, Persian #20.
[315] Bahá'u'lláh, *Gleanings*, LXI, pp. 118-119.
[316] Ibid., CXXI, p. 257.

Purpose of God's Religion
[317] Bahá'u'lláh, *Tablets of Bahá'u'lláh*, p. 168.
[318] Ibid., pp. 129-130.
[319] Ibid., p. 125.
[320] Bahá'u'lláh, *Kitáb-i-Íqán*, pp. 240-241.
[321] Bahá'u'lláh, *Tablets of Bahá'u'lláh*, p. 162.
[322] Ibid., p. 86.

Love for Mankind

323 Bahá'u'lláh, *Tablets of Bahá'u'lláh*, pp. 87-88.

324 Ibid., p. 167.

325 Ibid., p. 138.

Unity of Mankind

326 Bahá'u'lláh, *Tabernacle*, p. 7.

327 Bahá'u'lláh, *Summons*, p. 91, par. 176.

328 Bahá'u'lláh, *Tabernacle*, p. 9.

329 Bahá'u'lláh, *Proclamation*, p. 114.

330 Bahá'u'lláh, *Gleanings*, CXXXI, p. 286.

331 Ibid., pp. 286-287.

332 Bahá'u'lláh, *Epistle to the Son of the Wolf*, p. 14.

333 Bahá'u'lláh, *Hidden Words*, Arabic #68.

334 Bahá'u'lláh, *Tablets of Bahá'u'lláh*, p. 36.

335 Ibid., pp. 67-68

336 Bahá'u'lláh, *Tablets of Bahá'u'lláh*, p. 222.

337 Bahá'u'lláh, *Gleanings*, C, p. 203.

338 Ibid., CLVI, pp. 333-334.

339 Bahá'u'lláh, *Tabernacle*, p. 8.

New World Order

340 Bahá'u'lláh, *Kitáb-i-Aqdas*, par. 181.

341 Bahá'u'lláh, *Proclamation*, pp. 120-122.

342 Bahá'u'lláh, *Gleanings*, CXLIII, p. 313.

343 Bahá'u'lláh, cited in *The Promised Day is Come*, p. 117.

344 Bahá'u'lláh, cited in *Bahá'u'lláh and the New Era*, p. 173.

The Kitáb-i-Aqdas

345 Bahá'u'lláh, *Tablets of Bahá'u'lláh*, p. 262.

346 Bahá'u'lláh, *Kitáb-i-Aqdas*, par. 2.

347 Ibid., par. 45.

348 Bahá'u'lláh, cited in *God Passes By*, p. 216.

349 Bahá'u'lláh, *Kitáb-i-Aqdas*, par. 7.

350 Bahá'u'lláh, *Tablets of Bahá'u'lláh*, p. 126.

351 Bahá'u'lláh, *Gleanings*, CXXXIII, pp. 289-90.

352 Bahá'u'lláh, *Kitáb-i-Aqdas*, p. 6.

353 Bahá'u'lláh, *Tablets of Bahá'u'lláh*, p. 132.

354 Bahá'u'lláh, *Kitáb-i-Aqdas*, par. 4.

355 Bahá'u'lláh, *Tablets of Bahá'u'lláh*, p. 200.

Houses of Worship

356 Bahá'u'lláh, *Kitáb-i-Aqdas*, par. 31.

357 Ibid., par. 115.

Local and Universal Houses of Justice
[358] Bahá'u'lláh, *Kitáb-i-Aqdas*, par. 30.
[359] Ibid., p. 91.
[360] Bahá'u'lláh, *Tablets of Bahá'u'lláh*, p. 68.

Justice
[361] Bahá'u'lláh, *Hidden Words*, Arabic #2.
[362] Bahá'u'lláh, *Tabernacle*, p. 54.
[363] Bahá'u'lláh, *Gleanings*, LXXXVIII, p. 175.
[364] Qur'án 4:129.
[365] Bahá'u'lláh, *Tablets of Bahá'u'lláh*, pp. 66-67.
[366] Ibid., p. 164.
[367] Bahá'u'lláh, *Hidden Words*, Persian #64.
[368] Bahá'u'lláh, *Kitáb-i-Aqdas*, par. 158.
[369] Bahá'u'lláh, *Tablets of Bahá'u'lláh*, p. 164.
[370] Bahá'u'lláh, *Epistle to the Son of the Wolf*, pp. 28-29.
[371] Ibid., p. 32.
[372] Ibid., pp. 12-13.

Universal Language
[373] Bahá'u'lláh, *Tablets of Bahá'u'lláh*, pp. 127-128.
[374] Ibid., p. 166.
[375] Bahá'u'lláh, *Kitáb-i-Aqdas*, par. 189.

Universal Education
[376] Bahá'u'lláh, *Tablets of Bahá'u'lláh*, pp. 161-162.
[377] Bahá'u'lláh, *Gleanings*, XCIII, pp. 189-190.
[378] Bahá'u'lláh, comp. *Bahá'í Education*, p. 2.
[379] Ibid., p. 3.
[380] Bahá'u'lláh, *Tablets of Bahá'u'lláh*, p. 68.
[381] Bahá'u'lláh, comp. *Bahá'í Education*, p. 4.
[382] Bahá'u'lláh, *Tablets of Bahá'u'lláh*, p. 168.
[383] Bahá'u'lláh, comp. *Bahá'í Education*, pp. 5-6.
[384] *Kitáb-i-Aqdas*.
[385] Bahá'u'lláh, *Tablets of Bahá'u'lláh*, p. 128.
[386] Bahá'u'lláh, *Gleanings*, CLVI, p. 333-334.

Wealth and Poverty
[387] Bahá'u'lláh, *Tablets of Bahá'u'lláh*, pp. 34-35.
[388] Bahá'u'lláh, *Gleanings*, C, pp. 202-203.
[389] Ibid., CXLV, pp. 314-315.
[390] Bahá'u'lláh, *Kitáb-i-Aqdas*, par. 147.
[391] Bahá'u'lláh, *Hidden Words*, Persian #54.
[392] Ibid., Arabic #57.
[393] Ibid., Arabic #56.

[394] Ibid., Persian #51.
[395] Ibid., Persian #53.
[396] Bahá'u'lláh, *Hidden Words*, Persian #55.
[397] Bahá'u'lláh, *Tablets of Bahá'u'lláh*, p. 156.

Equality of Men and Women
[398] Bahá'u'lláh, *Compilations*, vol. II, #2145, p. 379.
[399] Ibid., #2094, p. 358.
[400] Ibid., #2093, p. 357.

Racial Unity
[401] Bahá'u'lláh, cited in *The Advent of Divine Justice*, p. 37.
[402] Bahá'u'lláh, *The Promulgation of Universal Peace*, p. 322.

Loyalty and Obedience to Government
[403] Bahá'u'lláh, *Tablets of Bahá'u'lláh*, pp. 22-23.
[404] Bahá'u'lláh, *Gleanings*, CXV, p. 241.
[405] Ibid., CII, pp. 206-207.

World Peace
[406] Bahá'u'lláh, *Tablets of Bahá'u'lláh*, p. 165.
[407] Bahá'u'lláh, *Epistle to the Son of the Wolf*, pp. 30-31.
[408] Bahá'u'lláh, *Tablets of Bahá'u'lláh*, p. 126.
[409] Bahá'u'lláh, *Summons*, p. 93, pars. 178-181.
[410] Bahá'u'lláh, *Tablets of Bahá'u'lláh*, p. 23.
[411] Bahá'u'lláh, *Proclamation*, p. v.

Chapter 6 – Personal Character, Conduct and Spiritual Transformation

Detachment From the Material World
[412] Bahá'u'lláh, *Gleanings*, CXXIII, p. 261.
[413] Bahá'u'lláh, *Summons*, p. 82, par. 156.
[414] Bahá'u'lláh, *Gleanings*, CLIII, pp. 328-329.
[415] Ibid., CIII, p. 209.
[416] Ibid., CLIII, p. 327.
[417] Bahá'u'lláh, *Kitáb-i-Aqdas*, par. 40.
[418] Bahá'u'lláh, *Hidden Words*, Persian #12.
[419] Ibid., Persian #14.
[420] Ibid., Persian #11.
[421] Ibid., Persian #27.
[422] Ibid., Persian #73.

[423] Bahá'u'lláh, *Gleanings*, CLI, p. 321.
[424] Bahá'u'lláh, *Summons*, pp. 202-203, par. 42.
[425] Bahá'u'lláh, *Gleanings*, CXXVIII, p. 276.
[426] Ibid., CLII, p. 322.
[427] Bahá'u'lláh, *Tabernacle*, p. 67.

Life of the Spirit
[428] Bahá'u'lláh, *Kitáb-i-Íqán*, p. 120.
[429] Qur'án 15:21.
[430] Bahá'u'lláh, *Seven Valleys*, pp. 37-38.
[431] Bahá'u'lláh, *Prayers and Meditations*, CLXV, pp. 258-259.

True Seeker
[432] Bahá'u'lláh, *Seven Valleys*, p. 7.
[433] Qur'án 29:69.
[434] Ibid.
[435] Bahá'u'lláh, *Kitáb-i-Íqán*, pp. 192-195.
[436] Bahá'u'lláh, *Tabernacle*, p. 11.

Surrender to Will of God
[437] Bahá'u'lláh, *Gleanings*, CLX, pp. 337-338.
[438] Bahá'u'lláh, *Kitáb-i-Aqdas*, par. 161.
[439] Bahá'u'lláh, *Tablets of Bahá'u'lláh*, pp. 109-110.
[440] Bahá'u'lláh, *Gleanings*, CLII, pp. 322-323.
[441] Ibid., LXVIII, p. 133.
[442] Bahá'u'lláh, *Hidden Words*, Arabic #18.
[443] Ibid., Arabic #40.
[444] Ibid., Persian #19.
[445] Bahá'u'lláh, *Tablets of Bahá'u'lláh*, p. 116.
[446] Bahá'u'lláh, *Prayers and Meditations*, LXVI, p. 108.
[447] Ibid., CL, p. 241.

Certitude
[448] Bahá'u'lláh, *Tablets of Bahá'u'lláh*, p. 78.
[449] Bahá'u'lláh, *Kitáb-i-Íqán*, pp. 195-199.

Prayer and Meditation
[450] Bahá'u'lláh, *Hidden Words*, Arabic #16.
[451] Bahá'u'lláh, *Kitáb-i-Íqán*, p. 38.
[452] Bahá'u'lláh, *Gleanings*, CXXXVI, p. 295.
[453] Bahá'u'lláh, *Bahá'í Prayers*, p. i.
[454] Ibid., p. 147.
[455] Bahá'u'lláh, *Tablets of Bahá'u'lláh*, p. 143.
[456] Bahá'u'lláh, *Epistle to the Son of the Wolf*, pp. 18-19.

[457] Bahá'u'lláh, *Kitáb-i-Íqán*, p. 238.
[458] Bahá'u'lláh, *Prayers and Meditations*, XXIX, pp. 33-34.

Fasting
[459] Bahá'u'lláh, *Kitáb-i-Aqdas*, pars. 10, 16-17.
[460] Bahá'u'lláh, *Gleanings*, CXXXVIII, pp. 299-300.

Huqúqu'lláh
[461] Bahá'u'lláh, *Kitáb-i-Aqdas*, par. 97.
[462] Bahá'u'lláh, *Compilations*, vol. I, #1099, p. 489.
[463] Ibid., #1104, p. 490.
[464] Ibid., #1105, p. 490.

Recite the Verses of God
[465] Bahá'u'lláh, *Kitáb-i-Aqdas*, par. 149.
[466] Ibid., par. 116.
[467] Ibid., par. 150.

Deepen in the Cause of God
[468] Bahá'u'lláh, *Kitáb-i-Aqdas*, par. 182.
[469] Bahá'u'lláh, *Gleanings*, CXXIX, pp. 279-280.
[470] Bahá'u'lláh, *Tablets of Bahá'u'lláh*, p. 132.

Teach the Cause of God
[471] Bahá'u'lláh, *Gleanings*, CXXVIII, pp. 278-279.
[472] Ibid., CLIV, p. 330.
[473] Bahá'u'lláh, cited in *The Advent of Divine Justice*, p. 83.
[474] Bahá'u'lláh, *Gleanings*, CLVIII, p. 335.
[475] Ibid., CXXVIII, p. 277.
[476] Ibid., CLVII, pp. 334-335.
[477] Bahá'u'lláh, *Tablets of Bahá'u'lláh*, p. 200.
[478] Ibid., pp. 198-199.
[479] Bahá'u'lláh, *Gleanings*, CXXIX, p. 280.
[480] Bahá'u'lláh, cited in *The World Order of Bahá'u'lláh*, p. 106.
[481] Bahá'u'lláh, *Tablets of Bahá'u'lláh*, pp. 189-190.

Steadfastness in the Cause of God
[482] Bahá'u'lláh, *Tablets of Bahá'u'lláh*, p. 51.
[483] Ibid., p. 268.
[484] Bahá'u'lláh, *Gleanings*, CXXXIII, CXXXIV, pp. 289-290.
[485] Ibid., CLX, p. 338.
[486] Bahá'u'lláh, *Tablets of Bahá'u'lláh*, p. 123.
[487] Ibid., pp. 116-117.

Defend the Cause of God
[488] Bahá'u'lláh, *Gleanings*, CLIV, pp. 329-330.

Character and Conduct
[489] Bahá'u'lláh, *Gleanings*, CIX, p. 215.
[490] Ibid., CXXXVII, p. 299.
[491] Bahá'u'lláh, *Tablets of Bahá'u'lláh*, p. 172.
[492] Ibid., p. 36.
[493] Ibid., pp. 138-139.
[494] Bahá'u'lláh, *Epistle to the Son of the Wolf*, pp. 93-94.
[495] Bahá'u'lláh, *Tablets of Bahá'u'lláh*, p. 86.
[496] Bahá'u'lláh, *Gleanings*, CXXXI, p. 287.
[497] Bahá'u'lláh, *Tablets of Bahá'u'lláh*, p. 257.
[498] Bahá'u'lláh, *Gleanings*, CXXXIV, p. 290.
[499] Ibid., CXXVI, pp. 270-271.
[500] Bahá'u'lláh, *Hidden Words*, Arabic #36.

Selflessness
[501] Bahá'u'lláh, *Hidden Words*, Persian #40.
[502] Ibid., Arabic #8.
[503] Ibid., Persian #32.
[504] Ibid., Persian #38.
[505] Ibid., Persian #66.
[506] Ibid., Persian #22.
[507] Bahá'u'lláh, *Tablets of Bahá'u'lláh*, p. 245.
[508] Bahá'u'lláh, *Gleanings*, LXXXV, pp. 167-168.
[509] Ibid., CXXXVI, pp. 294-295.
[510] Bahá'u'lláh, *Prayers and Meditations*, CLXII, p. 255.

Purity and Chastity
[511] Bahá'u'lláh, *Hidden Words*, Arabic #1.
[512] Bahá'u'lláh, *Gleanings*, LIX, p. 117.
[513] Ibid., CXXXVI, p. 297.
[514] Bahá'u'lláh, cited in *The Advent of Divine Justice*, p. 32.
[515] Bahá'u'lláh, *Gleanings*, LX, p. 118.
[516] Bahá'u'lláh, *Tablets of Bahá'u'lláh*, p. 138.
[517] Bahá'u'lláh, cited in *The Advent of Divine Justice*, p. 23.
[518] Bahá'u'lláh, *Gleanings*, CXLI, pp. 307-308.

Wisdom
[519] Bahá'u'lláh, *Tablets of Bahá'u'lláh*, p. 66.
[520] Bahá'u'lláh, *Summons*, p. 79, par. 150.
[521] Bahá'u'lláh, *Hidden Words*, Persian #78.

Knowledge
[522] Bahá'u'lláh, *Tablets of Bahá'u'lláh*, p. 156.
[523] Bahá'u'lláh, *Gleanings*, LXXXIX, pp. 176-177.
[524] Bahá'u'lláh, *Kitáb-i-Íqán*, pp. 3-4.
[525] Qur'án 2:282.
[526] Bahá'u'lláh, *Kitáb-i-Íqán*, p. 69.
[527] Bahá'u'lláh, *Tablets of Bahá'u'lláh*, p. 50.
[528] Ibid., pp. 51-52.
[529] Ibid., pp. 96-97.
[530] Ibid., p. 96.
[531] Bahá'u'lláh, *Tabernacle*, pp. 27-28.

Human Words and Utterance
[532] Bahá'u'lláh, *Tablets of Bahá'u'lláh*, pp. 172-173.
[533] Bahá'u'lláh, *Tabernacle*, pp. 8-9.
[534] Bahá'u'lláh, *Hidden Words*, Arabic #43.
[535] Bahá'u'lláh, *Tablets of Bahá'u'lláh*, pp. 197-198.

Words and Deeds
[536] Bahá'u'lláh, *Gleanings*, CXXXIX, p. 305.
[537] Bahá'u'lláh, *Hidden Words*, Persian #69.
[538] Ibid., Persian #76.
[539] Bahá'u'lláh, *Tablets of Bahá'u'lláh*, p. 156.
[540] Bahá'u'lláh, *Tabernacle*, p. 69.
[541] Ibid., p. 73.

Trustworthiness
[542] Bahá'u'lláh, *Compilations*, vol. II, #2013, p. 327.
[543] Bahá'u'lláh, *Tablets of Bahá'u'lláh*, pp. 37-38.
[544] Bahá'u'lláh, *Compilations*, vol. II, #2024, pp. 329-330.
[545] Bahá'u'lláh, *Tablets of Bahá'u'lláh*, p. 38.
[546] Bahá'u'lláh, *Gleanings*, CXXXVI, p. 297.
[547] Bahá'u'lláh, *Compilations*, vol. II, #2037, p. 334.
[548] Bahá'u'lláh, *Summons*, p. 210, par. 60.
[549] Bahá'u'lláh, *Compilations*, vol. II, #2033, p. 332.
[550] Ibid., #2039, p. 334.

Humility
[551] Bahá'u'lláh, *Tablets of Bahá'u'lláh*, p. 64.
[552] Bahá'u'lláh, *Gleanings*, V, p. 7.
[553] Bahá'u'lláh, *Summons*, p. 203, par. 43.
[554] Bahá'u'lláh, *Epistle to the Son of the Wolf*, p. 44.
[555] Bahá'u'lláh, *Gleanings*, V, p. 9.
[556] Bahá'u'lláh, *Hidden Words*, Arabic #42.

557 Ibid., Persian #47.
558 Ibid., Persian #48.

Courtesy
559 Bahá'u'lláh, *Tablets of Bahá'u'lláh*, p. 88.

Charity
560 Qur'án 59:9.
561 Bahá'u'lláh, *Tablets of Bahá'u'lláh*, p. 71.
562 Bahá'u'lláh, *Gleanings*, CXXVIII, p. 278.
563 Bahá'u'lláh, *Hidden Words*, Persian #49.
564 Bahá'u'lláh, *Tablets of Bahá'u'lláh*, p. 156.

Golden Rule
565 Bahá'u'lláh, *Hidden Words*, Arabic #29.
566 Bahá'u'lláh, *Summons*, p. 203, par. 44.
567 Bahá'u'lláh, *Tablets of Bahá'u'lláh*, p. 71.
568 Ibid., p. 64.
569 Bahá'u'lláh, *Hidden Words*, Persian #44.
570 Bahá'u'lláh, *Prayers and Meditations*, LXVI, p. 107.

Loving Fellowship
571 Bahá'u'lláh, *Gleanings*, CXLVI, pp. 315-316.
572 Bahá'u'lláh, *Kitáb-i-Aqdas*, par. 57.

Companionship with the Righteous
573 Bahá'u'lláh, *Hidden Words*, Persian #3.
574 Ibid., Persian #56.
575 Ibid., Persian #57.
576 Ibid., Persian #58.

Consultation
577 Bahá'u'lláh, *Tablets of Bahá'u'lláh*, p. 168.
578 Bahá'u'lláh, *Compilations*, vol. I, #168 and #170, p. 93.

Occupation
579 Bahá'u'lláh, *Kitáb-i-Aqdas*, par. 33.
580 Bahá'u'lláh, *Hidden Words*, Persian #80.
581 Ibid., Persian #82.

Marriage
582 Bahá'u'lláh, *Bahá'í Prayers*, p. 118.
583 Bahá'u'lláh, *Summons*, pp. 70-71, par. 136.
584 Bahá'u'lláh, *Kitáb-i-Aqdas*, par. 65.

Divorce
585 Bahá'u'lláh, *Kitáb-i-Aqdas*, par. 70.
586 Ibid., par. 68.

Loving-Kindness Towards Parents
587 Bahá'u'lláh, *Kitáb-i-Aqdas*, par. 106.
588 Bahá'u'lláh, *Compilations*, vol. I, #824, pp. 386-387.

Cleanliness
589 Bahá'u'lláh, *Kitáb-i-Aqdas*, pars. 74, 76.
590 Ibid., par. 106.
591 Ibid., par. 152.
592 Ibid., par. 151.

Music
593 Bahá'u'lláh, *Kitáb-i-Aqdas*, par. 51.

Moderation
594 Bahá'u'lláh, *Tablets of Bahá'u'lláh*, p. 69.
595 Ibid., p. 169.
596 Bahá'u'lláh, *Gleanings*, CLXIII, pp. 342-343.

True Liberty
597 Bahá'u'lláh, *Kitáb-i-Aqdas*, pars. 123, 125.

Prohibited Behaviors
598 Bahá'u'lláh, *Epistle to the Son of the Wolf*, p. 38.
599 Bahá'u'lláh, *Kitáb-i-Aqdas*, par. 17.
600 Ibid., par. 19.
601 Ibid., par. 73.
602 Ibid., par. 148.
603 Ibid., par. 153.
604 Ibid., par. 72.
605 Ibid., par. 119.
606 Bahá'u'lláh, *Compilations*, vol. II, #1783, p. 245.
607 Ibid., vol. I, #139, p. 54.
608 Bahá'u'lláh, *Kitáb-i-Aqdas*, par. 155.
609 Bahá'u'lláh, *Tablets of Bahá'u'lláh*, p. 71.
610 Bahá'u'lláh, *Kitáb-i-Aqdas*, par. 34.
611 Ibid., par. 33.
612 Ibid., par. 147.
613 Ibid., par. 159.
614 Bahá'u'lláh, *Summons*, p. 23, par. 42.

615 Bahá'u'lláh, *Kitáb-i-Aqdas*, par. 145.
616 Bahá'u'lláh, *Gleanings*, CXXXVII, pp. 298-299.
617 Bahá'u'lláh, *Kitáb-i-Aqdas*, par. 187.
618 Ibid., par. 130.
619 Bahá'u'lláh, *Hidden Words*, Arabic #27.
620 Bahá'u'lláh, *Kitáb-i-Aqdas*, par. 64.
621 Ibid., pars. 162-163.
622 Bahá'u'lláh, *Hidden Words*, Arabic #39.

Fear of God

623 Bahá'u'lláh, *Tablets of Bahá'u'lláh*, p. 155.
624 Ibid., p. 63.
625 Ibid., p. 120.
626 Ibid., p. 198.
627 Bahá'u'lláh, *Epistle to the Son of the Wolf*, p. 23.
628 Ibid., p. 27.
629 Bahá'u'lláh, *Tablets of Bahá'u'lláh*, p. 126.
630 Bahá'u'lláh, *Summons*, p. 201, par. 38.
631 Bahá'u'lláh, *Tablets of Bahá'u'lláh*, p. 93.
632 Bahá'u'lláh, *Gleanings*, XV, p. 38.

Tests and Difficulties

633 Bahá'u'lláh, *Hidden Words*, Arabic #51.
634 Qur'án 29:2.
635 Bahá'u'lláh, *Kitáb-i-Íqán*, pp. 8-9.
636 Bahá'u'lláh, *Summons*, p. 204, par. 47.
637 Bahá'u'lláh, *Hidden Words*, Arabic #50.
638 Ibid., Arabic #48.
639 Ibid., Arabic #49.
640 Ibid., Arabic #55.
641 Bahá'u'lláh, *Kitáb-i-Íqán*, p. 52.
642 Bahá'u'lláh, *Prayers and Meditations*, I, p. 3.
643 Ibid., CXXII, p. 208.
644 Bahá'u'lláh, *Gleanings*, CLIII, p. 329.

Repentance and Divine Forgiveness

645 Bahá'u'lláh, *Tablets of Bahá'u'lláh*, pp. 24-25.
646 Bahá'u'lláh, *Summons*, pp. 207-208, par. 54.
647 Bahá'u'lláh, *Prayers and Meditations*, XXV, pp. 29-30.
648 Bahá'u'lláh, *Gleanings*, C, p. 204.
649 Bahá'u'lláh, *Tablets of Bahá'u'lláh*, p. 25.

Physical Death

650 Bahá'u'lláh, *Hidden Words*, Arabic #32.
651 Ibid., Arabic #14.

[652] Bahá'u'lláh, *Gleanings*, CLXIV, p. 345.
[653] Bahá'u'lláh, *Hidden Words*, Persian #44.
[654] Bahá'u'lláh, *Kitáb-i-Aqdas*, par. 148.

Called to an Accounting
[655] Bahá'u'lláh, *Gleanings*, LXXXVI, p. 171.
[656] Bahá'u'lláh, *Summons*, p. 200, par. 36.
[657] Ibid., p. 226, par. 99.
[658] Ibid., p. 213, par. 69.
[659] Bahá'u'lláh, *Hidden Words*, Arabic #31.
[660] Bahá'u'lláh, *Gleanings*, LXXV, p. 143.
[661] Bahá'u'lláh, *Hidden Words*, Persian #35.

Paradise and Hell
[662] Bahá'u'lláh, *Gleanings*, XXIX, pp. 70-71.
[663] John 3:5-6.
[664] Bahá'u'lláh, *Kitáb-i-Íqán*, p. 118.
[665] Bahá'u'lláh, *Tabernacle*, p. 6.
[666] Bahá'u'lláh, *Tablets of Bahá'u'lláh*, p. 156.
[667] Ibid., p. 189.
[668] Bahá'u'lláh, *Proclamation*, p. 99.
[669] Bahá'u'lláh, *Gleanings*, CXXXIX, pp. 302-303.
[670] Ibid., LXXV, p. 143.
[671] Ibid., LXXXI, pp. 157-158.
[672] Bahá'u'lláh, *Tabernacle*, pp. 61-62.
[673] Bahá'u'lláh, *Hidden Words*, Arabic #6.
[674] Bahá'u'lláh, *Tablets of Bahá'u'lláh*, p. 118.

O People of Bahá
[675] Bahá'u'lláh, *Gleanings*, CXXXIX, p. 304.
[676] Ibid., C, p. 200.
[677] Ibid., CXV, p. 241.
[678] Bahá'u'lláh, *Gleanings*, CXXVIII, p. 276.
[679] Ibid., p. 278.
[680] Bahá'u'lláh, cited in *The Advent of Divine Justice*, p. 31.
[681] Ibid., pp. 75-76.
[682] Bahá'u'lláh, *Kitáb-i-Aqdas*, par. 120.

Essence of the Wisdom of Bahá'u'lláh
[683] Bahá'u'lláh, *Tablets of Bahá'u'lláh*, pp. 153-157.

Additional Quotations:
The quotation on page XI is from: Bahá'u'lláh, *Hidden Words*, Persian #33.
The quotation on page 307 is from: Bahá'u'lláh, *Gleanings*, XIV, p. 33.

Bibliography

'Abdu'l-Bahá. *The Promulgation of Universal Peace*, Talks Delivered by 'Abdu'l-Bahá During His Visit to the United States and Canada in 1912. Comp. Howard McNutt. Wilmette, IL, USA: Bahá'í Publishing Trust, 2nd ed. 1982.

Bahá'í International Community, Office of Public Information, New York, Statement on Bahá'u'lláh, May 29, 1992.

Bahá'í Publishing Trust (U.S.), *comp. Bahá'í Prayers*: A selection of Prayers Revealed by Bahá'u'lláh, the Báb, and 'Abdu'l-Bahá. Wilmette, IL, USA: Bahá'í Publishing Trust, 2002 ed.

Bahá'í World Centre Research Department, *comp. Bahá'í Education* (extracts from the Bahá'í writings, the utterances of 'Abdu'l-Bahá, and letters written by or on behalf of Shoghi Effendi). Haifa, Israel: Bahá'í World Centre, sent from the Universal House of Justice to all National Spiritual Assemblies in a letter dated 21 August 1976 (revised July 1990).

------. *Bahíyyih Khánum, the Greatest Holy Leaf:* A Compilation from Bahá'í Sacred Texts and Writings of the Guardian of the Faith and Bahíyyih Khánum's Own Letters. Haifa, Israel: Bahá'í World Centre, 1980.

------. *The Compilation of Compilations*, 2 vols. (Individual compilations prepared by the Bahá'í World Centre, 1963-1990). Bundoora, Victoria, Australia: Bahá'í Publications Australia, 1991.

Bahá'u'lláh. *Epistle to the Son of the Wolf*, trans. Shoghi Effendi. Wilmette, IL, USA: Bahá'í Publishing Trust, 1988. ps ed. 1988.

------. *Gems of Divine Mysteries (Javáhiru'l-Asrár)*, Haifa, Israel: Bahá'í World Centre, 2002 ed.

------. *Gleanings from the Writings of Bahá'u'lláh*, trans. Shoghi Effendi. Wilmette, IL, USA: Bahá'í Publishing Trust, 1983. ps ed. 1990.

------. *The Hidden Words of Bahá'u'lláh*, trans. Shoghi Effendi. Wilmette, IL, USA: Bahá'í Publishing Trust, 1970. rev. ed. 1985 reprint.

------. *The Kitáb-i-Aqdas: The Most Holy Book*. Haifa, Israel: Bahá'í World Centre, (authorized annotated English ed.) 1992.

------. *The Kitáb-i-Íqán: The Book of Certitude*, trans. Shoghi Effendi. Wilmette, IL, USA: Bahá'í Publishing Trust, 2d ed. 1950. ps ed. 1989.

------. *Prayers and Meditations by Bahá'u'lláh*, trans. Shoghi Effendi. Wilmette, IL, USA: Bahá'í Publishing Trust. ps ed. 1987.

------. *The Proclamation of Bahá'u'lláh*. Haifa, Israel: Bahá'í World Centre, 1972. US Bahá'í Publishing Trust 1978 reprint.

------. *The Seven Valleys and The Four Valleys*, trans. Marzieh Gail and 'Ali-Kuli Khan. Wilmette, IL, USA: Bahá'í Publishing Trust, 3d ed. 1986. ps ed. 1991.

------. *Summons of the Lord of Hosts: Tablets of Bahá'u'lláh*. Haifa, Israel: Bahá'í World Centre, 2002.

------. *The Tabernacle of Unity*: Bahá'u'lláh's Responses to Mánik<u>ch</u>í Saḥíb and Other Writings. Haifa, Israel: Bahá'í World Centre, 2006.

------. *Tablets of Bahá'u'lláh Revealed after the Kitáb-i-Aqdas*. comp. Research Department of the Universal House of Justice, trans. Habib Taherzadeh, et al. Haifa, Israel: Bahá'í World Centre, 1978. ps ed. 1988.

Esslemont, John E. *Bahá'u'lláh and the New Era*: An Introduction to the Bahá'í Faith. Wilmette, IL, USA: Bahá'í Publishing Trust, rev. paper ed. 2006.

Nabíl-i-Zarandí. *The Dawn-Breakers: Nabíl's Narrative of the Early days of the Bahá'í Revelation*, trans. and edited by Shoghi Effendi. Wilmette, IL, USA: Bahá'í Publishing Trust, 1932.

Shoghi Effendi. *The Advent of Divine Justice*. Wilmette, IL, USA: Bahá'í Publishing Trust, 1990 imprint. ps ed. 1990.

------. *God Passes By*. Wilmette, IL, USA: Bahá'í Publishing Trust, 1979; second printing.

------. *Messages to America: Selected Letters and Cablegrams Addressed to the Bahá'ís of North America, 1932-1946*. Wilmette, IL, USA: Bahá'í Publishing Trust, 1947 (Revised with additional cables, notes, a glossary, an index, and republished in 2002 as *This Decisive Hour: Messages from Shoghi Effendi to the North American Bahá'ís, 1932-1946*).

------. *The Promised Day Is Come*. Wilmette, IL, USA: Bahá'í Publishing Trust, 1980 revised edition.

------. *World Order of Bahá'u'lláh: Selected Letters by Shoghi Effendi*. Wilmette, IL, USA: Bahá'í Publishing Trust, 2nd rev. ed. 1974. ps ed. 1991.

www.ingramcontent.com/pod-product-compliance
Lightning Source LLC
Chambersburg PA
CBHW060455090426
42735CB00011B/1988

9 781876 322892